Haiti
a country study

Foreign Area Studies
The American University

Coauthors
Thomas E. Weil, Jan Knippers Black,
Howard I. Blutstein, Kathryn T. Johnston,
David S. McMorris, Frederick P. Munson
Research Completed February 1973

On the cover: Artist's sketch of the
    Citadelle Laferrière, prepared by
    Marty Ittner

First Edition, 1973; Fifth Printing: 1985.

Library of Congress Catalog Card Number: 73-600155

Headquarters, Department of the Army
DA Pam 550–164

For sale by the Superintendent of Documents, U.S. Government Printing Office
Washington, D.C. 20402

FOREWORD

This volume is one of a continuing series of books written by Foreign Area Studies, The American University, under the Area Handbook Program. The last page of this book provides a listing of other country studies published. Each book in the series deals with a particular foreign country, describing and analyzing the economic, national security, political, and social systems and institutions and examining the interrelationships of those systems and institutions and the ways that they are shaped by cultural factors. Each study is written by a multidisciplinary team of social scientists. The authors seek to provide a basic insight and understanding of the society under observation, striving for a dynamic rather than a static portrayal of it. The study focuses on historical antecedents and on the cultural, political, and socioeconomic characteristics that contribute to cohesion and cleavage within the society. Particular attention is given to the origins and traditions of the people who make up the society, their dominant beliefs and values, their community of interests and the issues on which they are divided, the nature and extent of their involvement with the national institutions, and their attitudes toward each other and toward the social system and political order within which they live.

The contents of the book represent the work of Foreign Area Studies and are not set forth as the official view of the United States government. The authors have sought to adhere to accepted standards of scholarly objectivity. Such corrections, additions, and suggestions for factual or other change that readers may have will be welcomed for use in future revisions.

William Evans-Smith, Director
Foreign Area Studies
The American University
5010 Wisconsin Ave., NW
Washington, D.C. 20016

PREFACE

The Republic of Haiti, which occupies the western third of Hispaniola, a near neighbor of the United States strategically located between the Atlantic Ocean and the Caribbean Sea, has attracted the attention of foreign powers throughout its turbulent history. Economic and political conditions in this densely populated country have been of particular interest to the United States. In the latter half of the nineteenth century and the early years of the twentieth century, the United States undertook to prevent intervention in Haiti by European powers; and between 1915 and 1934 the United States carried out a military occupation in the course of which projects designed to improve living conditions were introduced. In early 1973 the United States was extending technical and economic assistance.

This book represents an effort to provide a compact and objective exposition and analysis of the dominant social, political, and economic characteristics of Haitian society. Consultants with first-hand knowledge of the country have provided data not available in printed sources. The authors alone are responsible for the final draft.

English usage follows *Webster's Seventh New Collegiate Dictionary*. French and Creole words and phrases, used only when adequate English equivalents are lacking, are defined at first appearance. If employed frequently, they are listed in the Glossary. French is based on *The New Cassell's French Dictionary* (revised). Unless otherwise stated, production and commodity tonnage figures are in metric tons.

COUNTRY SUMMARY

1. COUNTRY: Republic of Haiti (République d'Haïti).

2. SIZE, TOPOGRAPHY, AND CLIMATE: Land area of about 11,000 square miles. Occupies western one-third of Hispaniola, second largest island in Caribbean; Dominican Republic occupies eastern two-thirds. Mountainous country in which only 20 percent of territory lies below 600 feet; topography dominated by five ranges with generally east-west axis. Generally well watered, but rivers have uneven flow. Prevailing temperatures vary with elevation, and sea breezes temper tropical heat in coastal lowlands; little seasonal change. Rainfall limited by fact that most of country lies in rain shadow. Precipitation generally heaviest in north, and heavier in highlands than in lowlands, but considerable local variation. Seasonal incidence also varies by locality.

3. POPULATION: One of most densely populated countries in the world. Population exceeded 4.2 million in 1971 census. Estimated growth rate averaged about 2 percent during 1960s. Urbanization proceeding slowly, and in early 1970s some 75 to 85 percent of population remained rural. Port-au-Prince, with at least half of urban population, was only large city.

4. ETHNIC GROUPS AND LANGUAGES: Great majority of the people are of African descent. Remainder are principally mulattoes—of mixed African-Caucasian ancestry—who, as a group, have occupied an elite position in the society. A small number of Haitian citizens are of Levantine or European origin. French is the official language but is spoken by less than 10 percent of the people. Creole, spoken by virtually all the people, is a combination of French dialects and certain African forms. The two languages are not mutually intelligible.

5. RELIGION: State religion is Roman Catholicism. All religious faiths tolerated. Protestant missionaries active throughout the country. Most of the people profess Roman Catholicism, but voodooism, based largely on West African religious practices, exerts profound influence on lives of the people.

6. EDUCATION: Enrollment of about 300,000 at all levels in 1970s; 90 percent of total in primary system. Most of primary and virtually all secondary and higher schools in urban localities. Only university is public institution in Port-au-Prince. Moderate increase in primary and secondary enrollments during 1960s; university enrollment declined. School instruction conducted in French, but most of rural population

speak only Creole; as consequence, rural enrollments low, dropout rates high. National rate of literacy estimated at 20 percent or less in 1970.

7. HEALTH: Medical personnel and facilities concentrated in Port-au-Prince and a few urban centers. Demand for modern medical care in rural areas limited by survival of traditional health attitudes and practices. Principal health hazards aggravated by poor nutrition and inadequate sanitation. These include malaria, tuberculosis, dermatosis, diseases of early infancy, parasite worms, and respiratory ailments. Yaws, formerly a major hazard, virtually eliminated; intensive anti-malaria campaign resulted in sharp decline in its incidence during 1960s.

8. GOVERNMENT: Constitutional democracy, but power is centered in hands of president. Executive, legislative, and judicial branches. Constitution changed in 1964 to make President François Duvalier president for life. Upon his death his son Jean-Claude became president for life. Unicameral legislature with fifty-eight members.

9. INTERNATIONAL MEMBERSHIPS: The country is a party to the Inter-American Treaty of Reciprocal Assistance and a member of the Organization of American States, the Inter-American Development Bank, and the United Nations and many of its specialized agencies.

10. CURRENCY: Gourde; symbol is G. Rate of exchange is 5 gourdes equal US$1. Currency stable.

11. AGRICULTURE AND INDUSTRY: Agriculture is basis of economy. Coffee is major export crop, but many other crops grown for both domestic and export markets. Industry, second leading sector of economy; small plants assembling imported components for re-export have been fastest growing segment.

12. LABOR: In 1970 estimated at 2.78 million, or a little over half of population in labor force. Proportion among highest in Latin America and nearly twice that in some Latin American countries. Over 80 percent believed engaged in agriculture and most of remainder in service activities. Women and girls made up nearly half of total. Organized sector of labor force small and of limited significance; confined largely to Port-au-Prince.

13. TRANSPORTATION: Inadequate for needs of country. Roads in poor condition, and many towns connected only by animal trails. Domestic aviation fills a small part of gap, but larger role is played by hundreds of small craft engaged in coastal trade. One nonfunctioning government-owned railroad of three-feet-six-inch-gauge track.

14. COMMUNICATIONS: About 5,000 telephones in country in 1972. Some domestic telegraph service as well as international telephone and telegraphic service.

15. IMPORTS AND EXPORTS: Exports consist mainly of coffee, cacao, sugar, light manufactures, and bauxite. Imports are varied and

include consumer durables, machinery, food products, chemicals, and fuels.

16. ECONOMIC AGREEMENTS AND AID: Some bilateral agreements have been negotiated with a few countries, including France. Foreign aid provided by United States, international lending agencies, and foreign governments.

17. ARMED FORCES: Security forces consist of army, small coast guard, and air force (totaling about 6,000) and a militia estimated at 7,000 to 10,000. Unified command system by which army controls navy, air force, and police. Army units primarily infantry-type battalions.

HAITI

TABLE OF CONTENTS

LIST OF ILLUSTRATIONS

LIST OF TABLES

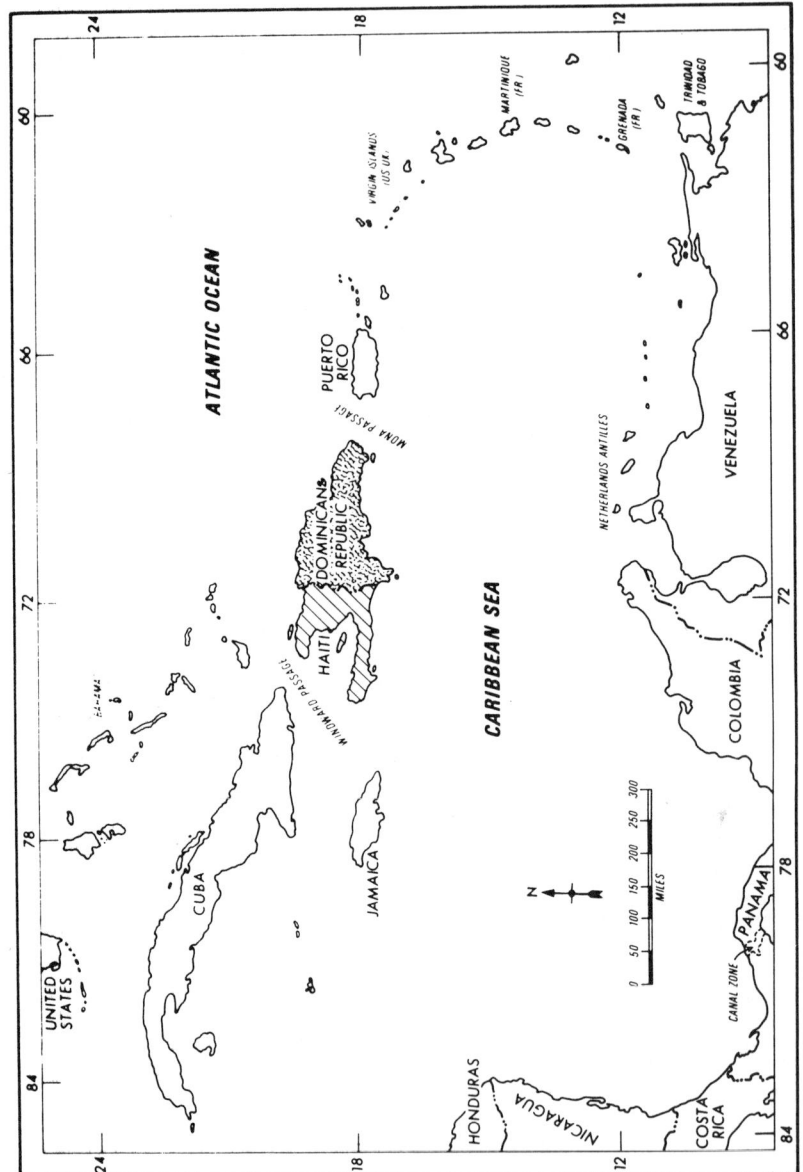

Figure 1. Haiti: Hispaniola and Its Position in the Antilles

SECTION I. SOCIAL

CHAPTER 1

GENERAL CHARACTER OF THE SOCIETY

In early 1973 the people of Haiti lived in a transitional period following the death of President Francois Duvalier, whose authoritarian regime had lasted for thirteen and a half years. Repressive measures were somewhat less in evidence; there were signs of an upturn in the economy after years of quiescence; and foreign relations were improving. After the death of Duvalier in 1971 conditions in the country had been relatively tranquil, but rivalry for political power continued among Duvalier's former followers.

Ever since the discovery in 1492 of the island of Hispaniola—the western third of which is occupied by the Republic of Haiti—the people of this territory have felt the effects of foreign intervention in one form or another. When Christopher Columbus, searching for a route to Asia, landed on Hispaniola and claimed it for the Spanish crown, what is now Haiti became part of a Spanish colony; and during the early years of Spanish occupation the indigenous peoples—Arawak Indians—were virtually destroyed by the cruel treatment inflicted by the colonists. As a result the population of modern Haiti, unlike those of most Latin American countries, shows virtually no trace of its indigenous peoples.

More than 90 percent of the people of modern Haiti are descended from African slaves, most of whom were brought in by French colonists to work on plantations. Ceded to France by Spain in 1697, the territory became one of the richest colonies in the French Empire, and the use of the French language and admiration for French culture shown by educated Haitians today had their origin in the French colony. Likewise Creole, the language spoken by virtually all Haitians, although characterized by the syntax of West African languages, is based largely on French dialects.

Present-day Haitians take pride in the fact that they gained their independence in 1804 after defeating French forces sent by Napoleon to put down a slave rebellion; and they are proud of the fact that in 1820 the country became the first Negro republic in the world. Although the economy of the country suffered badly after the departure of the French, the modern-day Haitian peasant, despite his poverty, cherishes his self-reliance and economic independence.

1

Ever since pirates, operating from what is now Haitian territory, preyed on Spanish galleons carrying treasure from the American mainland to Spain, foreign powers have recognized the importance of the Windward Passage, which separates Haiti from Cuba and serves as an important link connecting Central America and South America with North America and Europe. Through the years Haitians have witnessed shows of force by foreign powers anxious to protect their interests in the country; and between 1915 and 1934 the United States intervened militarily to protect the lives of its citizens and their property and to prevent intervention by European powers. In 1973 Haitians were receiving economic, technical and military assistance from abroad.

Haitians inhabit one of the most densely populated countries in the world. A large proportion of the population lives virtually outside the money economy; and agriculture, typically practiced on small, individual, family subsistence plots, is the mainstay of the country's economy. The proportion of the population that is economically active is substantially larger than the average in Latin American countries; and the participation rate of women is almost as high as that of men. Women play an important part in the rural economy—particularly in their role of vending or bartering produce in the village markets. At least 80 percent of the people live in rural areas, and most of the people working in urban localities are engaged in service occupations.

The people face the problem of extracting their living from plots of land, which are not only small but which have been overcultivated. Roughly two-thirds of the country is mountainous and unsuitable for cultivation. The rough terrain not only limits the amount of arable land but also renders internal communications difficult.

By 1973, although Haiti continued to be one of the poorest countries in the Western Hemisphere, the government had attained a more favorable fiscal position; foreign investment was increasing, along with growing confidence among businessmen; and the tourist trade was reviving. Exports—principally coffee, sugar, handicrafts, bauxite, and manufactured goods—contributed to unusually high reserves of foreign exchange. A promising development was the increasing number of small factories in and around Port-au-Prince, the national capital, in which imported raw or partially finished materials were processed for export—largely to the United States. Light industries were producing, among other things, baseballs, athletic goods, and electric components.

In a country with one of the lowest literacy rates in Latin America, the number of pupils attending secondary schools in 1972—primarily in urban areas—was increasing rapidly. In most parts of the nation, however, educational facilities were extremely limited; and the fact that instruction was given in French, in a country in which the great majority of the people understood only Creole, inhibited the effectiveness of education in public schools. Nevertheless, Haitians have developed a literary tradition; and among the people, folk music and painting play an important part in their lives. Artists and writers have created a consciousness of a distinctively Haitian culture, and emphasis has, in the twentieth century, been on aspects of Haitian life rather than on French models used in the past.

Freedom of expression, although guaranteed by successive constitutions, has often suffered under tyrannical governments. In 1973 newspapers and broadcasting stations avoided publishing or transmitting material that might be offensive to the government, but official censorship was not apparent. Because very few people were able to read, radio was the most influential mass medium in the country.

The small percentage of the population who enjoy the advantages of education and who are mainly responsible for intellectual activity are, for the most part, successors to the wealthy whites who constituted the elite in colonial times. When the whites were expelled at the end of the eighteenth century, the mulattoes—descendants of Africans and whites—became the elite. They preserved their position through generations of changing governments, whether the government was controlled by mulattoes or Negroes. In 1973 they continued to revere French culture and to support the Roman Catholic Church, but a society that had been sharply divided between the elite and the masses was changing. The beginnings of a middle class were apparent; and educated, wealthy nonelites were joining the old elite to form an upper class with a broader base. At the same time the masses in the countryside lived much as they had a hundred years earlier. Although the great majority were Roman Catholics, their lives were profoundly affected by voodooism—the Haitian religion based on West African religions—whose priests exercised a significant influence throughout the country.

In 1973 the people lived under a highly centralized government. Although the constitution provided for a system of checks and balances—with executive, legislative, and judicial branches—the president, supported by the armed forces, exercised strong executive power. In late 1972 legislative elections, which had not been held since 1967, were scheduled for February 1973. Various factions were jockeying for positions, as were individuals close to President Jean-Claude Duvalier, who had been designated president-for-life by his father, President François Duvalier. Meanwhile, in the countryside the people continued, for the most part, to live under conditions that had existed since the beginning of the nineteenth century.

CHAPTER 2

GEOGRAPHY AND POPULATION

The approximately 11,000 square miles that make up the territory of Haiti occupy the western one-third of Hispaniola, the second-largest island in the Caribbean; the eastern two-thirds is occupied by the Dominican Republic. Lying about 600 miles southeast of Florida, the island is separated from Puerto Rico on the east by the Mona Passage, and from Cuba on the west by the Windward Passage (see fig. 1). Because these two seaways are the principal water routes linking North America and Europe with Central and South America, the histories of Haiti and the Dominican Republic have been affected by external influences with unusual frequency.

In the aboriginal language, the word *haiti* means high land. The name is appropriate, for although the highest crests do not reach elevations as great as those of neighboring Dominican Republic, intricately convoluted mountains and hills cover most of the countryside. Less than 20 percent of the land lies at elevations below 600 feet, and about 40 percent is at elevations in excess of 1,500 feet. The mountain ranges, which follow a roughly east-west axis, make internal communication difficult and have contributed to the development of regionalism.

Once largely covered with tropical rain forest and Caribbean pine, the country has been subjected to extensive clearing of its woodlands for farming and for provision of timber and firewood. Erosion has been severe, and in the early 1970s very little commercial forest remained. Rodents of various kinds are the only native mammals, but there are numerous species of birds, reptiles, and fresh-water and salt-water fish. Mineral resources are limited.

One of the smallest of the American nations, Haiti is also one of the most densely populated countries in the world. During the 1960s and early 1970s the annual population growth rate was moderate in comparison to that registered in most other Latin American countries, but the limited amount of arable land coupled with massive erosion had resulted in severe rural crowding. A migration from country to town had been in process during the years since World War II, but its volume had been restricted by the urban economy's inability to develop industries in sufficient number to provide an increasing number of new jobs for the migrants. In 1972 four-fifths or more of the population continued to live in rural localities; a preponderant majority engaged in subsistence farming.

In the early 1970s more than half of the population was economically active, as compared with a proportion of less than one-third in Latin America as a whole. The participation rate for women, which was only slightly less than that for men, was the highest in the region. Most of the small urban labor force was engaged in service occupations, and — in the country as a whole—the number working for wages and salaries was far smaller than the number of employers and self-employed persons or the number of unpaid family workers.

BOUNDARIES AND POLITICAL SUBDIVISIONS

The 193-mile border between Haiti and the Dominican Republic, the island country's only international frontier, was agreed upon in a treaty signed in 1929. Some 80 percent of its demarcation was completed by 1930, and five remaining disputed border sections were settled by a 1936 protocol. For the most part, the frontier follows mountain ridges and courses of streams. There are also several short distances that follow straight lines, and in a portion of the interior highlands it is defined by the International Route (Route Internationale), a highway that parallels the course of the Libon River (Rivière Libon), a stream that had served as the border before the road was built.

Because of the dense rural population in Haiti and the relative emptiness of the frontier zone in the Dominican Republic, there has been considerable pressure on the border. During the nineteenth century the line in some places shifted substantially to the east, a circumstance that explains the occurrence of Spanish names such as Los Palos and Los Pozos for places on the Haitian Central Plateau (Plateau Central). Haitian farmers occupying miniature farms close to the border have looked enviously at the relatively empty lands on the Dominican side, and the Dominican government has established a string of frontier-zone agricultural colonies in order to make the border secure. The Haitian government, on its part, has endeavored to minimize friction by forbidding the construction of homes within one kilometer (0.62 miles) of the border in certain localities. Illegal migration of Haitians seeking employment in the neighboring country has continued, however, and the border had been closed for most of a five-year period when it was reopened at the beginning of 1972. At the middle of the year, however, it was reported to be closed again.

On the eve of a conference on the law of the sea held in Santo Domingo early in 1972 and attended by fifteen states with Caribbean interests, Haiti issued a decree fixing the limits of its territorial waters at twelve nautical miles, plus a contiguous three-mile zone in which fishing rights were reserved. It also asserted the right to control the exploration of natural resources of its continental shelf, a principle later adhered to by the states attending the Santo Domingo conference.

The Constitution of 1957 and subsequent legislation call for the internal division of the country into nine departments (*départements*).

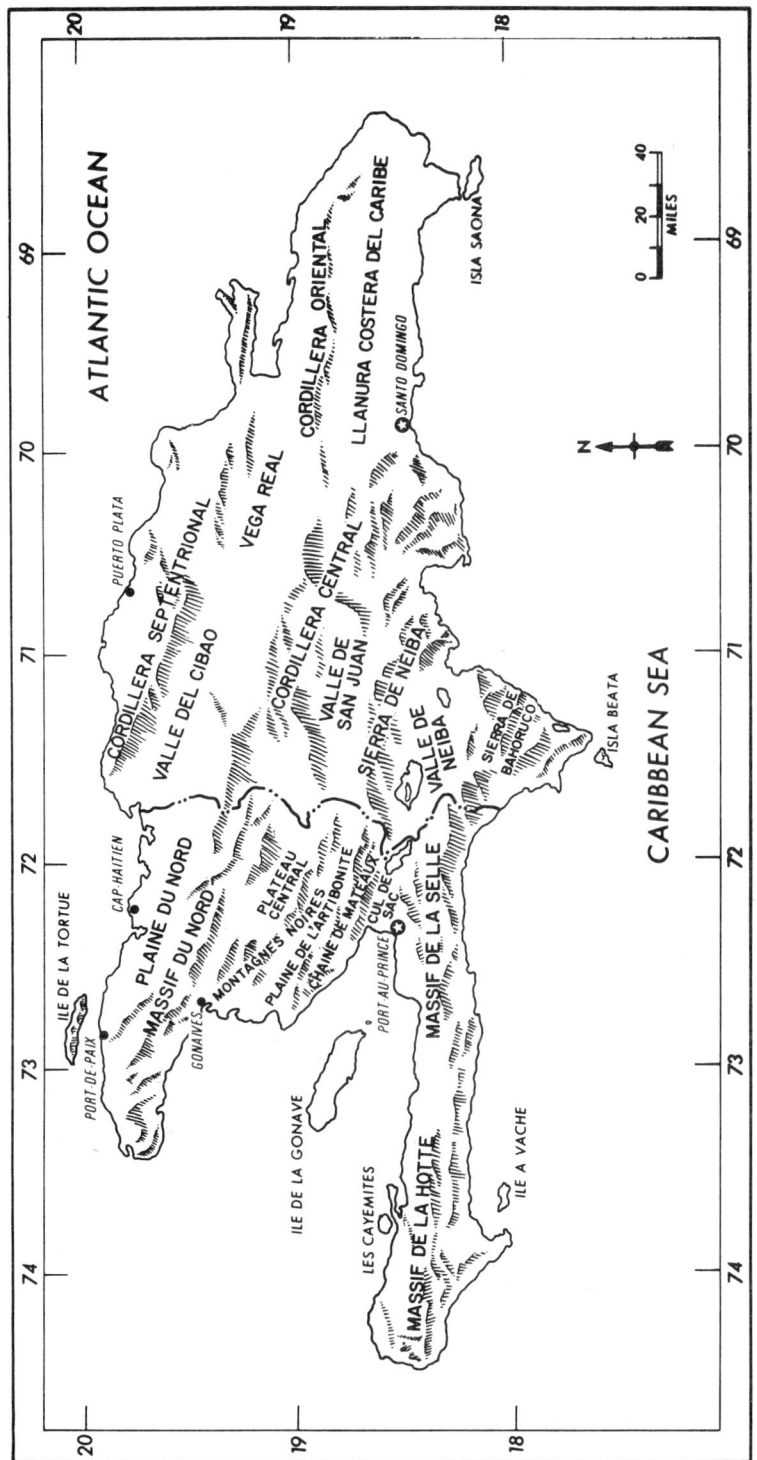

Figure 3. Haiti: Relief Features of Hispaniola

9

Massif du Nord, which slants southeastward from the Atlantic Ocean near Port-de-Paix across the Dominican border to become the Cordillera Central. This range forms part of the Caribbean Antillean system that extends from Puerto Rico and the Virgin Islands westward across Hispaniola to Cuba. Nowhere in Haiti does it reach 4,000 feet in elevation, but it is rugged and intricately dissected. Its complex geology includes sedimentary, magmatic, and plutonic rock, and limestone cliffs scar its slopes. To its west at the extremity of the island, satellite ranges extend to Môle-St.-Nicolas. To the southwest, the range called the Montagnes Noires has altitudes up to 2,000 feet and extends laterally across the country to a point where its approaches are separated by the Artibonite River (Rivière de l'Artibonite) from the Chaîne de Mateaux, a range with a southwesterly axis that extends from the Gulf of Gonâve to the frontier and into the Dominican Republic as the Sierra de Neiba.

The Chaîne de Mateaux is separated by the Cul-de-Sac from a mountain system in the far south that extends the full length of the long southern peninsula of Haiti to the frontier and into the Dominican Republic as the Sierra de Bahoruco. In the west it is the Massif de la Hotte, and in the east it is the Massif de la Selle. The latter range has several peaks with elevations of over 7,000 feet, and the Morne de la Selle at 8,793 feet is the country's highest peak. Extensive pine forests on the higher slopes of this range constitute the country's principal remaining timber reserve.

Lowlands

The most important of the lowland regions of the country are the Northern Plain (Plaine du Nord), the Central Plateau, Artibonite Plain (Plaine de l'Artibonite), and the Cul-de-Sac. There are also scattered stretches of narrow coastal plain and small coastal basins, as well as pockets of level land tucked into the mountains where small groups of people practice subsistence agriculture in virtually complete isolation.

The Northern Plain, which has an area of about 150 square miles located between the Atlantic Ocean and the Massif du Nord, extends eastward from near Cap-Haïtien to the Dominican border. Its rich soils are formed in part by abrasion and in part by alluvial deposition. The heartland of the plantation economy of the French colonial era, the plain is a geographical extension of the Cibao Valley in the Dominican Republic.

Southward from the Massif du Nord, the Central Plateau extends eastward from the Montagnes Noires to the Dominican frontier, where it joins the San Juan Valley. Its more than 840 miles of rolling terrain make it the largest of the country's flatlands. Slightly dissected and composed of consolidated and unconsolidated sediments, the plateau has an average elevation of about 1,000 feet, and its relatively thin soils are useful principally for pasturage.

Separated from the Central Plateau by the Montagnes Noires and located to the north of the Chaîne de Mateaux, the funnel-shaped Artibonite Plain has an area of about 300 square miles. Drained by the Artibonite River that crosses the central part of the country after rising in the Dominican Republic, it is broadest along the coast of the Gulf of Gonâve and narrows progressively to the east as the adjacent mountains encroach progressively on the river valley. The region is generally fertile, but near the coast its soils are too alkaline for intensive agriculture. In the early 1970s its rural population remained somewhat less dense than that of the Northern Plain and of the Cul-de-Sac, and there was promise of expanding its acreage of arable land through irrigation.

In the far south, the 150 square miles that make up the Cul-de-Sac lie between the Chaîne de Mateaux and the Massif de la Selle. Extending eastward from Port-au-Prince to the frontier, the Cul-de-Sac becomes the Neiba Valley in the Dominican Republic. It is a downfaulted depression once filled by the waters of an ocean channel that separated the mountain ridges to the south from the mainland. Later, alluvial fans formed gradually by rivers at both ends blocked off the waters of the channel, causing them to evaporate and to leave a series of sedimentary terraces and brackish lakes.

According to the Haitian Statistical Institute, there are sixteen other plains, valleys, and basins, ranging in extent from seventeen to 115 square miles. These, together with other smaller lowland areas including those on the adjacent islands, have a total area of a little more than 300 square miles. In all, the lowlands cover about 22 percent of the country's territory.

Hydrography

More than 100 rivers and streams form an intricate tracery as they flow from their mountain headwaters into the Atlantic, into the Gulf of Gonâve which is formed between the extended arms of the northern and southern peninsulas, and into the Caribbean Sea. None of any size flows eastward into the Dominican Republic. In the highlands the flow is rapid and permanent, but the movement tends to slow and to meander as the watercourses reach the lowlands. The flow becomes subject to considerable seasonal change, and in many instances it is dissipated by evaporation before reaching tidewater. None of the rivers is navigable, but they are important for crop irrigation and for their hydroelectric power potential.

Much the largest of the streams is the Artibonite River. It is shallow, as are the other Haitian watercourses; but it is the longest, and its flow averages ten times that of any of the others. Second in length is the Trois Rivières, which spills into the Atlantic at the town of Port-de-Paix at the gap between the Massif du Nord and the smaller ranges that cover the tip of the northern peninsula. Next is the Grande Anse, which reaches tidewater near the town of Jérémie on the southern peninsula. The Massacre River (Rivière du Massacre, better known as the Rio Dajabon) and the Pedernales River (Rivière Pedernales), both of which rise in the Dominican Republic, form portions of the Haiti-Dominican Republic border before they flow into the Atlantic Ocean and the Caribbean Sea, respectively.

The largest of the lakes, seventy square miles, is the brackish Lake Saumâtre (Etang Saumâtre), which is located in the Cul-de-Sac close to the frontier and is the habitat of many exotic species of tropical wildlife. There are also several smaller natural lakes and a reservoir known as Lake Péligre (Lac de Péligre), formed by the damming of the upper Artibonite River at the point of convergence between the Montagnes Noires and the Chaine de Mateaux. Initiated in the 1930s as a flood control project, the project also involves irrigation and hydroelectric schemes that have progressed slowly. Completion of the dam in 1956 resulted in the creation of a massive artificial lake and made possible some control over the flow of the Artibonite River, which had previously changed seasonally from a raging torrent to an uncertain trickle. Work on the entire project continued on an off-and-on basis after 1956, and the hydroelectric operation was finally inaugurated early in 1971.

Coastal Waters and Islands

Much of the Haitian coastline is rimmed by an underwater sedimentary platform that extends around the island of Hispaniola. There are many protected anchorages, but waters close to the shoreline tend to be shallow. These depths range from about four feet at Port-de-Paix on the Atlantic coast to ten feet or more at Les Cayes on the Caribbean coast and Gonaïves on the Gulf of Gonâve. The platform is widest at Port-au-Prince—the country's principal port—where it spreads across most of the adjacent bay as far as Gonâve Island (Ile de la Gonâve). The platform extends continuously along the Atlantic coast where, off the port towns of Cap-Haïtien and Port-de-Paix, there are also coral reefs. A reef adjacent to Cap-Haïtien is believed to hold the remains of the flagship of Columbus, the *Santa Maria*.

The Haitian government classifies six places as maritime ports, four places as secondary maritime ports, and an additional sixteen as ports for coastal traffic. About half are located on the Gulf of Gonâve, and the remainder are distributed equally between the Atlantic and Caribbean coasts. They tend to be shallow, however, and port improvements, including dredging, might be of considerable importance to the transportation system in a country where internal transportation is notably deficient (see ch. 8).

The largest of the islands is Gonâve, located in a gulf of the same name off Port-au-Prince. Its area of approximately eighty square miles is made up of rugged terrain, and its highest point, Morne la Pierre, rises to more than 2,500 feet. Second in size is Tortue Island (Ile de la Tortue), better known by its Spanish name of Tortuga. Having an area of seventy square miles, it lies in the Atlantic Ocean off Port-de-Paix.

It was a major pirate stronghold during the colonial era.

Among the remaining islands, the largest are Vache Island (Ile à Vache) located off the town of Les Cayes in the Caribbean, and the Cayemites (Les Cayemites) in the Gulf of Gonâve west of the town of Jérémie. Both are surrounded by dangerous coral reefs. In 1972 all of these islands were inhabited, but only Tortue Island was of particular economic importance. A large part of it was being developed as a multimillion-dollar tourist resort complex and free port.

Climate

Prevailing temperatures vary with elevation, and sea breezes temper the tropical heat in sea-level localities near the coast. The annual average temperature of about 81°F in the lowlands drops to 76°F in the elevated interior. In some intermontane basins, however, protecting mountain walls coupled with the direct heating effects of the sun produce what are sometimes the country's highest temperatures. Nowhere is the mean annual temperature range greater than 10°F. Within the limits of this range, the highest temperatures are recorded from June through September and the lowest in February through April.

Port-au-Prince, at the western terminus of the Cul-de-Sac, is sheltered both to the north and to the south by mountain walls; the result is that average temperatures are among the highest recorded in cities of the Antilles. Temperatures in the mountain vacation resort of Kenscoff, some fifteen miles from Port-au-Prince, may be 15°F cooler than in the capital city. Eastward in the mountain-girded Cul-de-Sac, however, there is a hothouse climate with little air movement and stifling humidity exceeding that of Port-au-Prince.

Rainfall is produced primarily by the moist north and east trade winds slanting across the mountainous eastern part of Hispaniola. As a consequence, most of the country lies in a rain shadow that makes it drier than the Dominican Republic. For the most part, highlands receive more precipitation than plains, and the north- and east-facing slopes receive generous precipitation. The heaviest rainfall tends to occur in the north of the country, but local variations are such that the annual total varies from twenty inches to more than 100 inches.

The seasonal incidence of rain varies by locality. Near the north coast there is more rain in winter than in summer, but farther south the winter is a relatively dry season, and Port-au-Prince has its heaviest rains in two seasons—April through June, and August through November. In the capital city, rain occurs most frequently at dusk and during the night, and even in the rainy months the days tend to be clear and sunny.

Thunderstorms account for much of the country's summer precipitation, and hurricanes contribute considerable but irregular amounts of rainfall during the summer and fall. Haiti lies in the hurricane belt but is less exposed than the Dominican Republic, and the two paths of maximum hurricane frequency pass to the north and to the south of Hispaniola. The surrounding mountains leave Port-au-Prince relatively free of hurricane effects, but in 1963 the eye of hurricane Flora passed over Haiti, causing heavy rains and widespread damage.

Particularly in the southern part of the country, a high rate of solar evaporation occurs when temperatures exceeding 80°F result in arid or semiarid conditions in many localities that have moderate amounts of rainfall. As a consequence, much of the Cul-de-Sac and much of the Artibonite Plain support only natural desert growth, and irrigation is needed for farming.

Vegetation and Wildlife

In few countries of the world has the destruction of the natural woodland cover been so nearly complete. In the mountain areas there is still the occasional stand of mahogany, lignum vitae, pine, or other commercially valuable woods. Where forests remain, Caribbean pine tends to be the principal tree species, along with various hardwoods. Only in the higher levels of the Massif de la Selle in the south, however, is there a situation in which the pine forest and its undergrowth constitute the prevailing mountain cover.

Aside from pine forests of the south, little of the Haitian countryside remains where the forest has not been cut over. Remaining scatterings of the original cover include rosewood and sapin, such fruit trees as avocado, orange, lime, and cherry. In some places, there are still giant tree ferns, and the native forest includes some twenty species of trees and plants useful for nutritional or medical purposes. Mangroves fringe the Gulf of Gonâve and the north coast to the east of Cap-Haïtien, and guava thickets everywhere figure prominently among the second-growth species.

The natural vegetation closely reflects conditions of climate. Wetter areas were originally covered with dense rain forest, but drier slopes supported only scrub woodland. In the southern lowlands, the moderate rainfall and high atmospheric humidity are insufficient to counter the effects of a high rate of evaporation. The soils of the Cul-de-Sac support only a scrub woodland natural cover, and for the most part the naturally rich soils can fully be exploited only under irrigation.

The Northern Plain supports scattered patches of desert-type growth and wide stretches where trees grow only along the margins of watercourses between which lie stretches of open grassland. A similar pattern obtains in the northwestern part of the Central Plateau where the grassland is dotted with scattered semideciduous trees and conifers; toward the southeast, there is scrub woodland and cacti. In the Artibonite Plain thorny scrub woodland near the coast gives way to grassland savanna and mixed woodland toward the east.

The island of Hispaniola has no indigenous land mammals other than rodents. There are, however, several species of reptiles, including three varieties of crocodile, the rhino-horned iguana, many small lizards, and several species of nonpoisonous snakes. There are many insects, arachnids such as spiders and scorpions, and centipedes. All of these are poisonous, but their stings are rarely fatal. Among the forms of birdlife are parrots, four kinds of wild pigeon, guinea hens, ducks, and weaverbirds. Egrets and flamingos are found in the brackish lakes of the Cul-de-Sac.

Minerals

The country's known mineral wealth is limited both in scope and extent, and the degree to which man has traversed all parts of Haiti leaves little hope that there is much mineral wealth yet undiscovered. Bauxite, the most important, has been mined since 1957 from a locality at about the midpoint in the southern peninsula. Copper ore— sedimentary and in veins—has been mined from the Massif du Nord since the early 1960s. The ores have yielded some gold and silver. Some copper is known to exist in the vicinity of Cap-Haïtien, and copper explorations have been carried out in the Terre-Neuve district of the Artibonite Department. In various parts of the country moderate quantities of limestone, sand, gravel, clay, building stone, and salt are intermittently produced for local consumption.

There are undeveloped manganese deposits in the Morne Macaque region of the Massif du Norde, and lignite deposits are extensive in the Central Plateau. Other minerals known or believed to exist in some quantity include iron, antimony, lead, zinc, nickel, coal, sulfur, marble, porphyry, and gypsum. Unsuccessful petroleum drillings have been undertaken in the Central Plateau, the Cul-de-Sac, and off Gonâve Island. In general, mineral resources appear far scantier in Haiti than in the Dominican portion of Hispaniola.

SETTLEMENT PATTERNS

The prevailing settlement pattern is one in which every acre of usable land is used; there are no frontier lands awaiting the machetes and plows of adventurous frontiersmen, and in the early 1970s the acreage not already under cultivation was left idle, not because of its remoteness from markets, but because it did not appear to be worth cultivating. The population density averaged nearly 500 per square mile, as compared with less than thirty-six per square mile for the Latin American region as a whole. Farms were estimated to average no more than 2.5 acres in size, and many comprised less than one acre. Significantly, the myriad little plots from which the operators battled for subsistence living were referred to not as farms but as "gardens".

A few large plantations remained, primarily in the northern plains and in the Cul-de-Sac, but the characteristic pattern was one of small holdings. By department—the principal political subdivision—the heaviest concentration was in the Cul-de-Sac in the Department of the

West. Next in order were the Department of the North, the Department of the South, the Department of the Artibonite, and the Department of the Northwest.

The pattern was one of rural villages strung out along a road, nuclear villages clustered haphazardly in a mountain basin or on a coastal indentation, or of isolated farms located wherever a patch of tillable soil could be found. This pattern had evolved after the destruction of the French plantation economy that had supplied half of Europe with sugar and cocoa, as well as with cotton, indigo, and coffee. The revolution that expelled the French colonials destroyed both the symbols and the substance of their rule. Manor houses and cane fields were put to the torch; the highways and irrigation systems were sabotaged and fell gradually into disuse.

A different and simpler kind of life emerged in an atmosphere where agriculture was pursued on a basis of subsistence rather than for large-scale commerce. Land resources diminished rather than increased, and in the early 1970s no more than 10 percent of the cultivated lands were in plantations. The rural population clusters characteristic of the plantations had been replaced by the patchwork gardens of the subsistence farmers.

The little farms were established first on the easily accessible lowlands where the plantations had been located. Later, the subsistence farmers moved progressively higher into the uplands—wherever land capable of producing food crops could be found. The villages that developed were relatively few. Central market towns were fewer still, and few roads were constructed to bring produce to central markets and to ports. Trade was too limited to encourage urban growth. Towns were not needed as population nuclei for defense purposes, and the voodoo priests who provided religious and civic leadership had no need of any regional central organization of their own.

With the passage of time, the already small farms were subdivided because of inheritance, and by the time of the 1950 census some 23 percent of the farm holdings consisted of multiple parcels of land located at some distance from the farmer's residence. This circumstance entailed spending some time in travel to and from the fields, but the possession of noncontiguous plots of land sometimes had the advantage of making it possible to produce different crops at different times of the year.

The movement of people during the twentieth century has taken the form of unplanned expansion, which has reached in every available direction in order to fill up the remaining empty places. A discernible change in the rural settlement pattern has evolved only to the extent that during the late 1930s several agricultural colonies near the frontier were established for the benefit of returned illegal emigrants to the Dominican Republic.

Throughout the nineteenth century, and during much of the twentieth century, there was very little urbanization. The colonial capital of Cap-Haïtien stagnated, while Port-au-Prince grew moderately. In general, however, the breakdown of the colonial system had been accompanied by a disintegration of the beginnings of urban life in the interior. Coastal fishing communities survived better, and in the early 1970s all Haitian urban localities with populations in excess of 10,000 were located at tidewater. Even at the few internal crossroads, market or communications centers of importance had not developed.

POPULATION STRUCTURE AND DYNAMICS

Preliminary results of a census conducted in 1971 showed the population of the country to have been 4,243,926. The figure, however, was so much lower than had been anticipated that a considerable under-enumeration appeared to have occurred. Population estimates previously released by the government for 1969 and 1970 had been 4,768,010 and 4,876,200 respectively, and an increase to 5,399,400 by 1975 had been projected. Other estimates for 1970 had ranged as high as 5.5 million, and the consensus was a little over 5 million.

Censuses have been few. A largely forgotten survey taken during 1918 and 1919 indicated that there were about 1.9 million people in the country, and the first formal census—taken in 1950—showed the population to have reached 3,097,000. The 1950 census, however, suffered from a variety of deficiencies, some of which may also have affected the 1971 tabulation. The participating officials lacked training and experience, and many of the persons enumerated lacked fixed places of residence. Women, in particular, tended to disguise their ages in the belief that certain ages were luckier than others, and some men were believed to have avoided enumeration in order to escape military service. Perhaps more important, there was a general suspicion of visiting strangers asking questions. The total number reported in 1950 was later calculated by United Nations demographers to have represented an underenumeration of 8.3 percent; other estimates of the magnitude of the shortfall reached as high as 30 percent.

Before the preliminary results of the 1971 census were announced, demographers of the Haitian government, the United Nations, and the International Labor Organization (ILO) had estimated the rate of population growth during the 1960s to have averaged about 2 percent annually, considerably lower than the 2.9 percent average for all Latin American countries. The actual census figures for 1950 and 1971 indicated a population increase during the twenty-one intercensal years of 1,146,000 or about 37 percent of the 1950 total, and an annual average of substantially less than the previously estimated 2 percent. A mid-1972 publication of the Haitian government, however, estimated the growth rate during 1972 as 2.5 percent. The various data available are speculative to a degree that limits their usefulness, but they lead to the general conclusion that population growth during the 1960s and early 1970s was at a moderate but probably increasing rate.

Between the 1950-55 and 1963-70 periods the birth rate was estimated by the United Nations to have declined from 45.5 to 43.9 per 1,000, and death rates from 25.5 to 19.7 per 1,000. Between the two periods cited, life expectancy at birth was estimated to have risen from 32.6 to 43.9 years. The United Nations life expectancy data did not differentiate between the sexes, but other estimates indicated an expected lifespan of 39.4 years in 1950. A lifespan of 38.7 years was estimated for males and 40.1 years for females; the lifespan was estimated to increase to forty-seven or forty-nine years during the early 1970s.

Infant mortality was estimated to have been as high as 190 per 1,000 babies in the late 1960s, and the limited data available indicated that it might have shown a slight rise during the decade. This proportion was at least double the average for Latin America and, as a consequence, the country's fertility ratio was relatively low. This ratio (the number of children under the age of five years per 1,000 women between the childbearing ages of fifteen and forty-nine) was an estimated 732 in 1970—about the average for Latin America. Given the very high Haitian birth rate, the country's fertility ratio would have been correspondingly high had it not been for the high toll of infant mortality.

Both the 1950 census and 1970 estimates by the ILO show the median age of the population to have been about nineteen years, the age of females averaging slightly higher than that of males. Age data collected in the 1950 census suffered badly from technical deficiencies and from fears and prejudices of the people counted, and therefore do not point to reliable conclusions. A 1970 United Nations estimate shows males in a small majority through the age of twenty-nine years, and females in a majority in subsequent age groups. A 1970 ILO estimate shows males in a small majority in all age groups from birth through the age group of forty-five through fifty-four years and females in a majority in all older groupings. Both series, in showing males substantially outnumbering females through the age of twenty-nine, suggest a fairly high rate of maternal mortality.

The preliminary 1971 census report showed the urban population to have represented 19.4 percent of the total as compared with the 12.2 percent counted in 1950. The populations of cities and towns grew much faster than those in rural localities during the twenty-one-year period, but in 1971 the proportion living in the countryside remained among the highest in Latin America. Moreover, the proportion overlooked by the census takers was presumably much higher in the rural than in the urban sector. In addition, the census definition that categorizes all administrative centers of communes as urban localities is a generous one that includes some very small population clusters with predominantly rural characteristics. The preliminary 1971 census data did not include detailed tabulations, but in 1950 the smallest locality classified as urban had a population of seventy-two, and only 8 percent lived in places with populations in excess of 2,500.

For the most part, the growth of Port-au-Prince and the few other major urban centers was relatively faster than that of other urban localities. According to one series of estimates, between 1960 and 1970 the overall population growth rate of 2 percent annually was made up of a 5.2 percent rate for the capital city; 3.8 percent for all urban localities; 2.7 percent for urban places other than Port-au-Prince; and 1.6 percent for rural Haiti.

The effect of this movement was to cause a relative increase in the size of the larger centers. The 1950 census had counted Port-au-Prince as having a population of 134,117. Cap-Haïtien, which had a population of 24,617, was the only other city with more than 20,000. One source estimated that in the early 1970s the population of Port-au-Prince had reached 500,000—including the satellite towns of Pétionville and Carrefour, which had been counted separately in 1950. Cap-Haïtien was estimated to have reached 50,000, and Gonaïves, to have reached 29,000. The towns of Les Cayes, Jérémie, and Saint-Marc were estimated to be next in size, with populations of between 10,000 and 20,000.

The 12.2 percent proportion of the national population defined as urban in the 1950 census was refined to show that females outnumbered males. In 1972 no more recent data or estimates were available, but there was no reason to believe that the proportions had changed. Essentially, there were relatively few jobs available for girls and young women in the countryside, and there was a relative abundance available in untrained domestic and other service activities for young females migrating from town to town.

The urbanization that has been characteristic of Latin American countries during the years since World War II has tended to consist of a push-pull process. The push provided by rural overpopulation and the lack of amenities in rural life is coupled with the pull that consists of the promise of better jobs and better lives in urban places, the latter often underlined by glowing letters received from relatives or friends who have migrated earlier. The hopes of migrants are seldom fully realized, but in most countries the people who have migrated do, in fact, find their new urban lives superior in quality to the old rural existences that they have abandoned.

This has not been entirely true in Haiti. Migration from country to town has been predominantly a push movement that has not been accompanied by a strong urban lure. Urban Haiti in 1972 had yet to develop an industrial base sufficient to make jobs available to the migrants from the countryside, and the limited information available does not indicate that the urban migrants have found their lives improved by the change.

Movement between rural places has been insignificant. For example, the 1950 census showed that in the Department of the North some 92 percent of the population outside of the department's one large urban center of Cap-Haïtien resided in the commune in which they had been born. In addition to the fact that there is no remaining rural frontier offering new lands, countryfolk continue to be strongly influenced by the local voodoo pantheon. A departure from the place of birth may be resented by these spirits.

The irregularity of land tenure also plays a part in discouraging mobility. No comprehensive cadastral survey has ever been executed, and those country people who hold deeds to their farms seldom have legal means for establishing the boundaries of their properties. These are occupied largely on the basis of general recognition by neighbors of property claims. Titles cannot readily be transferred, and they can best be confirmed by continuous occupancy.

External migration appears to have been large enough to have had some effect on the population level. Immigration since World War II has been negligible, but emigration may have resulted in a net population loss through external migration of as many as 20,000 people annually during the 1960s.

Historically, the principal outflow has followed the bottoms of the east-west valleys leading into the Dominican Republic. Haiti's smaller territory, larger population, and lower standard of living have resulted in a continuing flow of jobseekers across the border. For the most part they have migrated seasonally in order to serve as field hands in the sugar harvest, but an undetermined number have remained. In 1968 Dominican immigration authorities were quoted as reporting that fewer than 25,000 Haitians had received alien registration documents, but that as many as 200,000 were living in the country. Although the actual number is a matter for conjecture, the presence of cheap Haitian labor in the Dominican Republic has been a cause for continuing friction between the two countries, and in December of 1971 the Dominican State Sugar Council announced that it would no longer employ Haitian workers in the sugar harvest.

Many Haitians have emigrated by legal or other means to the United States, a considerable number reportedly having entered informally through Puerto Rico. Estimates of the number during the early 1970s ranged from 80,000 to 200,000, most of them apparently living in New York City.

Between 1915 and 1930 as many as 300,000 may have migrated to Cuba. During the onset of the world depression in the 1930s most of this number returned to Haiti, but a 1953 Cuban census counted nearly 28,000 remaining in that country. In addition, in the early 1970s as many as 50,000 were estimated to be residing in the Bahamas, and a sizable Haitian colony was reported in Venezuela.

The substantial emigration has been useful in the sense that it has had a moderating effect on population growth in the already crowded country. Qualitatively, however, it has resulted in a relatively heavy loss of professional and skilled personnel. According to a report by the

Organization of American States, between 1959 and 1967 an average of 288 professional and skilled workers emigrated each year. Of these, a little more than one-third was reported to have had a university education, the second-highest proportion among emigrants from seventeen Latin American countries surveyed.

POPULATION PROBLEMS

Many Latin American countries during the early 1970s faced potential or emerging problems of overpopulation, but in Haiti the problem had already materialized. Its 2 percent annual population growth rate during the 1960s was very moderate by Latin American standards, and the twenty-nine years estimated in 1969 as required for doubling of the population was considerably longer than the Latin American average. Its birth rate was not among the highest, and despite remarkable gains in longevity during recent years, the death rate remained among the highest in the hemisphere. The rural population density of some 350 persons per square mile in 1970 was the highest among the independent countries in the hemisphere, however, and had reached the qualitative and quantitative limits that were viable in terms of the available amount of arable land.

To meet the problem entailed by these circumstances, a small private Family Planning Association was formed in 1962 but ceased activities in 1964 when the Haitian government installed a department for family planning in what was then the Ministry for Social Affairs. The president of the country in 1968 requested technical assistance in family planning as well as in other health matters from the Pan American Health Organization. During the same year, a new private planning body was formed, which received assistance from the Western Hemisphere office of the Planned Parenthood Federation, even though it did not become a formal participant in that organization's activities.

External assistance for the public and private programs has come from several sources. Among these have been the Pathfinder Fund, the Church World Service, the Unitarian Universalist Service Committee, the Mennonite Central Committee, and World Neighbors. In general, family planning was being presented less as an independent program than as a part of larger programs for advancement of family welfare. For the most part, it had been made available only in urban localities, and its potential effectiveness depended largely on an increase in the general level of education.

LABOR FORCE

The labor force in 1970 was estimated by the ILO to consist of 2,780,000 workers, or 53 percent of the total population. An increase to 3,468,000 by 1980 was projected. The only statistics available in 1972 came from the 1950 census, which counted 1,747,000 workers, or 56.7

percent of the total. Adjusted data prepared by the ILO for the same year showed a figure of 1,942,000, or 57.4 percent. All these rates were far higher than the Latin American average, estimated by the ILO to have been about 31 percent in 1970. Other ILO estimates show that in 1960 82.75 percent of the labor force was engaged in agriculture and related activities, 6.75 percent in industry, and 10.5 percent in personal and other services.

The elevated rate of participation in the labor force was primarily a reflection of remarkably heavy participation by females who, according to the 1960 ILO estimates, made up nearly 46 percent of the total, as compared with slightly under 20 percent for Latin America as a whole. Girls and women made up 44 percent of the number engaged in agriculture and related activities, 44 percent of those in industry, and nearly 60 percent of those in personal and other services. This heavy female participation is explained at least in part by the traditional role of the Haitian woman as a worker as well as a housewife. This derives from the origin of the people in Africa, where women shared work equally with their men, and from a harsh early history where the loss of many men in combat made it necessary for women to work the fields. In addition, in primarily agricultural Haiti where much of the soil is barren and badly eroded, a very high input of manpower is required. Moreover, it is traditionally the farm wife who—in addition to working in the fields—performs the task of selling the produce that is brought to market. Both husband and wife may be considered underemployed, but both contribute their labor to support of the family.

Estimates by the ILO indicate that the participation rates for the population as a whole remained at a near maximum between the ages of twenty and sixty-four. By five-year age groups the specific rates ranged from 86 to 89 percent of the total population. Participation varied between 93 and 98 percent for men, and between 78 and 81 percent for women. Among those over sixty-five years of age, participation of males dropped to about 81 percent and female participation declined more sharply to 55 percent. Between the ages of fifteen and nineteen, however, participation was almost equal for the two sexes; nearly 74 percent of the females and slightly more than 75 percent of the males were economically active. It was in this age grouping that the largest number of young women migrated from country to town to take jobs as domestic servants or in other untrained service occupations. Between the ages of ten and fourteen some 231,000, or a little less than 38 percent, were economically active; boys slightly outnumbered girls. No employment of children under the age of ten was reported.

According to the 1950 census, some 44 percent of the labor force were employers and self-employed persons. Twelve percent were wage and salary earners; 41 percent, unpaid family workers; and 3 percent not identified by category of employment. Males outnumbered females by nearly two-to-one among employers and self-employed, and by three-to-two among wage and salary earners. Among family workers, however, females were in a slightly greater than two-to-one majority. By sector of employment, nearly all of the unpaid family workers were engaged in agriculture and related activities. Among wage and salary earners the largest numbers were in agriculture and in services. Among the employers and self-employed a large majority were engaged in agriculture, and most of the remainder were in manufacturing and in commerce.

More recent data were not available in 1972, but it appeared likely that the proportions had changed only to the extent that urban migration might have brought about some decline in the number of unpaid family workers. The figure of 213,000 wage and salary earners reported for 1950 may, however, have been excessive. In the early 1970s estimates with respect to the number of persons earning wages and salaries ranged downward from 200,000 to as few as 80,000.

The information available in 1972 suggested that few members of the labor force had acquired any skills other than the father-to-son communication of traditional ways to farm the land and, correspondingly, traditional ways of creating artisan products. In the educational system, few secondary students were enrolled in vocational courses, and—at the university level—most of the students chose to specialize in medicine and law rather than in disciplines providing skills of immediate value to the economy (see ch. 6). In the absence of specialized training, the Haitian feels little incentive to familiarize himself with workaday technology, and an old creole maxim holds that if work were a good thing, the rich would long ago have taken to it.

The 1950 census indicated that about 1 percent of the entire labor force was engaged in the professional, technical, executive, administrative, and clerical activities that in a more developed society could have been expected to absorb a larger proportion of the working population. In 1970 the National Development and Planning Council estimated that there was one trained agricultural technician for each 5,000 rural inhabitants, and public administrators of the program for development of the Péligre dam system on the Artibonite River felt it necessary to establish a special schedule for training of the engineers and other professional and technical personnel that might be required for the maintenance and functioning of the hydroelectric and irrigation aspects of the project.

No fully satisfactory data on the extent of unemployment have been developed. The 1950 census found it to represent only 2.4 percent of the labor force, but a survey of working-class families in Cap-Haïtien during the late 1950s revealed that more than one-third of the people over the age of fifteen who were surveyed considered themselves unemployed on the date of the canvass. In 1972 an entity of the Haitian government noted that Port-au-Prince was still a preindustrial city and that, as a consequence, the city's economy lacked the capacity to absorb its heavy burden of unemployed labor.

The level of underemployment is also a matter for conjecture. According to one estimate, however, during the early 1970s it was rated at 50 to 60 percent of the labor force in the countryside and at 30 to 40 percent in Port-au-Prince. In general, the country's economy was still insufficiently developed for it effectively to utilize the services of its labor force.

CHAPTER 3

HISTORICAL SETTING

Haitian society reflects, for the most part, the historic impact of French colonization in the eighteenth century and the importation of slaves from Africa. There are virtually no traces of Spanish culture or of the culture of the Taino (Arawak) Indians. The official language is French, and the language spoken throughout the country is Creole, a dialect based on French. French influence is apparent in the educational system, and the elite mulattoes—descendants of black and French progenitors—traditionally regard Paris as the world's cultural capital. The agricultural economy is based mainly on small plots carved out of the French plantations that flourished in the eighteenth century. The transition from a prosperous plantation economy to a nation of peasants, proud of their landownership, began early in the nineteenth century, when rulers of the newly independent country cut up large estates and parceled the land out to people who had recently freed themselves from slavery.

West African influences are apparent in the religion of the majority of the people who, despite nominal adherence to Roman Catholicism, believe in voodooism, the Haitian version of West African religious beliefs. Throughout the countryside the voodoo priests are community leaders who exercise significant power over the people.

Haiti was discovered by Christopher Columbus in 1492 when, in the course of his first voyage in search of a route to Asia, he landed on the northern shore of the island, which he named La Isla Española, later known as Hispaniola. This island became the first permanent European colony in the Americas (Santo Domingo). The western part of the colony of Santo Domingo was to become a French colony (Saint-Domingue), which in 1804 became the Republic of Haiti, while the eastern part eventually became the Dominican Republic.

Unions of French and blacks in colonial times produced a mulatto element that became an elite class. Throughout the history of the republic the rivalry of mulattoes and blacks has resulted in struggles for power and prestige involving assassinations, insurrections, and civil wars. Interest in Haiti's strategic position on the Windward Passage has brought foreign warships into Haitian waters. The United States concern for the territorial integrity of Haiti during World War I and its desire to protect investments in a country that was in a state of chaos triggered the military occupation that lasted from 1915 to 1934. The occupation forces brought many benefits to the people in the form of public works, health programs, and public utilities, but after the departure of the United States forces these were allowed to deteriorate.

During the early years of the republic, powerful leaders undertook to direct economic and political life along definite lines, but it soon became obvious that planned social structures would not remain intact. Subsequent developments in the political and economic life of the country were largely unplanned, and in the twentieth century standards of living, compared with those of many other countries, were low.

Turbulence has played a prominent role in the history of Haiti, beginning with the annihilation of the Tainos by the Spaniards and the establishment of the first permanent settlement by French and English pirates. The slave rebellion that drove out the French at the end of the eighteenth century, invasions of the Dominican Republic, revolutions supported by mercenary Haitian guerrillas, and rulers who have exercised dictatorial powers ruthlessly—all have contributed to instability and uncertainty in the lives of the people. After the rise to power of Rafael Leónidas Trujillo Molina in 1957, the peasant continued to cling to his small plot of land; the mulatto elite maintained its prestigious position; and black leaders remained politically powerful.

DISCOVERY AND CONQUEST

It was in Hispaniola that Columbus conceived a colonial policy for Spain that left a lasting imprint on the life in the New World. Finding friendly Taino Indians who wore golden ornaments, Columbus predicted that Europeans would gain "profitable things without number," and he speculated on the great opportunity for spreading Christianity that would result from his discovery.

After founding the town and fortress of Navidad on the northern coast, Columbus returned to Spain, leaving about forty men with instructions to avoid trouble with the Indians, to seek gold, and to explore the island. After an enthusiastic reception in Spain, Columbus sailed with seventeen ships; 1,500 settlers; soldiers and missionaries; and supplies of agricultural implements, cattle, and seeds. He found Navidad deserted. The settlers, who had treated the Indians ruthlessly, had been killed.

Columbus then founded Isabela on the northern coast of what is now the Dominican Republic. The settlers suffered from disease and fought off attacks by Indians, thousands of whom were killed. In an effort to build a handsome city, Columbus ordered his followers to perform manual labor—a command deeply resented by men who considered themselves gentlemen. These malcontents plotted against Columbus and denounced him to the authorities in Spain. The Spaniards' cruel treatment of the Indians generated revolts that were mercilessly crushed, and many Indians fled to the mountains.

Isabela, where Columbus' brother Bartolomé was serving as Columbus' deputy, was in a virtual state of anarchy, and the prospects for the colony were gloomy. In June 1496 Columbus, intent on defending himself against his detractors, returned to Spain, where he waited two years before obtaining ships for a third voyage.

When Columbus arrived at the town of Santo Domingo, a new settlement founded by his brother, many Spaniards in the northern part of the island were openly revolting against Bartolomé. In an effort to mollify the rebellious colonists, Columbus established a system of exploitation that was to become a basis for social institutions throughout the Spanish colonies in America. This was the scheme of *repartimientos*, under which a settler was granted a large tract of land, along with the Indians who lived on it, to exploit as he pleased. In order to rid themselves of a gold tribute that the Spaniards had been demanding, the Indian chieftains turned their subjects over to the colonists.

News of dissension among the colonists, however, had prompted the Spanish king and queen, Ferdinand and Isabella, to name Francisco Bobadillo chief justice to investigate conditions in the colony. On his arrival at Santo Domingo in August 1500 he found a number of colonists, who had revolted against Columbus, swinging from the gallows and several others about to be hanged. Bobadillo ordered the arrest of Columbus and his brother Bartolomé and sent them to Spain in chains.

Columbus was released six weeks after his arrival in Spain and was received by Ferdinand and Isabella; but, without consulting Columbus, the monarchs sent Nicolás de Ovando to Hispaniola as governor. Ovando imported the first blacks into Hispaniola, fought Indians who had managed to maintain their independence, and built up the city of Santo Domingo. Columbus, however, persuaded Ferdinand and Isabella to furnish ships for a fourth voyage, in the course of which he coasted the shores of Central America, was wrecked on the island of Jamaica, and was rescued by Ovando. The man who, in the words of Hubert Herring, had made the Caribbean Sea "a Spanish lake" returned to Spain and died in 1506.

The *repartimiento* system failed to improve the lot of the Indians, and in 1503 the Spanish crown instituted the *encomienda* system, under which all the land theoretically became the property of the crown, but the colonist to whom land was granted was entitled to certain days of labor from his Indian tenants. He was obliged to look after their physical well-being, to instruct them in Christianity, and to pay a tribute to the crown. Although the *encomienda* did not involve actual possession of the land, grantees were able in one way or another to become owners of the tracts assigned to them and to reduce the Indians to a state of virtual slavery.

Although it was to persist for many years in the Spanish colonies on the mainland and was not outlawed until the end of the eighteenth century, the *encomienda* system in Hispaniola did not last long. By the middle of the sixteenth century the Taino population, estimated at about 1 million in 1492, had been reduced to about 500. The need for a new labor force led to the importation of increasing numbers of Negro slaves, principally for the cultivation of sugarcane, and by 1520 Negro labor was used almost exclusively in Hispaniola.

Throughout the island each landowner exercised virtually complete authority over his estate, and there was little contact between the hinterland and Santo Domingo, the capital city. Santo Domingo was principally concerned with its relations with Spain, which furnished supplies, administrators, and settlers for the colonies, and with the continent, which provided treasure for the crown. It was a way station for traffic between Spain and continental America, and a jumping-off point from which the Spaniards explored the New World.

In 1509 Columbus' son, Diego, was appointed governor of the colony. With a view to curbing the power of the governor, the crown in 1511 established a new political institution called the *audiencia*—a tribunal consisting originally of three judges with jurisdiction over all the West Indian Islands, where it became the highest court of appeals. During the sixteenth, seventeenth, and eighteenth centuries *audiencias*, established in many parts of the Spanish Empire, became the continuing core of royal authority; but the failure of some to carry out administrative and disciplinary duties assigned to them led to the appointment of viceroys, who personified the power and the prestige of the king. In 1535 Hispaniola became part of the Viceroyalty of New Spain, which included Central America and much of North America.

After the conquest of Mexico by Hernán Cortés in 1521 and the discovery in Mexico and Peru of great wealth in gold and silver, the prestige of Santo Domingo began to decline. Alluvial deposits of gold were depleted, and the Indian labor force was dying off. Large numbers of colonists left for Mexico and Peru, and the population of Hispaniola declined sharply. Agriculture was neglected, and Spain became preoccupied with the larger and richer colonies on the mainland. According to the Haitian historian, J.-C. Dorsainvil, the population of the colony in 1545 amounted to no more than 1,100 persons.

SAINT-DOMINGUE

The Spaniards neglected Hispaniola, but French and English pirates, intent on attacking Spanish shipping, established a base on Tortue Island (Ile de la Tortue), better known as Tortuga, in or around 1625. In 1641 they founded Port Margot on the western end of Hispaniola and before long had gained a foothold in the surrounding territory. The French then drove out the English and, along with piratical operations, occupied themselves with hunting wild cattle and hogs and with farming. The settlement prospered in spite of Spanish efforts to destroy it, and in 1664 Louis XIV, king of France, placed the territory under the control of the French West India Company and appointed a former pirate, Bertrand d'Ogeron, as governor.

To build up the country the governor encouraged agriculture and brought young women from France to marry the men. Among a number of small towns founded in western Hispaniola, called Saint-Domingue by the French, was Cap Français (now Cap-Haïtien), laid out in 1670. In 1697, under the Treaty of Ryswick, Spain ceded Saint-Domingue to France; and a governor general, who served as the principal royal authority, and an intendant, the chief judicial and financial officer, established their authority over the inhabitants.

The population of Saint-Domingue at the end of the seventeenth century included about 6,000 adult white and mulatto males and approximately 50,000 black slaves. Although mulattoes were, strictly speaking, the first generation offspring of Negroes and whites, the term was applied to their descendants. By 1775 the slave population was estimated at approximately 250,000; and the resident white population, at more than 30,000. Under a decree issued by Louis XIV in 1685, certain mulattoes (*gens de couleur*) achieved their freedom and French citizenship; and at the end of the eighteenth century these mulattoes, also known as freemen (*affranchis*), numbered about 28,000.

During the eighteenth century Saint-Domingue became one of the richest colonies in the French Empire. The colonists raised sugar, coffee, cacao, cotton and indigo—products that were exported to France and eventually to the United States. Roads were built; handsome houses were constructed; and irrigation was developed. The planters lived in luxury, and many spent much of their time in Paris. Many freemen acquired great wealth and aroused the jealousy of the *petits blancs*, the whites who had failed to become *grands blancs*—whites who held high office, owned large plantations, or were wealthy merchants.

In the last quarter of the eighteenth century freemen owned plantations in all parts of the colony, and one fertile parish in the south (Jérémie) was almost entirely in their hands. They owned large numbers of slaves, sent their children to France for their education, and in many cases were accepted in the society of the *grands blancs*. Eventually the rising tide of color prejudice influenced *grands blancs*, and discriminatory laws were passed by the colonial authorities prohibiting most freemen from carrying firearms and imposing other restrictions. The freeman was not allowed to hold any office superior to those held by a white person and was barred from certain occupations. He was required to wear clothing different from that worn by white people and was segregated when he attended church or the theater.

When news of the French Revolution (1789) reached Saint-Domingue, the freemen hoped to win back their rights as French citizens. The whites, on the other hand, saw an opportunity to gain independence for the colony under white rule. Early in 1791 a young mulatto, Vincent

Ogé, encouraged by members of an organization in France called the Friends of the Blacks (Les Amis des Noirs), led a demonstration against the colonial governor and was put to death. Before long, the colony was torn with riots involving all groups. Slaves deserted their masters and organized bands that burned and pillaged throughout the colony. The insurrection that started in August 1791 resulted in the massacre of every white man, woman, and child on whom the slaves could lay their hands. All whites who escaped this fate fled the colony.

One of the leaders of the slave rebellion was Toussaint Louverture, an exslave whose French master had allowed him leisure for self-education and for the acquisition of a private fortune. He had considerable knowledge of military tactics and possessed significant qualities of leadership and political acumen. In the course of the slave rebellion Toussaint crossed the border from Saint-Domingue into Santo Domingo and joined Spanish troops in their battles with French forces—a consequence of the French revolutionary wars in Europe. He rose to high command in the Spanish forces; when France announced the emancipation of slaves in Saint-Domingue in 1793, however, he returned to that colony and joined the French units fighting British and Spanish forces, which had attacked Saint-Domingue by land and by sea. With the support of Negro forces led by Toussaint, the French drove out the Spanish and British invaders.

In 1795 Spain ceded Santo Domingo to France, and Toussaint had himself appointed commander-in-chief of all French forces in the colony. He assumed dictatorial powers and in 1801 promulgated a constitution that in theory emancipated all slaves in Hispaniola but in fact provided for further importation of African slaves. The constitution also provided that the Roman Catholic Church, which had been established in Santo Domingo by the Spanish and in Saint-Domingue by the French, would be the official church and that whites and blacks would be equal before the law. Toussaint declared the whole island of Hispaniola an independent nation and was made president for life.

INDEPENDENCE

Napoleon Bonaparte, who had become first consul of France in 1799, refused to recognize Toussaint's rule in the colony; he dispatched an expeditionary force of 23,000 men that, after meeting strong resistance from Toussaint's armies and suffering from the ravages of yellow fever, brought about Toussaint's defeat. Toussaint died in a French prison in 1803, but in November of that year the French forces remaining in the colony surrendered to General Jean-Jacques Dessalines; on January 1, 1804, Dessalines proclaimed the independence of Haiti—the first colony in Latin America to sever its political ties with the Old World. Virtually all the whites had left, and the blacks were in power. A struggle for position was about to begin between the mulattoes and the ruling blacks.

Dessalines, an exslave who assumed the title of governor general for life, had no followers with experience in government. On his orders, most of the few whites who were left were killed. The fighting in 1802 and 1803 had virtually ruined agricultural projects and plantations. The population of the country had dropped to about 380,000; and women outnumbered men by almost three to two. Dessalines established an economic organization that was, in effect, based on serfdom. All people except soldiers were "attached as cultivators to a plantation," a system which gave the people no opporutnity to become familiar with occupations other than tilling the soil. Dessalines' system, sternly administered, furnished the roots for the peasantry that would soon become a typical form of Haitian life.

Dessalines used his troops to enforce discipline among the workers on the land and forbade individual enterprise. He tried to gain control of most of the land in the country, but when he died many of the mulatto landowners who had held estates in colonial times retained their properties. Dissatisfaction with his callous, autocratic rule burgeoned, and in October 1806 he was ambushed and killed near Port-au-Prince. Utilizing a display of force, which created fear among the people, Dessalines had succeeded in establishing a state.

After the death of Dessalines, the country was split under separate rulers. In the north Henry Christophe, the last of the revolutionary generals, ruled from 1808 to 1820. Born a black slave in the English Caribbean island of St. Christopher, he had settled in Haiti and was one of 800 Haitians who had volunteered for service under the Marquis de Lafayette in the American revolutionary war. An admirer of things English, he spelled his first name in the English manner rather than the French. He invited English scientists to visit his kingdom and tried, without success, to introduce English agricultural methods. In 1811 he had himself crowned King Henry I and established a royal court filled with barons, counts, and knights. He built the magnificent royal palace of Sans Souci and, on a mountaintop, the imposing citadel of La Ferrière.

Christophe saw to it that everyone worked, and men assigned to the fields performed their tasks under military discipline. As a result of his energetic measures, profitable agriculture and commerce were revived, and the people probably enjoyed greater security than they had ever known before. Christophe's rule combined military despotism with certain paternalistic elements and territorial feudalism based upon the noble class that he had created. Christophe's stern discipline generated dissatisfaction, however, and, eventually, rebellion. In 1820, according to legend, Christophe, a benevolent despot, killed himself with a silver bullet.

The rival regime in the south was headed by Alexandre Pétion, a mullato, who served with the title of president from 1808 to 1818. Educated in France, Pétion had a certain admiration for democratic ideals and allowed the people to enjoy unprecedented liberty of action. He confiscated the large French plantations and parceled out small plots of land to soldiers and officers. Pétion's generosity, however motivated, changed the entire agricultural base of the society. No longer willing to cultivate coffee, indigo, and sugar, most of the people in the south grew garden crops for their own use. Although profits from export crops declined, the common man, secure on his small plot, probably considered himself better off than ever before. In terms of national prosperity, however, the results were calamitous. Customs and tax revenues declined; paper money without backing was issued; and a few foreign loans were obtained at excessive interest rates. Nevertheless, the people in the south enjoyed freedom, while the people in Christophe's kingdom lived as serfs. Pétion, who died in 1818, was popular with the people he endeavored to serve.

After the death of Christophe, Jean Pierre Boyer, who had succeeded Pétion in the south in 1818, reunited the north and the south and, in addition, annexed the eastern part of Hispaniola where, in 1822, the people of the colony of Santo Domingo had driven out the Spaniards. Boyer, like Pétion, was a mulatto educated in France, who had served in the Pétion government. When he took office, he continued the distribution of small parcels of land and left the people to their own devices. When, in 1825, Boyer's government approved a French ordinance that recognized Haiti's independence in return for trade privileges and a large indemnity, Boyer hoped to ward off another invasion by the French, but black leaders were enraged by the fact that these concessions had been made by a mulatto-dominated government. The blacks were also angered by Boyer's negotiation of a French loan to pay the indemnity, a transaction that made it necessary to issue paper money to meet domestic needs.

When the internal situation continued to deteriorate, Boyer abandoned his moderate rule and adopted the stern tactics of Dessalines and Christophe, forcing the peasants to plow and harvest under armed guard. His inept rule lasted until 1843, when he was overthrown and exiled by a conspiracy of members of his own social group—urban mulattoes. In the ensuing turmoil the people of Santo Domingo threw off Haitian rule, and the Dominican Republic was established in the eastern part of Hispaniola. After trying unsuccessfully to establish a stable government, the mulattoes in Haiti lost their power to unlettered Negro leaders, and for the next seventy-two years Negroes were in almost complete control of the country.

In the middle of the nineteenth century Haiti reached an economic impasse. Toussaint Louverture's system of forced labor had generated a temporary increase in the colony's productivity, but many peasants had fled to the hills and settled on land that they regarded as their own. A system of sharecropping had been initiated by white émigrés whom Toussaint had encouraged to return. Under Dessalines certain freemen who were allowed to possess plantations had continued the system of sharecropping instituted by Toussaint. Thus for many years forced labor, squatting, and sharecropping had persisted as the bases of agricultural production. Pétion's large-scale distribution of land, continued by Boyer, had contributed to the deterioration of the country's agricultural economy. Most individual holdings were too small for sugar and indigo cultivation, and sugar had all but disappeared from the country's list of exports. The major export was coffee, a crop that was more easily cultivated on small farms.

The lives of the people were profoundly influenced by voodooism (*vodun*), the religion based largely on West African beliefs and practices, including ancestor worship, performance of propitiatory rites, and belief in communication by trance with deities. Although the Catholic missionaries brought to Hispaniola by the Spaniards and to Saint-Domingue by the French had made nominal converts of many of the slaves, voodooism's hold on the blacks was usually stronger than the influence of the church and was to continue into the twentieth century as a major element in Haitian life.

By the middle of the nineteenth century the stratification of society that was to last into the twentieth century had clearly evolved. The elite were, for the most part, the descendants of the freemen, or *gens de couleur*, of the colonial era. When the French colonial aristocracy was destroyed, they had acquired much of the wealth of the colonial elite and under Pétion and Boyer had enjoyed social and political dominance. When the Negroes came to power in 1843, the elite were compelled to console themselves with a belief in their social superiority. A deep chasm separated the elite from the masses, who now constituted a peasant society largely illiterate and poor.

At the end of the Boyer regime it was apparent that the mulatto effort to rule the country as an elite class while making economically damaging concessions to the predominantly black population had ended in failure. Not only had organized cultivation of cacao, cotton, and sugarcane for export ceased, but irrigation works had fallen into disrepair, tidy coastal towns had become villages of wooden houses, and the countryside was dotted with African-type huts of mud and wattles. The elite mulattoes had abandoned their plantations and, lacking any direct involvement in agriculture, had shown little interest in maintaining irrigation systems and roads or in promoting rural education. Crowding into the cities, they turned their backs on the peasants. Color prejudice grew and became a permanent feature of Haitian life.

YEARS OF TURMOIL, 1843-1915

The seventy-two years following the exile of Boyer were marked by the rise and fall of twenty-two dictators and recurring civil distrubances. Between 1844 and 1859 the Negro army, determined to reduce the power of mulattoes in government, placed four Negro presidents in office. One of these was Soulouque (1847-59), who, assuming the title of Emperor Faustin I, made two unsuccessful attempts to reconquer Santo Domingo, killed many Haitian mulatto leaders, and assigned illiterate blacks to public positions. He practiced voodoo openly and devoted hours to elaborate court ceremonies daily. Opposed by forces led by General Fabre Nicolas Geffrard, Soulouque fled the country in 1859.

Fabre Geffrard, described as "neither black nor mulatto" (the son of a black father and a mulatto mother), served as president from 1858 to 1867. He encouraged the cultivation of cotton; established an agricultural credit corporation; promoted public works such as reservoirs and gaslight companies; and opened schools of architecture, painting, and law. He favored the Concordat of 1860, under which the breach with the Vatican, created by Dessalines at the beginning of the century, was mended; and educational and charitable orders such as the Sisters of St. Joseph de Cluny (Soeurs de Saint-Joseph de Cluny) and the Brothers of Christian Instruction (Frères de l'Instruction Chrètienne) were allowed to establish themselves in Haiti. Geffrard's efforts to improve the lot of the people failed to prevent an insurrection, however, as he was driven into exile in 1867.

Louis Félicité Lysius Salomon, president between 1879 and 1888, who had served as Soulouque's minister of finance, introduced monetary reforms, but these were offset by the issuance of quantities of paper money that led to inflation. His efforts to effect agricultural reforms were unsuccessful. Among constructive projects inaugurated during his term of office were improvement of communications with the outside world, effected by the laying of a submarine cable. Nevertheless he was bitterly opposed by the mulattoes, who mounted an insurrection in 1883. In reprisal, Salomon executed so many mulattoes in Port-au-Prince that business came to a virtual standstill. Then, in 1889, when he attempted to extend his tenure of office beyond the constitutional limit, he was faced with another civil war and was forced into exile.

Another president during the 1843-1915 period who is remembered for efforts to improve conditions is Florvil Hyppolite, in office from 1889 to 1896. A dark-skinned member of the elite, he established the Ministry of Public Works, which built bridges, introduced telegraph and telephone systems, and constructed new marketplaces in Port-au-Prince and other cities. As a result of an increase in the price of coffee, the country enjoyed a short period of relative prosperity, which prompted the government and merchants to indulge in extravagant expenditures. This led to a deteriorating financial situation and growing dissatisfaction among Hyppolite's rivals. In 1891 Hyppolite mercilessly suppressed an uprising in Jacmel, in the south; but five years later, he died while leading his troops to punish the rebellious Jacmelians again.

During a period of almost three-quarters of a century after the Boyer regime, only three of the twenty-two presidents were mulattoes. The mulatto elite of necessity adjusted to existing conditions—controlling the business sector, indulging in cultural pursuits and, because of their superior education, serving in certain government positions. Political consciousness and activity were confined almost entirely to the army, the townspeople, the elite, and those who aspired to elite status. The great mass of the peasants were little affected by reform movements, revolutions, counterrevolutions, financial disasters, or foreign relations. During this period Haiti evolved into a country of peasants cultivating small plots of land, which, when divided among heirs, became increasingly smaller.

At the end of the nineteenth century Haiti lacked a significant educational system. No president had seen fit to introduce universal education, and some powerful members of the elite expressed doubts regarding the educability of the black masses. Lacking education, the people had no opportunity to compare Haiti with other countries or to participate in political discussion, and they were easily swayed by agitators who opposed the incumbent president. A politician planning a revolution could raise an army and take the field against the government after borrowing money from a merchant at approximately 100 percent interest, to be paid when the revolution succeeded.

During the latter half of the nineteenth century and the early years of the twentieth century an important factor in the political life of the country was the use of mercenary guerrillas by revolutionary politicians aspiring to the presidency. Certain peasants, who found fighting and rapine an occupation more profitable than any other, were known as *cacos* in the north and as *piquets* in the south. Known as "kingmakers," the *cacos* would make an agreement with a presidential aspirant under which, for a certain sum to be paid after a successful revolution and an opportunity to loot towns on the way to the capital, they would move down from the mountains and place a revolutionary leader in power. During the American intervention, initiated in 1915, *caco* leaders organized an uprising, which was suppressed by United States Marines after several years of guerrilla warfare. The marines' success was generally regarded as a death blow to the *cacos*.

Between 1843 and 1915 Haiti received little aid from foreign countries in solving its domestic problems, and for many years after independence it had been virtually isolated in the field of foreign relations. The first nation to recognize the country's independence was France— in 1825. At about the same time a British consul general was appointed, but the United States did not extend recognition until 1862, after which a coaling station for the United States West Indian Squadron was established at Cap-Haïtien. Between the termination of the United

States Civil War and the intervention in 1915 Haiti was affected by the opposing interests of Great Britain, the United States, Germany, and France and by strained relations with the Dominican Republic.

Between 1908 and 1915, a period characterized by revolutions, assassinations, and insurrections, Haitian governments raised money through bond issues and unorthodox financial operations, driving the republic into political and financial bankruptcy. During this period seven men served briefly as president, most of them having seized power with the support of *cacos*. One was killed when the presidential palace was blown up; others fled the country; and the last was hacked to pieces by an infuriated mob. In 1915, when Germany was winning victories in World War I, there were rumors that Germany sought a naval base in Haiti, and Germans in Haiti who had lent large sums to finance *caco* revolts were asking their government for help. French owners of Haitian securities were pressing the Haitians for payment, and United States financial interest controlling Haiti's railroads and banking were concerned over the danger to their investments. In the face of these threats to United States interest in the Caribbean and bearing in mind United States responsibility for the Panama Canal, President Woodrow Wilson made the decision to intervene in Haiti.

UNITED STATES INTERVENTION, 1915–34

In 1914 there were frequent visits to Haitian ports by United States naval vessels. Marines from French, British, and German warships also went ashore to protect their countries' interests. In January 1915 Vilbrun Guillaume Sam marched toward Port-au-Prince at the head of a *caco* army and by March had established himself as president. An American admiral, William Caperton, whose ships were standing by, had warned Sam against violence but, when a rival *caco* army was reported on its way to the capital to overthrow the president, Sam threw his principal critics into prison and fled to the French Legation. More than 160 prisoners, including respected members of the elite, were killed, probably on Sam's orders. A mob then dragged Sam from the French Legation, tore his body apart, and marched through the city with the pieces. Admiral Caperton then landed with 300 marines from his cruisers.

Supported by additional forces the marines spread out over the country, disarmed the Haitian army, and opened recruiting offices for a native constabulary. This police force of about 2,400, commanded at the outset by 100 marine officers, was the nucleus of the future Haitian Guard (Garde d'Haiti). Roads connecting the principal towns were built; clinics, hospitals, and telephone systems were established; and reservoirs and sewerage systems were constructed. Between 1915 and 1930, under presidents installed in office by the occupying forces, United States officials eliminated graft, collected taxes, introduced economies, and managed the treasury. The Haitian Guard proved to be the best constabulary in the history of the country, and United States engineers oversaw the construction of much-needed public works. The Americans organized a public health program and opened a school for farm leaders. The American presence was, however, resented by Haitians, who were angered by the affront to Haitian sovereignty, by Haitian army officers and politicians whose usual sources of income had dried up, and by *cacos* who, resenting the drafting of peasants for roadbuilding, staged an insurrection that was said to have cost the lives of 2,000 Haitians.

Haitians were angered by the terms of a treaty with the United States, reluctantly accepted by the Haitian government in 1915, which gave the United States control over the customs and over the gendarmerie. Most Haitians were unhappy over the fact that the occupying forces seemed to favor the mulattoes and to discriminate against blacks. In 1930 a commission appointed by President Herbert Hoover recommended that the incumbent Haitian president step down in favor of an interim government that would supervise a free election. The election brought Sténio Vincent to the presidency in 1930. The United States minister appointed by President Hoover was given the responsibility for bringing to an end the American occupation as rapidly as possible. When Franklin D. Roosevelt became president in 1933, the process was well underway. In 1934 President Roosevelt ordered withdrawal of the marines, and in 1941 a financial commission that had remained to protect United States investments was finally withdrawn.

DEVELOPMENTS, 1934-57

The United States occupying forces had shifted political responsibility from the blacks to relatively enlightened mulatto leaders, who ruled until 1946. The black masses, however, worked for a return to black leadership. Backed by the Haitian Guard, which had been organized by the United States occupying forces, black leaders ousted a mulatto president and installed Dumarsais Estimé, who purged the government of mulatto officials and replaced them with blacks and who initiated reforms designed to benefit urban workers and to improve agriculture. He discharged the American debt and signed an agreement with the United States Export-Import Bank to finance a US$6 million irrigation and land-reclamation project in the Artibonite Valley. When, in 1950, he attempted to have the constitution amended to allow him to succeed himself, the army removed him from office and sent him out of the country.

Estimé's successor was Colonel Paul E. Magloire, a black leader and a powerful figure in the army, who seemed to enjoy the tacit approval of the elite along with the enthusiastic support of the black masses. In his inaugural address of December 6, 1950, President Magloire promised to safeguard rights guaranteed by the constitution, to give priority to irrigation projects, soil conservation, cooperatives, and independent planters, and to grant assistance to education. He took a stand against communism, persuaded the United States to expedite aid programs, and encouraged foreign investment. Total foreign trade increased in 1951 and 1952, largely as a result of high prices for exports stimulated by the Korean War. Magloire was accused of despotic rule and corruption, however, and in December 1956 he was overthrown. For nine months thereafter there were seven shaky governments, and in September 1957 François Duvalier, a former follower of Estimé who had refused to accept Magloire in 1950, was elected president (see ch. 7).

CHAPTER 4

SOCIAL SYSTEM

Throughout its history the social system of Haiti has been marked by a dual heritage—that of the French colonial and that of the African slave. The social and racial configuration was introduced during the colonial period when a small minority of wealthy whites held sway over the lives of their black slaves. A rigid, color-based stratification system evolved that enhanced initial cultural differences. As independence was ushered in, the white elites were ushered out, giving Haiti the opportunity to develop new values and institutions. The new mulatto elite opted for the social model of their predecessors, however, and kept Roman Catholicism, the French language and culture, and light skin color as criteria of high social position.

The slave masses that fought alongside the mulattoes gained little more than emancipation and subsistence plots after independence. The lifestyles that had evolved during slavery were adapted to their new peasant status with only minimal changes. They maintained their own religion (voodoo) and their own language (Creole) and continued to center their lives on African and slave-based family and market patterns. Little has changed in the peasants' isolated, rural existence since slave days; they remain outside the national economy and political life and are virtually untouched by modern technology or social change.

The twentieth century has seen the initial erosion of the traditionally dichotomous society and the emergence of a nebulous middle class. The rise in black consciousness and nationalism has brought an increased awareness of the African heritage by Haitian intellectuals—as witnessed by the liberalizing of official attitudes towards voodoo and the sporadic attempts to bring greater prestige to Creole. Expanding economic opportunities have caused differentiation within social strata, and political awareness has given impetus to the incipient middle sector. Geographic isolation and regionalism are breaking down as rural inhabitants become more mobile and seek opportunities outside their ancestral villages. Although members of the elite retain their exalted position as the last bastion of prestigious French culture, the group has opened its ranks to wealthy, educated nonelites, forming a broader based upper class.

In spite of these signals of change, the overall social structure has not been deeply affected. At the base of the social pyramid the peasants' life is unchanged. Observations of rural life made in the nineteenth century were only slightly updated by the social scientists of the 1930s and 1940s; in general, these commentaries are still a fairly accurate picture of the peasant in 1972. Power and wealth have not been diffused throughout the society. New groups are developing, but the balance of power has remained with the 5 to 10 percent of the population possessing wealth, education, and social prestige. Finally, there has been no effective amalgamation or adoption of lower class norms. Creole and voodoo, despite their pervasiveness, have never been officially acknowledged by the upper class, who remain culturally segregated. Traditional class criteria are still employed to designate status. The middle class is ambivalent about its double heritage and has developed little class solidarity.

COLOR AND CLASS

Racial and Ethnic Heritage

The evolution of Haitian class structure and ethnic configuration may be seen in terms of three periods: the colonial and early independence period; the period of the American occupation (1915-34); and the revolution of 1946. The racial composition was established during the first of these periods, and subsequent history served to reinforce rather than to change the early colonial configuration. Although the colonial period technically began in 1492 with the Spanish conquest of the Taino Indians on Hispaniola, little of lasting cultural importance was to take place on the western half of the island until the arrival of the first French planters and their African slaves in the middle of the seventeenth century (see ch. 3).

The French presence in Haiti was of shorter duration than that of any other colonial power in the New World, yet the cultural transmission was extensive and especially affected the elite. The values of wealth, light skin color, Roman Catholicism, education, and cultural refinement were introduced by the French. Haitian society has never successfully shaken the legacy left by the early planters. Although the outlines of social values and institutions were drawn by the French, the details of daily life were often supplied by the black slaves. The blacks developed lifestyles that incorporated their African background and their experience as slaves, and they passed on this legacy to their offspring. The differences between the French and African cultural backgrounds have never been fully reconciled nor amalgamated, however; and the result has been the development of parallel institutions, values, and lifestyles of the mulatto elite and the peasant masses.

The French imposed a stratification system composed of three classes and based on color and French-derived class criteria. At the top of the social ladder were the white elite, who were further subdivided between those born in France and those born on the island and between government officials, planters, and the poor whites. The bottom rung was occupied by the black slave masses who had been taken from more than 100 African tribes. They, too, were differentiated between those born in Africa and those born on the island and between house servants and field hands. Finally, due to the extensive miscegenation between the slaves and their masters, a third group arose to occupy the middle stratum. Referred to as freedmen, people of color, or mulattoes, many of these individuals held a relatively advantageous position in the society. Some prospered financially, owning slaves and land; others attained a high level of education in France. This group effectively reinforced the French culture throughout the colony by emphasizing the positive values of wealth, education, and light skin color.

The issues of race and ancestry were an integral part of the white-oriented class system, further fragmenting the colonial society. Numerous terms were employed to categorize mulattoes according to their parentage. Even the courts of Saint-Domingue came to recognize as many as ten major, and 200 minor, blood combinations. Racial prejudice increased as whites began to fear the power, wealth, and rising numbers of the free, colored people. Not a solidified class under any other circumstances, the white population united in their efforts to draw and maintain the color line. Mulattoes were deprived of their civil rights as stated in the Code Noir of 1685 and were barred from positions in the court and the militia. Every effort was made to keep mulattoes from gaining authority over white men. Mulattoes were eventually barred from the more profitable occupations as well as from the professions and public service. Finally, in an effort to maintain social distance, the whites enforced segregation in churches and theaters and ostracized any white who married a person of color (see ch. 3).

By the end of the eighteenth century, racial and class strife affected all classes of Haitian society. Virtually no group felt secure in its status. Hatred, fear, and envy dominated social relations and eventually erupted into a slave revolt that led to the expulsion of the whites and to the independence of the Haitian republic in 1804.

The stratification system shaped during the colonial period settled into two caste-like strata in the years following independence. The vacuum created by the exodus of the white elite was rapidly filled by the educated, wealthy, and powerful mulattoes. The black slaves gained both freedom and land, yet the majority continued to live outside the realm of national affairs as they had under the French. Consequently, Haitian values and institutions remained much the same as before independence. French language and culture were still emulated by the urban upper class, whereas the black peasant masses remained poor, rural, and powerless. Lighter skin was still an indicator of upper class status, and elite families were careful to preserve the color distinction through intermarriage.

Despite the politically favorable position of the mulatto elites, many Haitian leaders rose from the disadvantaged and darker lower classes. The most outstanding of these leaders was Jean-Jacques Dessalines (see ch. 3). All Haitians revere him as the national hero who established independence and effectively discouraged the return of white overlordship. The folk saying "Dieu, Dessalines, Duvalier" (literally, "God, Dessalines, Duvalier") expresses the loyalty Haitians feel towards the country's first president. Historians have described him as an illiterate man who hated whites and persecuted mulattoes: nevertheless, he equated being black with being Haitian and engendered national pride within the world's first black republic. His rule emphasized absolutism, authority, and a strong military ethic, and these values were still evident in 1972. The term "Dessalinian" has evolved to describe certain personality traits and indicates the respect and admiration accorded the individual manifesting these traits.

For the first hundred years of its independence Haiti remained one of the most isolated states in the hemisphere. Except for continued contact with France, there was little foreign cultural input, and few foreigners intermarried with Haitians. The preexisting fissures between the peasantry and the elite deepened. The hatred and mistrust that had characterized relationships between whites and nonwhites came to exist between mulattoes and blacks as the divergent lifestyles solidified.

The second important period of social history was the American occupation (1915–34). For the first time in over a hundred years, Haitians found themselves under the political jurisdiction of a white foreign power. The nineteen years of occupation had several effects on the class structure. The United States Marines and the supremacy of the occupation forces helped to strengthen both the value given militarism in government and the military ethic initiated under Dessalines. More importantly, the color stratification system was reinforced and the inherent racial prejudices of both countries were brought to the fore. The white administrators were both envied and resented for their light skin.

Although the American occupation forces supported the mulatto elites for government positions, they tended to treat the upper class as social inferiors. Furthermore, they introduced cultural influences that clashed with traditional Haitian values and presented alternative lifestyles. New educational and occupational opportunities opened up as a consequence of the occupation, and these fostered an incipient middle class. Finally, appreciable numbers of lighter skinned Haitians of lower class status were born during the United States occupation, thus creating a second mulatto group. When they reached maturity, these lighter skinned individuals found the opportunities for economic and social betterment more readily available than did their darker contemporaries.

The third period, beginning with the revolution of 1946, was in part a reaction to the American occupation. This era brought the most radical change to the traditional stratification system. The backlash of antiwhite sentiment that followed the American occupation was accompanied by a rise in black consciousness and an awareness of Haiti's African heritage among the educated and progressive. The new wave of black nationalism was strikingly reflected in artistic and intellectual endeavor (see ch. 6). The revolution was also experienced at the political and social levels, as educated and experienced blacks from lower and middle class origins emerged to fill the presidency and other important government posts. Under the influence of these men the middle class grew in numbers and strength, their social status paralleling the growing power of the government.

Upper Class

The Haitian upper class traditionally constituted less than 10 percent of the total population and in 1972 composed from 2 to 5 percent. In the past it existed as the elite of a closed, caste-like society. Social position was determined by birth, and class solidarity was reinforced by traditional values and marriage within the group. This fragment of the society was cosmopolitan and possessed education, wealth, and social prestige. It directed the destiny of the country and that of the peasant mass below. The criteria that distinguished elite status were economic, social, physical, and geographic.

A prestigious occupation and relative wealth historically characterized the elite's economic position. The elite disdained manual labor, industry, and commerce in favor of the more gentlemanly professions of law, medicine, and architecture. The elite woman never worked, devoting all her time to home and family. In sharp contrast to other Latin American countries, the Republic of Haiti has not had a landed oligarchy. A few wealthy citizens have owned homes in the country, but the land itself has belonged to the peasant since the days of Dessalines. Property ownership has existed, but it was urban land that brought in the rental income.

Traditional elite status presupposed descent from freed mulattoes followed by several generations of legal marriage. The highest elite traced their ancestry to the famous "Two Hundred Families" of revolutionary times. Class solidarity was rooted in a strong family system, blood relationships, and common heritage. The interlocking family ties were carried to such an extent that all elite appeared to be related. The elite adopted the French social institutions and exhibited extreme francophile attitudes, manifesting elegant deportment, fiery patriotism, and European savoir faire.

Light skin was highly prized and was accompanied by the notion of the superior intelligence of the white race. On the other hand, the prejudice lodged against the black peasants was far more cultural than racial in nature. Rural dwellers exhibited the characteristics that the elites found most degrading about their country—illiteracy, poverty, slave heritage, belief in voodoo, and a lack of cultural refinement, that is, French culture. It was practically impossible for someone of humble origin to move up through the society but, providing he could adopt the other requirements for social acceptance, he was not denied elite status because of his blackness.

A final determinant of elite status was geographic. From the earliest days of the republic the elite formed an exclusively urban enclave in the predominantly rural society. There were few wealthy landowners among the elite, and the majority of the land was left to the peasants. The geographic split enhanced the cultural differences between the elites and the masses, keeping the former in the mainstream of national and world trends at the expense of rural isolation.

In the past few decades, however, there has been a marked relaxation of social boundaries as a result of the weakening position of the elites. In the 1960s and early 1970s the elite was still considered the paragon of Haitian society, although political persecution and extensive emigration had undermined the significance of the traditional elite. Their political power was rapidly declining, and their social and economic position was weakening. As a consequence, this stratum is no longer recognizable as an elite caste. It has opened into an upper class composed of the elite and nonelite elements sharing a similar standard of living and prestige but not a common social life.

The criteria for upper class status reflect the change in its composition. Increased immigration from Europe and intermarriage with foreigners has brought German, Danish, and Syrian surnames to rosters once exclusively French. Broader opportunities for education and wealth have introduced individuals of humbler origin into the ranks of the upper class. The value assigned to commercial activity increased, and enterprising persons of nonelite status have moved upward through wealth accrued in industry or the export-import business. Many members of the traditional elite, faced with economic ruin, have been forced into commercial enterprises despite social taboos concerning manual labor. Wealth, always vital in maintaining a high standard of living, has done much to weaken the color barrier and raise personal status. A famous Haitian proverb expresses it—"The rich black is a mulatto; the poor mulatto is a black." Women, foreigners, and blacks have found more career opportunities than did their forebears. In addition to receiving the vote and certain property rights, it is now common for upper class women to be employed, especially as bilingual secretaries.

For members of the upper class, the family has remained the focal point for love and loyalty. Social life revolves around an extended kinship system and interaction through upper class social clubs. Norms encouraging intraclass marriage have appreciably weakened, however.

Financial security has become as attractive a quality in a potential mate as light skin and family background once were, and members of the elite have intermarried with wealthy nonelites or foreigners. Haitian men studying abroad exhibit a distinct preference for white women of European extraction and often make matches abroad.

Although many norms have been relaxed to broaden the base of upper class membership, other standards have been maintained and even reinforced. The value of French culture, language, Roman Catholicism, and education has remained constant. Individuals aspiring to high status must adopt these standards and emulate the life-styles and customs of the traditional elite. Despite the increase in black consciousness in the arts, little genuine affinity with Africa is felt among the upper class; the psychological and cultural ties remain with France. Moreover, as French culture is found only in the urban areas, the upper class has remained concentrated in the cities, thus reinforcing the rural-urban dichotomy.

Middle Stratum

There was little room for a middle class in the two-caste system existing in Haiti before the twentieth century. Anthropologists conducting studies as late as 1940 described the elite and the masses and make only casual reference to a middle sector. They portrayed it as being neither elite nor mass and neither distinct nor functional as a separate class. Individuals of this category were found to be urban, literate, legally married, and regularly employed, but having little effect on the national society. They were upwardly mobile and were considered to be aspirants to elite status who did not reach their goal.

The middle stratum has become more sharply defined since the 1940s because of changes that occurred during the American occupation and thereafter. Educational change in the 1920s, the upsurge in black consciousness, and the wave of industrialization and economic prosperity that followed the wars, resulted in the strengthening of the middle stratum. It has continued to grow in numbers and political power; the regime of former President François Duvalier reflected his middle class origins through numerous political appointments.

The middle stratum is still a residual segment caught between the upper and lower classes and constitutes only 2 to 4 percent of the entire population. It is culturally ambivalent and insecure, a factor that makes it a suspicious and sensitive group. Class solidarity and identity are virtually nonexistent, as are common class values and traditions. It remains an essentially urban catchall category. The majority of its members is concentrated in the capital, is of provincial or foreign extraction, and includes Syrian, Lebanese, Corsican, and some Europeans; yet a great many are also found in the smaller provincial towns.

The chief distinctions between the middle class and the lower class are economic and cultural. Criteria for membership include a non-manual occupation, a moderate income, education, and a mastery of French. More than half the middle class is dependent upon the government for its occupational security. The other half is variously employed as professionals, businessmen, shopkeepers, and teachers. Regardless of the amount of income or how it is earned, members of this class generally live beyond their economic means.

Family heritage and color are of less importance among members of the middle stratum than among their upper class contemporaries. Their marriage and family patterns are more flexible, allowing them to choose spouses from other classes. Middle class Haitians are upwardly mobile, as are their children, and they perceive education and urban residence as two essential keys to achieving higher status. They attempt to emulate the lifestyles of the elite, while resenting their social prestige and light skin color.

Lower Class

Urban Lower Class

The urban lower class constitutes about 6 percent of the total population and about half the urban population. It is concentrated in Port-au-Prince and the other coastal towns. (Because towns of the interior have a much more rural orientation, their residents are classified with the peasantry.) The urban lower class has grown in the last few years because of increased migration from the countryside. Realizing that moving to the city is the only viable means of upward mobility, these rural individuals have come in search of education for their children and employment for themselves.

Within the urban lower class there are several strata, all dependent upon the status criteria of regular employment. Jobs are scarce within this category because there is little industry to absorb the burgeoning migration; consequently, there is much unemployment or marginal employment. The service sector is taken from this group, comprising domestics, shoe shiners, and day laborers. Others are self-employed as shopkeepers, artisans, lottery ticket vendors, and market women.

The urban lower class displays social heterogeneity and a lack of class consciousness. They are a group whose orientation is changing from a rural to an urban way of life, and they still manifest many of their peasant characteristics. There are higher percentages of legal unions, strict Roman Catholics, and French-speakers than in the rural areas. Most members of this group display a preference for speaking Creole, and common law marriage and voodoo are still prevalent.

The political nature and strength of the urban lower class is subject to debate. Both labor and communist movements draw from this stratum, although the great majority identified with François Duvalier who recruited his militia from their ranks. Nevertheless, members within this group are subject to political manipulation by those more powerful than they. Their degree of political articulateness and their ability to effect economic reform has not been determined.

One of the outstanding characteristics of this group is their pre-occupation with educating their children. Despite economic hardships for their parents, a real effort is made to keep these children in school for the duration of the official six-year curriculum. A significant and growing percentage of the urban lower class is Protestant, perhaps because of the educational facilities provided by the Protestant groups. Through education and through political participation, some of the more ambitious individuals in this stratum are achieving mobility into the middle class.

Peasants

At the bottom of the social ladder, constituting 88 percent of the population, are the peasants. Of these only about 5 percent are relatively well off and merit the Creole distinction of *gros habitant* or *gros neg* (expressions for rural persons of wealth and power). The *gros habitant* subclass derives its status from its large landholdings and leadership positions within the community. In spite of greater wealth, this group is categorized with the peasants for several reasons. First, the *gros habitants* identify with the rural masses much more than they do with the urban classes. Although they may have absolute political, social, and economic control within their area, their status is regional, and they wield no power on a national level. In contrast to urban dwellers, this group does not rely on a cash income to maintain a certain lifestyle, and it possesses few, if any, modern conveniences.

The status of these individuals is related to their place in the rural economy and in local politics. In addition to possessing more land, the *gros habitants* may bring in more income by renting oxen or by conducting a local business, such as a coffee or corn mill. They are also in a position to hire day laborers and specialize in certain crops. The *gros habitant* manifests his wealth by having a larger home or more common-law wives than his poorer neighbors. He is careful not to appear too prosperous, however, for he then may become the target of black-magic spells cast by jealous peasants. Politically, the *gros habitant* controls rural Haiti. Many become the *chef de section* (sheriff) of their community and serve as a liaison between the national and local governments.

Despite their rural orientation *gros habitants* are not unaware of the city, and many of its members have urban goals. The degree of adult education may range from complete illiteracy to a few years of primary education, yet the children of upper class peasants may be enrolled in urban schools. The more ambitious of these children may remain in the city and thus provide a primary source for the incipient middle class.

On the national level Haitian peasants are politically impotent, economically substandard, and socially ostracized; yet the other 17 percent of the Haitian population is dependent upon them. Not only is the country's economy almost entirely dependent upon the export crops that the peasants produce, but also the world's image of Haitian folk customs, religion, and language is based on the African slave heritage. On the other hand, the peasant is not dependent upon the activities of the rest of the population for his existence. He consumes little that he does not produce himself and is the most self-sufficient member of the society.

The lifestyle of the rural Haitian has remained virtually unchanged throughout the history of the republic. His technology has not evolved much beyond that of his African ancestors, and the social structure of his community is reminiscent of the slave society. Customs may vary from region to region, but generally speaking the peasant's portrait remains the same: his language is Creole; his religion is voodoo; his marriages are common law; and his value system and livelihood are based on the land.

Unlike peasants in most of Latin America, the majority of rural Haitians have owned their land since independence in the early nineteenth century. Throughout the years this pattern has remained fairly stable despite the increased pressure and excessive fragmentation accompanying population growth. Land is the most valuable rural commodity, and the peasant and his family will go to great lengths to accumulate a few more acres. His family will aid him financially and give him moral support by participating in voodoo ceremonies to gain the favor of the local gods and family spirits. The desire for property is not likely to decrease in the future, as it is propagated within the family, attached to other positive values, and reinforced by proverbs and songs.

Nevertheless, there is some evidence that family units in the northwest are breaking down because of the difficulties in the struggle for existence. Elder members of the community express an unwillingness to part with their land, thus forcing the younger members to seek a livelihood elsewhere. This in turn is breaking down the static condition that grew out of an immobile slave society. Some landless individuals may resort to sharecropping, the lowest status occupation for a rural resident, whereas others may effect the move to an urban center in the hope of improving their lot in the city.

Peasants within an average fifty- to 100-member community are a closely knit group and are often interrelated. In this and other ways their life styles bear a striking resemblance to African social patterns. Men may have several common-law wives living in relative proximity to one another. Although monogamous legal marriage is the ideal, common-law marriage is the rule and is not censured by the community. Because of the character of marital unions, the resultant family is centered on the mother's permanent presence and stability.

The sense of cooperation and togetherness within the community is reinforced by the prestige of the eldest male family member and by the household gods, as well as through the *combite*. The *combite* is an agricultural mutual aid society whose basic purpose is the communal cultivation of crops (see ch. 8). It encompasses all adult males and combines the practical and utilitarian aspects of a communal work society with the recreational and ceremonial aspects of a social club.

The peasant woman also plays a prominent role in the economic activities of rural Haiti. Her work and social life are combined in the market system in which she—not the male—is the key figure. Any profit or accumulation of capital will be used in a number of ways. If it is not used to buy more land, it may be invested in sweets or soft drinks to be resold at a public function. If the peasant family is upwardly mobile, the extra income may be used to educate children. Because of her status as a link between the rural community and the urban market, the peasant woman is an important instrument in potential modernization.

RELIGION

Roman Catholicism

A popular Haitian folk expression claims that "Haiti is 90 percent Catholic and 100 percent voodoo." Although Roman Catholicism has been the official religion, it has never been a prominent influence outside the urban areas. Only about one-third of the 90 percent is practicing and active. The other two-thirds are peasants who practice their own brand of folk Catholicism heavily laced with voodooism.

Catholicism did not penetrate French colonial Haiti to the same degree it did the Spanish colonies, largely because of the attitude of the colonials. The buccaneers and planters were chiefly interested in enriching themselves and were unconcerned with making converts among their slaves. They were indifferent and insolent towards the church and regarded the priests working among the slave masses as a potentially subversive force. The Vatican became disillusioned, first with the attitude of the French colonials and later with that of the new republic. (The Constitution of 1805 had separated church and state and had declared marriage to be a civil rather than a religious contract.) For fifty-five years after independence no priest entered Haiti.

Nevertheless, for the newly installed mulatto elite, Catholicism was an integral part of the French culture that they adopted. They officially reinstated Catholicism as the national religion with the Concordat of 1860 and welcomed the French and Belgian priests whose life-style and values were so similar to their own. It was too late for the Roman Catholic Church to develop into a powerful or wealthy institution, however. The land—often a source of church revenue in Latin America—had already been apportioned to the peasants. The elite themselves retained the nonchalant attitudes of the colonial planters and, although anxious to set a good example, exerted no social pressure to attend mass. For the elite, and later the upwardly mobile middle class, the church was a symbol of their link with the outside world and a bulwark against the voodoo of the black masses.

Voodoo flourished during the period of isolation (1805-60), and became inextricably fused to Catholicism. The Haitian peasant came to regard the two as interwoven and inseparable and considered himself a member of both religions. The Concordat of 1860 provided for parochial organization and an annual government subsidy, but it made no mention of the complications voodoo presented for the incoming clergy.

The majority of priests have been French-speaking Europeans who confronted a profound cultural gap between themselves and their rural parishioners. Roman Catholic values were respected by the peasants, but actual compliance with these norms—such as legal monogamous marriage—was sporadic. The expense of dressing oneself for mass or preparing for a church wedding or other rite was often prohibitive for the average peasant. Consequently, Catholicism and the priests came to be associated with the elite and the *gros habitants* who could afford to participate fully in church activities. Finally, and most importantly, the peasants felt that for all practical purposes they were already Roman Catholic. They possessed neither the value orientation nor the religious sophistication to comprehend the theological arguments against voodoo.

Whereas the church has been openly favored by the elite and taken for granted by the peasants, it has been opposed or deemphasized by black nationalists. They associated the European-born priests with exploitation and cultural imperialism, fearing the ultimate aim of the clergy was reunification with France and sublimation of Haitian values and culture, particularly voodoo. The conservative and paternalistic attitude of many priests towards poorer Haitians discouraged the more progressive and educated nationalists. The hierarchical, centralized organization of the church was thought to lend itself to political organization and was consequently feared by those in power. President François Duvalier exemplified this negative attitude, and during much of his time in office he kept a running battle going with the Roman Catholic clergy. His opposition culminated in the expulsion of several provincial bishops and the archbishop of Port-au-Prince and eventually in his own excommunication by the Vatican.

Owing to the controversial position of the church in some sectors of the Haitian society, many priests are striving to reorient and redirect the church and its values. They have begun to take a more practical attitude toward voodoo and its believers and the position of the church in a poor community. More priests are becoming interested in the peasant and are moving from the domain of the urban upper class to the countryside. More Roman Catholic vocational training centers, hospitals, and rural schools have been the result of their efforts. An increasing number of priests are Haitian-born and, as of 1972, the archbishop was Haitian.

Voodoo

Voodoo is the living religion of the Haitian masses, although it is not officially recognized and is denigrated by the upper classes. As do all religions, it encompasses a set of beliefs and practices dealing with the spiritual forces of the universe and serves as an intermediary between these forces and mankind. It lacks a formal theology, printed scriptures, a hierarchical clergy, and a system of catechism. Rather, it is an informal religion of action, created by and suited to the rural life of the peasant. It functions as a spiritual release, a vehicle for socializing and recreation, and a loose form of social control.

The word voodoo comes from the Dahomean term meaning "god," but the religion itself cannot be identified with a particular tribe. It is an amalgam not only of African beliefs but also of certain Roman Catholic practices. It began to emerge in the years between 1730 and 1790 when the importation of slaves was at its zenith. The traditional African religious concepts it incorporated included invocation and placation of numerous spirits or gods, water rites, magic, cults of the dead, music, and dance. The dance was the most important of the early elements, for it served as a nucleus to unify the slaves under the auspices of entertainment and religion. This seemingly harmless outlet actually provided an important means of communication for the discontent that erupted into the slave rebellion. During the revolution voodoo supplied vital moral support, as well as special charms that purportedly made the wearer invulnerable to bullets.

Voodoo was suppressed under the first three rulers because of its potential for sedition. When the mulatto elite presidents rose to power they did not deign to recognize voodoo. During these years voodoo became diffused throughout the society, developing to the form that presently exists. In the years since the mid-nineteenth century there have been a few efforts by the Roman Catholic clergy and the elite to expunge voodoo and its influence, but these have been completely unsuccessful. Until the François Duvalier regime, the governments chose either to ignore it or to disdain it. Duvalier adopted a new stance and openly favored voodoo. He used it effectively to buttress his regime among the lower class. As he always wore a dark suit and talked in a low key, many peasants took him to be the living personification of Baron Samedi—a voodoo god characterized as a nineteenth century undertaker. François Duvalier retained many voodoo priests as advisers and elevated one priest to the position of secretary of state.

Voodoo is based on a belief in the Christian God and lesser Haitian and African deities, called *loa*. God is ultimately good and omnipotent but is conceived to be rather remote and not to be bothered with the small details of everyday human existence. This is the realm of

51

the *loa*, who are consequently closer to the Haitian peasant. The *loa* possess the same desires and weaknesses as do mankind. As neither man nor *loa* are entirely good or bad, sin and moral law are not dictated by the gods and are not a part of voodoo. There are hundreds of these gods, and some are directly linked to Roman Catholic saints through a similarity in characteristics or physical appearance.

Possession is one of the most vital aspects of voodoo. It occurs at public religious gatherings when a participant feels himself to be entered—influenced or controlled—by one of the *loa*. At such times the individual personality becomes subverted, and the possessed manifests the characteristics of the deity. Under the influence of the snake god, for example, a man may seem to glide up a tree in serpentine fashion in apparent defiance of the laws of gravity. When an individual is first "mounted" by a *loa*, be becomes his "horse," or servant and is baptised to solidify the relationship. Throughout his lifetime, the individual will pay particular allegiance and homage to that god. Only at death is the *loa* removed so that the man's soul may ascend to God—the Christian God.

Possession is a profound experience because it is believed to be the revelation of divine will of the *loa* through the medium of the common man. Rural Haitians accept it, and those possessed by it, as a normal part of the community's religious life. Peasants welcome the experience and express neither surprise nor fear if a fellow dancer suddenly sheds his own personality for that of a *loa*. Although possession is a fairly common occurrence, its frequency does not diminish its prestige or that of the individual possessed. After an individual is mounted by a *loa*, he is treated with deference and respect by other community members.

The priests and priestesses of voodoo—*houngans* and *mambos*, respectively—receive their training as apprentices. There is no hierarchy, and each priest informally establishes himself in an area, his reputation and prestige growing with his proven effectiveness as curer and diviner. The *houngan* and *mambo* more closely resemble medicine men than they do Roman Catholic priests. Their duties include cures and divination, in addition to acting as officiant at voodoo services. The majority have lives outside their religious calling and are full, if not prominent, participants in the community affairs. They are highly respected members of their society and often rise to a position of political eminence.

The rites and services are based to a large extent on the Roman Catholic mass. The ritual encompasses benedictions, genuflections, and responses. It is conducted within a special building decorated with images of saints identified with the *loa*. The service itself is entirely religious and dedicated to pacifying or gratifying certain gods. The service is not held on a regular basis but as the need arises. It is attended by family members and is followed by a dance, which is a community affair.

The dance serves both a social and religious purpose (see ch. 5). Friends come to exchange gossip and to enjoy dancing. Nevertheless, there is a religious undercurrent throughout, and the eventual outcome is a religious experience. Both the dancing and singing have sacred themes, and the drum itself is a sacred object. Inspired by the drumbeat, a believer may become possessed by one of the *loa*.

The Roman Catholic Church has had a greater influence on the cult of the dead than on any other element of voodoo. In the preparation of the corpse, the wake that follows, the burial in consecrated ground, and the concern for the spiritual peace of the deceased the practices closely resemble those of Roman Catholicism. Contrary to Christian beliefs, however, it is thought that the spirit retains worldly powers after death and continues to play an important role in the ongoing lives of his family. Should they be neglectful or disrespectful, he may possess and persecute the offender, often to the point of death. Consequently, peasants take utmost precaution in revering and attending their dead.

Certain magical beliefs and practices are closely intertwined with voodoo. A *houngan* may prepare a cure for a sick follower, but he will not participate in black magic—the practice that may bring harm to another. This is the realm of the *bocor*, or sorcerer. Like the priests, the reputation of the *bocor* rests on the exhibition of his powers. Occasionally he is engaged by a jealous peasant to cast a spell on a more prosperous neighbor; but more typically his magic is in the form of charms. These are worn for good luck or protection against the evil eye or other evils—such as flying bullets—or as an amulet to ward off disease.

Voodoo is still one of the strongest influences in rural Haiti. It serves to enhance family solidarity on the one hand, whereas on the other it enhances the mistrust of those outside the kin group. It exercises a form of local social control and organization through common belief and participation in voodoo rites. On the national level the low status of voodoo and its exclusive nature—as opposed to the international character of Roman Catholicism and Protestantism—have served to reinforce the isolation of the peasant believers. Because of its magic and dancing, it is effective for releasing aggression and frustration, as well as for providing entertainment and recreation. Finally, it provides the peasant with a workable explanation of his universe and gives him meaning and direction.

Protestantism

Protestantism is the third religion in Haiti and estimates of its strength vary from 10 to 30 percent of the total population. It was introduced in the mid-1800s by American missionaries who concentrated their efforts mainly among the lower class. A few peasants were converted to the evangelical and fundamentalist denominations because of similarities to the emotional form of worship and the possession of voodoo. Protestantism did not flourish in rural areas, however, because it could not coexist with voodoo. The Protestant clergy encouraged education and economic development. They viewed voodoo and its beliefs as a temporary opiate that served to reinforce the peasants' low status.

Although Roman Catholicism has always been the religion of the elite, the Protestant Episcopal Church has also held appeal for the upper stratum. It was introduced in 1861 by black slaves emigrating from the United States. Some of the elite traditionally resented the Roman Catholic Church, partially because the services were not held in French, and they regarded Episcopalianism simply as Roman Catholicism practiced in their language. Through its foothold among the elite and through the efforts of missionaries in the rural areas, the Protestant Episcopal Church rose to be the most powerful Protestant denomination in Haiti. Leadership emphasis has been transferred from the United States, and today most of the clergy are native Haitians. Many organizations and facilities have stemmed from the Protestant Episcopal Church, among them the Boy Scouts and educational programs.

Numerous Protestant denominations, including Seventh Day Adventists, Methodists, Presbyterians, and Baptists, have sent missionaries to the country. They tend to take on a uniquely Haitian character with the passage of years. Some Protestant sects have been backed by small groups or by individuals.

In the last few years there has been a rapid growth of Protestantism, stemming from the efforts of the clergy and the changing attitudes among the lower classes. As of the early 1970s, few rural towns were without their own Protestant church. The clergy have made practical and much needed improvements through schools, clinics, and cooperatives. Their focus is on Creole rather than French. Their schools are free, and the programs are adapted to the lives of the lower class. They compete with the Roman Catholic clergy by performing marriages and baptisms gratis, and they live in the rural areas that may be visited by a Catholic priest only twice a year. Many Protestant denominations are particularly well entrenched in some of the lower class slums around Port-au-Prince. The converts are zealous and upwardly mobile, and many are strongly antivoodoo.

LANGUAGES

Haiti has two national languages. Creole is the language of the common people but is understood and spoken throughout the society. French is the official national language and is understood and spoken only by upper and middle class urbanites. The differences in prestige, usage, and governmental policy surrounding the two languages highlight the polarity of the society and offer a partial explanation for the continuing isolation of 90 percent of the population.

Linguists have identified several factors influencing the users and usages of Creole and French. Approximately 7 percent of the population is bilingual, and the rest are monolingual in Creole. For this 7 percent, the two languages are used side by side and are frequently interchangeable within a sentence. French is always used in formal public occasions and is preferred in formal private situations as well. In informal situations, both public and private, Creole predominates. In addition to these social contexts, personality differences and change of style or mood will determine which language the speaker employs. A more relaxed and progressive bilingual indicates his identification with the black consciousness and the native culture through the usage of Creole, whereas a more conservative individual or a member of the rising middle class may insist on French in all situations.

The legendary stories attached to the origins of Creole reflect the deprecatory attitude manifested by most Haitians. Until recently, it was felt that Creole arose as a corrupted, Africanized version of French during the early years of the slave trade in Haiti. Settlers supposedly simplified their language to facilitate comprehension by slaves, who in turn supplied West African grammar. The result was the pidgin French of the lower class, which was considered a patois without the rights or status of a separate language.

Although this theory has some basis in fact, most linguists now consider Creole a full-fledged language arising from the French maritime trade dialect existing prior to colonization but characterized by the syntax of West African tribal languages. The striking similarities of the Caribbean Creole dialects would indicate that Creole did not develop in an insular fashion in each colony. It was an amalgam of the dialects of several French provinces, and it served as the lingua franca for whites and blacks in the slave collecting centers in Africa and in the French colonies alike.

The use of French and Creole during the colonial and independence period set speech patterns and attitudes for the next century. French was established as the language of culture and refinement, and it was spoken only by whites and educated mulatto freedmen. When the slaves became free, the greatest barrier between the various classes of colored peoples was broken down, and all Haitians became legally equal. Thus, the maintenance of the French language and life-style became a vital distinction between the two groups and a necessary means of ensuring the mulattoes' superior status over the former slaves.

Traditional attitudes towards Creole began to change during the twentieth century. The first attempt at a Creole text appeared in 1925 and the first Creole newspaper, in 1943. The black consciousness and nationalistic movements have always been tied to the desire to extend Creole usage, and social protest literature has used the peasant's language for both practical and ideological reasons. There was, however, no official reference to Creole until 1957. The constitution of that year stated that Creole would be recommended over French where there was insufficient knowledge of the latter. In 1969 a law was passed acknowledging the existence of Creole and granting it legal status; it could be used in Congress, law courts, and clubs but not in accredited educational institutions.

CHAPTER 5

LIVING CONDITIONS

Living conditions in Haiti form a distinctive pattern, somewhat different from that found elsewhere in Latin America. In other countries, the conditions prevailing in urban localities differ sharply from the simpler ones found in the countryside. In Haiti, the distinction is between the conditions under which the mulatto elite live and those experienced by the Negro majority. In other countries the urban working-class people live more simply than the well-to-do, but their lives tend to be much more varied than those of country people. In Haiti the average urban worker's diet is better and his housing is somewhat inferior to that of the subsistence farmer, but low income, his lack of education, and the fact that in many instances he is a new arrival from the countryside prescribe for him living conditions that are otherwise not very different from those of the subsistence farmer. They have their origin in Africa; those of the elite are patterned after the way of life in Paris.

Almost all of the elite live in Port-au-Prince. There is no rural landholding aristocracy, and the relatively few well-to-do in the other urban localities do not constitute an identifiable provincial elite. In Port-au-Prince there are the private clubs, the French boutiques, the well-stocked markets, most of the limited theatrical fare that the country has to offer, and the small private hospitals that serve the elite and, to some extent, an emerging middle class that remains relatively far smaller than in most other countries of Latin America.

Sports play only a limited part in recreational life, although soccer is played in Port-au-Prince, and cockfighting is the national pastime. In very different forms, however, clubs are of unparalleled recreational importance to the elite and to peasants alike. For the elite, the private clubs in and around Port-au-Prince offer dances and banquets, as well as golf, tennis, and swimming. For the peasant, the house of the local voodoo priest serves a corresponding purpose. It is a kind of community center, and the voodoo rites have an importance that dwarfs in significance all other forms of recreation available to the peasant. Voodoo, moreover, is practiced in urban as well as rural localities and is scarcely less significant to the urban worker than to the subsistence farmer.

The concentration of power and wealth in Port-au-Prince results in a corresponding concentration of amenities and services. Over half of the medical personnel of all kinds practice in the capital. It has the country's most extensive water and electricity services and the only sewer service. It also has the comfortable modern or ornate Victorian homes of the elite, but much of its working-class population lives in jerry-built shacks without public services of any kind.

Rural housing tends to be somewhat better than that found in urban working-class districts. There is no electricity, however; and a near absence of sanitary facilities contributes to a general level of health that is among the lowest in the Americas. Peasants, like urban workers, dress simply in brightly colored cotton garments made at home from purchased cloth, but garments are few in number and more worn. The diet of urban workers is fairly adequate, but in the countryside it is so deficient both in quality and quantity that malnutrition is sometimes cited as the most serious of Haiti's many health problems. In the early 1970s, however, public and private programs in nutritional education were achieving considerable success.

DIET

As estimated in 1966 by the Food and Agriculture Organization of the United Nations, the Haitian daily per capita food consumption averaged 1,633 calories and forty-seven grams of protein. Higher and lower figures have been cited for approximately the same period, but all are well under the daily intake of 2,654 calories and sixty-eight grams of protein quoted by the Organization of American States (OAS) as the average for seventeen Latin American countries during the late 1960s. The Haitian diet, however, included a relatively high proportion of edible oils.

Nutritional deficiency in terms both of the quantity and variety of foods consumed is of such proportions that malnutrition may represent the country's most serious health hazard (see Health, this ch.). During the summer season when few crops are reaching maturity, country people can often afford no more than a single starchy meal per day, and some are said to subsist from time to time by eating mangoes and chewing on sugarcane.

Relatively little is known about the specific deficiencies. Vitamins, minerals, and other nutrients have been so seriously inadequate, however, that the height and weight as well as the health of much of the population have been adversely affected.

In order to combat this inadequacy, the government in 1962 established the Office of Nutrition, charged with responsibility for the study of nutritional problems and the formulation of solutions. A series of nutritional surveys was initiated, and by 1969 some fifteen public centers and an equal number of private units had been established. The annual cost of each center is no more than G5,000 to G10,000 (5 gourdes equal US$1), depending on the extent of community support. Their work is primarily educational, and it involves teaching rural people to upgrade the quality of their diets by such measures as the

58

increased use of dishes made from beans, corn, and other high-protein vegetables. The program is regarded as an effective one and has been praised as offering better long-run prospects than much more expensive food distribution undertakings.

According to the Haitian Statistical Institute, in 1960 some 71.2 percent of the estimated market value of all comestibles consumed consisted of fruit and vegetable produce. Stockraising represented 8 percent; poultry raising and apiculture, 1.4 percent; and fishing, a scanty 0.5 percent. Domestically processed food products represented 11 percent of the total cost, and the remaining 7.9 percent was in the form of edible imports.

The food crops most in demand are high in starch content. Of the eight principal crops, the tonnages produced in 1969 were highest for corn, followed in order by millet, manioc, rice, and bananas. Bread made from imported wheat is seldom eaten outside urban localities. Green vegetables grow well in Haiti, and a wide variety is available seasonally in Port-au-Prince. The acceptance of green vegetables in the countryside is limited, however, and even onions and tomatoes appear less frequently on rural tables than do the wild greens that are gathered. In addition, citrus fruits, avocados, breadfruit, and mangoes are eaten extensively. Mangoes are of particular importance because of their richness in vitamin A but are available only seasonally.

Because of their relatively high cost, beef and lamb are usually beyond the reach of most of the population; most of the meat consumed is in the form of locally slaughtered goat and pork. Many farmers keep a few chickens, but eggs and poultry are usually reserved for the urban market; during the late 1960s the annual per capita consumption of milk was less than ten quarts annually. Fish and shellfish abound, but are not popular outside Port-au-Prince. Canadian salt cod is probably the most widely accepted form of seafood.

Sugar is consumed in great quantities, much of it in the form of *rapadou*, a syrup produced in the refining process. It is also the base for *clairin*, the raw Haitian rum that is the most popular alcoholic beverage of the countryside. In addition, an undetermined but probably very large amount is consumed by chewing cane stalks taken from the field. For the Port-au-Prince elite, sweets and pastries are as important to the well-stocked buffet table as are ham and turkey.

The urban well-to-do have diets that are satisfactory both in quantity and variety. Even the working class, however, fares much better in urban than in rural localities. In a 1951 survey, the Haitain Statistical Institute found the daily caloric intake of a representative group of city workers to have averaged 2,450 calories daily; at the same time, the diet in the countryside was reported to average a daily intake of 1,471 calories. A similar survey conducted in 1966 by an unidentified organization found urban and rural caloric intakes to have been 2,100 and 1,600 calories, respectively. Urban-rural data are not available with respect to protein content, but the variety of meats available in urban markets coupled with the much greater urban purchasing power indicates a still greater balance in favor of the urban family. The pattern for consumption of fats and oils is different. The Haitian peasant who consumes little in the way of butter and cheese shares with his urban counterpart the custom of using a relatively large amount of oil in cooking.

In the countryside, the farmer rises at dawn to breakfast on a cup of strong, locally grown coffee, which is sometimes accompanied by a disk of sour bread baked from bitter manioc flour. A light luncheon is brought to him in the fields, and the principal meal of the day—a plate of rice and beans or some kind of stew—is eaten late in the afternoon, soon after his return from work. The poorest farm family is sometimes able to afford only a single meal a day, but etiquette dictates that food be served a visitor who arrives near mealtime.

The monotonous peasant diet contrasts with the diet enjoyed by the urban elite. The Creole cuisine has a variety and elegance unmatched in the Caribbean area and combines elements of French, African, and Spanish cookery. Among the Creole specialties are spiced shrimp, pheasant with orange sauce, green turtle steaks, wild duck, and hearts of palm salad. One of the most renowned of the many sauces is *ti malice*, an onion and herb concoction. Among the better known traditional Haitian dishes is *calalou*, a mixture of salt pork, crabmeat, pepper, onions, spinach, okra, and chili pepper. The ingredients are simmered for an hour or more and served with rice. Among the other traditional dishes are a preparation of grilled meat called *tassot* and a pudding made of grated sweet potato, figs, bananas, and seasoning.

DRESS

The clothing of the Haitians, both Negro and mulatto, is perhaps the most colorful worn in the Caribbean region. The urban mulatto elite dress with considerable elegance. The accent is on informality, although men are expected to wear coats and ties for dinner, and formal dress is worn in the exclusive clubs. Women wear shorts and slacks in the home and for recreation, but shorts are not seen on the streets of Port-au-Prince. The tropical-weight garments worn year around by the men and the brightly colored cottons of the women are cut according to European style; particularly popular are styles from France, where many of the elite were educated. There are numerous dressmakers in Port-au-Prince, and a variety of boutiques offer clothes designed by personnel purportedly trained in Paris.

Male city dwellers of the working class dress simply in light-weight shirts and trousers for everyday wear. Women wear simple wide-necked blouses and full skirts, often gathered at the waist with a sash; bandanas are standard headgear. There is no home weaving in either town or countryside, and much of the material purchased for dressmaking in the home is imported. Shortly after Alaska received statehood, one enterprising United States exporter found in Haiti a ready market for obsolete forty-eight-star flags as clothing material. Wardrobes are limited, but both sexes usually have clothing reserved for special occasions, and garments are usually neat and freshly laundered. Ordinances requiring the wearing of shoes in the larger urban centers are survivals of a regulation originated by Henry Christophe.

The dress of the country people who make up most of the population is similar to that of the urban working class, although older and less varied. Rural women also are fond of bright colors, and most of the clothing is made at home from purchased yard goods, which represent an important cost item in the rural budget (see Patterns of Living and Leisure, this ch.).

Both men and women customarily wear wide-brimmed straw hats at work in the fields, and adults as well as children invariably go barefoot or are shod in sandals fashioned at home of such materials as old automobile tires. Proper shoes are luxury items, and country folk going to Port-au-Prince are often seen carrying their footwear to the edge of the city.

HOUSING

The 1950 census counted some 693,000 housing units in the country. In 1972 this figure remained the most recent statistical figure available, but the pace of construction during the 1950s and 1960s had been slow, and in the early 1970s it appeared that housing starts had not kept pace with population growth. The 1950 census had resulted in a conclusion that 100,000 of the units in existence did not meet the basic conditions for habitation. In 1965 the Haitian Statistical Institute estimated that there was a housing shortage of 392,000 units. The estimate did not include an explanation of how the word *shortage* was defined. Squatter settlements proliferated around Port-au-Prince during the late 1960s, however; and the Inter-American Development Bank reported that early in the 1970s no more than one-fifth of the population could be considered adequately housed.

Some 80.5 percent of the units counted in 1950 were owner occupied, and 11 percent were rented. Many of the remainder were occupied by *gérants* (agents), occupants in both countryside and town who, for any of several reasons, resided in dwellings without paying rent. Owner occupancy was more common in country than in town. A 1949 survey of a Port-au-Prince working-class neighborhood found that 76 percent of the occupants were tenants. Land titles in Haiti are often not well established, and many of the owner-occupied dwellings are built on lands of uncertain title or on state-owned property for which rent is seldom charged.

Some 14.8 percent of the housing units counted in 1950 consisted of one room, 68.9 percent had two rooms, and only 3.5 percent had as many as four rooms. As defined in the census, hallways and utility areas, such as kitchens, bathrooms, and storage areas, were excluded. The houses were small by North American standards, but the proportion of one-room units was far smaller and the proportion of two-room units was much greater than the Latin American average. The one-room dwellings were found principally in urban localities where the housing unit was defined only as living space occupied by a family group. In urban Haiti, housing consists frequently of rooms in tenements or of squatter shacks.

The residences of the elite, for the most part located in Port-au-Prince and its more affluent suburbs, represent a mixture of the old and the new. The older dwellings are often frame or of limestone and have ornate gingerbread wood embellishments and ironwork filagree. The newer houses, suburban for the most part, are usually of stone or concrete construction and modernistic or European in style.

No quantitative data are available with respect to the materials used in housing construction, but a scattering of surveys indicates that in both the countryside and in working-class urban communities the most frequently encountered is *clissage* (wattle), which is usually— but not invariably—covered with a layer of mud or plaster and sometimes whitewashed. Limestone abounds in the country, and rural people often dig their own material for use in plastering the walls. Floors are usually of pounded earth, although cement or wood flooring is fairly common in urban localities. The roofs, usually gabled, are customarily either of thatched material or of sheet iron. The adobe walls and roofs of oval tile common to most of the Latin American countries are seldom encountered.

The stream of country people coming to Port-au-Prince during the years since World War II resulted in an occupany rate in dwelling units rising from 4.05 persons in 1950 to an estimated 6.1 in 1961. Makeshift homes, largely in squatter settlements, are fashioned of scrap materials selected at random. In some parts of the central city, the crowding in the early 1970s had grown so severe that the shanties were literally piled on top of one another.

Working-class furnishings are simple to an extreme. They consist of a few tables and chairs, which are often homemade, a cupboard, and one or two beds. In larger households, some of the younger members sleep on mats on the floor. Furnishings tend to be fewer in number in urban than in rural homes, possibly because of more effective tax collections in urban localities and the fact that there was at one time a tax levied on each piece of furniture.

Few dwellings are served by public utilities. According to a series of 1969 estimates by the Pan American Health Organization (PAHO), some 6.5 percent had access to piped water. This total included 44.9 percent of all houses in urban areas and 2.9 percent of all those in rural localities. About one in five had direct connections; the remainder were classified as having easy access to a public fountain. The PAHO also estimated that 18.5 percent of the urban homes had sewer connections.

Few of the urban and almost none of the rural housing units have electricity. International statistical summaries published in the early 1970s were able to quote only a 1949 survey that found 27.1 percent of the dwellings in Port-au-Prince to have electrical connections. In practice, however, a much larger proportion of the urban homes have gained uncertain access to electric current for many years. After dusk, in unlighted neighborhoods, bamboo poles with wires attached are hoisted by householders to powerlines in order to make an electrical contact and provide light. The number of dwellings is so considerable that in 1968 the loss of power in Port-au-Prince during peak consumption periods was estimated at more than 40 percent. To compensate for this attrition, each residential sector of the city was allotted a one-hour nightly blackout.

In the late 1960s and early 1970s a majority of the population relied for lighting on kerosine lamps, which were either homemade or of domestic manufacture. Water was obtained from streams or wells in the countryside. In the case of domestic households, some continued to rely on water vendors. A large proportion of the dwellings in Port-au-Prince had sewer connections or latrines, although many of the latter were simple pit privies. In other urban centers, however, there was probably considerable dependence on public toilets. Current statistics were not available, but in the late 1950s some 86 percent of the dwellings in a working-class neighborhood of Cap-Haïtien used public facilities. In rural localities, a few of the more substantial homes had outhouses, but probably a majority were without facilities of any sort.

Housing construction, an area of investment traditionally reserved to the small private sector of the economy, has been discouraged by a progressively rising cost in building materials coupled with a continuing shortage in both private saving and public investment directed toward new construction. In the early 1950s the regime of President Paul Magloire undertook several Port-au-Prince housing developments; they were initially conspicuously attractive but after a few years had suffered severe deterioration. Under President François Duvalier, the National Housing Office (Office National de Logement— ONL) was established in 1966, but the record of public housing during the 1960s was not impressive. The showcase project had been the Simone Duvalier project, which had involved the construction of some 1,000 units in 1964.

PATTERNS OF LIVING AND LEISURE

Holidays and Business Hours

Sunday is a day of rest, but Saturday is a regular business day. The Constitution of 1964 as amended in 1971 lists as national holidays:

Independence Day (January 1), Heroes' Day (January 2), Agriculture and Labor Day (May 1), Flag Day (May 18), National Sovereignty and Recognition Day (May 22), Birthday of the President for Life (June 22), Anniversary of the Battle of Vertierès and Armed Forces Day (November 18), and Discovery of Haiti Day (December 5). Religious holidays are: the moveable dates of Corpus Christi and the Ascension; and the Assumption (August 15), All Saints' Day (November 1), and Christmas (December 25). Pan American Day (April 14) and the Death of Dessalines (October 17) are holidays set by law.

Even in Port-au-Prince there is a wide variation in business times. Stores and offices open and close at varying hours, some occasionally remaining open until late in the evening. There is no regularly observed siesta at midday, but some establishments close for several hours during this period. In provincial towns, the irregularity of hours is more pronounced. In the smallest towns and in hamlets there are few business enterprises; the most important are the weekly open-air markets, which open soon after dawn and terminate when the wares have been sold or the flow of purchasers has ceased.

Social Activity

The manner in which leisure time is enjoyed in Haiti differs sharply from that encountered in most of the other countries of Latin America. The difference results from such factors as the predominantly rural character of the population, the breadth of the socioeconomic gulf between the mulatto elite and the remainder of the population, the extreme poverty of most of the people, and the pervasive influence of voodoo on all important aspects of the national life.

Sports do not have the recreational importance found elsewhere. Soccer games are scheduled regularly at the Sylvio Cator stadium in Port-au-Prince and are played in a few of the larger towns, but the progress of the teams is not followed with the fervor encountered in many other countries, and soccer is seldom played in the countryside. There are no other team sports of importance. There is no regular horseracing, and water sports have only limited popularity, although two fairly good artificial private beaches have been constructed within an hour's drive of Port-au-Prince. Tennis is available only at private clubs, and golf can be played only on a nine-hole course in the Port-au-Prince suburb of Pétionville.

The closest approach to a national sport is cockfighting. The encounters are staged informally throughout the country, but the best are those held regularly in Port-au-Prince at the Gaguère arena. Attended by people of all classes, the bouts evoke from spectators the frenzied enthusiasm that in other American countries is lavished on soccer or baseball.

Gambling plays an important part in the recreational life. Even the subsistence farmer occasionally makes a tiny wager on some game of chance. Tickets for the weekly lottery in Port-au-Prince are sold also in other urban centers. Casino gambling is available to the well-to-do in Port-au-Prince, and in 1972 plans had been made for a casino in the new resort complex on Tortue Island. Wagers are made on cockfights, in bezique and other card games, in dominoes, in a local dice game called *ouapi*, and in *wari*—a kind of draughts game of West African origin that is played in the capital but unknown in the countryside.

Private clubs play an important part in the recreational life of the urban working class as well as of the elite. A study in the late 1950s found that in a single working-class district of Cap-Haïtien there were seven clubs, including two operated by labor unions. For the urban poor as well as for the peasant in the countryside, a kind of club membership is provided by access to the voodoo center, which serves as a clubhouse, music hall, and theater combined.

Music and dancing are outlets of extreme importance to elite and peasant alike. Endowed with a sure sense of rhythm, even the Haitian child barely able to walk will spontaneously break into the dance on hearing the beat of a *méringue*.

The limited formal theatrical fare available consists principally of plays performed in French by a Port-au-Prince company, and dances and drumming performances by the Folklore Troupe of Haiti. Motion pictures are principally French films and North American offerings with dubbed soundtracks. Attendance is limited by the low average income as well as by the virtually complete absence of theaters in the countryside where most of the people live. In the mid-1960s the attendance rate was estimated at 0.3 performances per capita annually. Distribution of radio and television sets is also among the scantiest in Latin America.

All of this does not mean that the Haitian does not enjoy a relatively rich variety of recreational activities. A scattering of surveys suggests that the peasant as well as the urban working man devotes a proportion of his income to recreation that compares very favorably with that of people of corresponding income level in other Latin American countries. More important, the very fact of the extreme crowding of the countryside makes possible for the Haitian peasant a degree of community intercourse denied to people who live in more dispersed rural environments.

For its recreational value, the *combite* is of particular communal value. Essentially, the *combite* is a working party of neighbors assembled by the small farmer to help in needed tasks, which may involve reaping of a field or the raising of a dwelling. The volunteer workers are not paid, but they receive liberal amounts of food and drink while they engage in work that is accompanied by singing or the beating of drums. Work ends in midafternoon and the entertainment may include a dance that continues until late in the night. Where *combites* involve a great many workers, particularly in the north, the work may of itself become a contest; the participants divide into two teams and work in competition to determine which finishes first (see ch. 8).

The atomization of farms through inheritance has resulted in some decline in the *combite*. Moreover, the participants have tended increasingly to arrive late for work and to perform their jobs with less than extreme zeal. Because of the gradual extension into the hinterland of the cash as opposed to the barter economy, the cost of liquor and food involved represents an increasing part of the host's scanty income, and many farmers have chosen to engage the help of neighbors on a commercial basis. This change, however, has served to illustrate the extraordinary peasant ability to derive pleasure where he finds it. Where *combite* festivities have been replaced by commercial work groups, these elements also combine work with amusement. The groups are often regularly composed of teams that are identified by fanciful names. They are constituted along military and political lines and have presidents, officers, and soldiers who work at regularly assigned and specific tasks. Work is done in an atmosphere of conviviality not too different from that of the original *combite*, and the organization resembles a benevolent society in the sense that the farm of a disabled or ailing member is often cared for by his fellows.

All other forms of social activity are of far less significance than participation in voodoo rites to virtually all of the rural population and much of the urban working class. Voodoo is a serious matter—fashioned more in awe and fear than in fun—but the Haitian who is possessed by a spirit of the voodoo pantheon and who slithers, snakelike, up a tree is momentarily as completely freed from the immediate concerns of everyday life as are the natives of other American countries as they engage in cheering the winning goals in soccer. The voodoo ceremonies with their rituals, sacrifices, chants, libations, and dances are undeniably the high point in the day-to-day existences of most of the population of Haiti (see ch. 4).

The influence of voodoo on recreation and other phases of Haitian life is nowhere better exemplified than in the harvest festival that occurs, usually over a two-day period, in November. It is called the *manger-yam* (literally, "eat-yam"), a name derived from the significance of the yam as a dietary staple. Like harvest festivals throughout the world, it is a recreational high point in the year. *Manger-yam* is celebrated with feasting, libations, singing, and dancing. It is also, however, a voodoo rite, presided over by the voodoo priesthood and marked by incantations to the dead and to the voodoo spirits.

The nonsacred *bamboche* (literally, "a spree") is the customary means of family or community celebration of weddings, birthdays, and other ceremonial occasions. It is similar to voodoo assemblies but is not presided over by voodoo priests. Even wakes and funerals are occasions of social importance in which the departed is entertained by feasting and drinking of *clairin*, the performances of storytellers, and the playing of cards and other games.

Several annual occasions directly or indirectly related to the Christian religion are also festivals of importance. In the larger urban centers, Christmas is marked by stringing elaborate displays of lights, by singing and the music of orchestras, and by street dances. Preparations start early in December, and the festivities continue through the beginning of the New Year. Carnival brings work to a near halt during the three days preceding Ash Wednesday and is celebrated with parades, floats, ceremonial kings and queens, dances, and prizes. The concept of Carnival as a final celebration before the onset of the Lenten season of penance has been lost. Festivities continue to erupt on Lenten weekend evenings and reach their highest point during the final days of Holy Week. Special orchestral groups called *rara* bands (there are several ways of spelling the word), which have danced across the countryside throughout the season, converge on the larger urban centers, particularly the town of Léogâne, a few miles west of Port-au-Prince. The *rara* tradition derives from fifteenth- and sixteenth-century ceremonies in Europe that have long since been abandoned in their countries of origin.

Rara band leaders are accomplished dancers who wear elegant and sometimes costly costumes topped by towering headdresses of West African origin. When two bands meet, their leaders sometimes challenge one another to competitive dances. Near the town of Jérémie, *rara* festivities are associated with exhibitions by wrestlers, who sometimes are accompanied by their own musicians. Traditional personalities that appear as part of the functions include the juggler, the strong man, and the baton twirler. The most important of these is Monsieur Judas, an effigy of Judas Iscariot that is carried about from place to place during Holy Week. On Good Friday, the effigy is hidden and the community makes merry as it hurries about in search of the hiding place of the villain in order that the effigy be destroyed.

Haiti differs from the other Latin American states in the sense that local days of patron saints are seldom causes for celebration, although Saint Joseph's Day and Saint Anne's Day are noted in Port-au-Prince, Saint Pierre's Day is observed in Pétionville, and a few others are celebrated in major centers. The occasional Roman Catholic day of observation, however, is likely to have become obscured by festivities that have become inextricably mixed with those more concerned with the voodoo gods. Perhaps the best example of this mixing occurs in July at the village of Ville-Bonheur, where a celebration called the *saut d'eau* (waterfall) is observed. This celebration appears originally to have been set aside for Our Lady of Mount Carmel on July 16. In practice, it has become a celebration recalling the purported appearance of a miraculous virgin in a tree close to a waterfall. It is one of the major festivities in Haiti, one to which people come from great distances. It is, however, one in which Christianity is honored indiscriminately with the voodoo patheon.

Consumption Patterns

The composition of the Haitian demand for goods and services is strongly influenced by the low average cash income; in the late 1960s and early 1970s it was probably well under G400 a year. Miners and skilled factory workers could earn as much as G10 a day, and the minimum legal daily wage was G5. A maximum of 200,000 persons worked for wages, however, and the average for the self-employed workers in handicrafts and services activities was probably much lower (see ch. 2). A large majority of the labor force was made up of subsistence farmers who lived virtually outside the cash economy.

Specific data are scanty, but according to a government survey the proportion of disposable per capita income spent on food ranged irregularly, and within narrow margins of variation, between 57.4 percent of the total in 1950 and 56.1 percent in 1960. Scattered surveys, however, indicate that the poorest families spend nearly all of their income on food.

The pattern of food expenditure by urban families who are dependent primarily or entirely on their cash incomes is necessarily different from that of rural people who grow most of their own food and engage in barter for much of the remainder. Rural cash incomes are extremely low, however, and the proportion spent on food is not significantly lower than that spent by city dwellers. Amounts expended in the countryside on meat, dairy products, and green vegetables are negligible, but it was estimated by the United States Department of Agriculture that in the early 1970s the Haitian peasant spent as much as 20 percent of his cash income on soybean oil and other edible oils.

Clothing is the second expense in order of importance for rural families. An extensive 1954 survey of expenditure patterns involving rural families in twenty-four selected areas showed clothing to have represented 19 percent of all expenditures. It is probably somewhat lower in urban localities because of the higher average income and greater variety of goods and services available. The principal clothing item is yard goods for garments made in the home (see Dress, this ch.).

Housing is next in importance in urban localities, where many of the dwellings are rented. It is less important in the countryside, where a large majority of the people are owners of their simple dwellings (see Housing, this ch.). Cooking and eating utensils represent expenditures of appreciable importance in both country and town, but furniture is in large part homemade.

Miscellaneous expenses are few, particularly in the countryside. It is a measure of the low rural demand for miscellaneous items that country stores and markets rarely stock generally needed items, such as hammers and screwdrivers. Despite the low level of income, however, even the poorest Haitian is able to devote something to recreation. The expenditure may be only for a bottle of rum or for a contribution to a voodoo ceremony, but scattered urban and rural surveys conducted in the 1950s indicated that 4 to 5 percent of income was expended on recreation.

Few working-class families are able to amass savings, and many are forced to borrow periodically at very high rates of interest. In the rare instances where savings in any quantity are amassed, the money is seldom invested in a business enterprise. The Haitian peasant or worker tends to have a mistrust of mercantilism and prefers to devote his limited funds to the purchase of land or to the education of his children.

HEALTH

Administration of the Public Health Program

The public health program is a responsibility of the Secretariat of State for Public Health and Population. Administratively, the country is divided into a series of health districts, but in practice the administration tends to be centralized in Port-au-Prince. A health administrator in each of the districts is charged with medical supervision of the area, but most of these officials are physicians attached to the district hospitals who are for the most part concerned with medical practice and have little or no public health or administrative training. The facilities include the supervisory district hospitals, hospital-dispensaries, health centers, and rural clinics.

Public health costs are relatively high. Budget expenditures for public health as a proportion of all government expenditures rose irregularly from 11.2 percent for the total in 1964 to 13 percent in 1968. During the latter year, the proportion expended by Haiti ranked fourth among twenty countries counted in a PAHO survey. The estimated amount per capita expended for health (calculated at the equivalent of US$0.53) was the lowest among twenty-one Latin American countries surveyed by the PAHO.

Nearly all health work is at least in part government financed or sponsored. Even the Haitian Red Cross requires public financial assistance. Foreign assistance has also been important, particularly in the field of preventative medicine. The United States aid program has provided material help in the field of malaria eradication, and the World Health Organization (WHO) engaged in a successful joint program with the Haitian government in yaws eradication.

The Secretariat of State for Public Health and Population is responsible for a corps of sanitary engineers, who numbered fifty-six in 1968, but environmental sanitation construction projects are under other controls. Water supply for the Port-au-Prince metropolitan area is a responsibility of the Autonomous Metropolitan Potable Water Center (Centrale Autonome Métropolitaine d'Eau Potable—CAMEP). Elsewhere in the country, water supply responsibility rests with the Hydraulic Service of the Republic of Haiti (Service Hydraulique du Républic D'Haïti—SHRH), an agency of the Secretariat of State for

Public Works, Transportation and Communication. Within the SHRH, an agency called the Cooperative for Potable Water Supply to Communities of the Interior (Coopérative pour l'Alimentation en Eau Potable Pour les Comunités du Arrier-Pays—COALEP) provides installations for areas not able to finance the services. It depends on contributions from various public and private entities for its funds and for cooperation in the form of personnel and services.

Health Hazards and Preventive Medicine

Diagnosed cases of disease are reported from hospitals and outpatient facilities, but the records are not complete, and no exact listing on causes of morbidity and mortality are available. The Annual Report of the Public Health Service—a series later discontinued because of lack of funds—cited statistics deriving primarily from 1954. Analysis of these data led to the conclusion that less than half of the hospital and outpatient cases cited could be specifically identified with respect to the causes of the deaths and diseases involved. Another government publication, however, listed as the most important health hazards (in order of incidence) malaria, dermatosis, respiratory ailments, parasitic worms, and ulcers.

With the exception of malaria, the most serious health hazards do not correspond to those most frequently encountered in tropical climates. Rather, they are directly or indirectly conditioned by poor nutrition and poor personal hygiene. The death toll is particularly high among infants as well as among small children. During the 1960s infant mortality was estimated to be as high as 20 percent of live births, and mortality among the young between the ages of one and four years was thought to be as high as 25 percent.

As many as 15 percent of all infant deaths during the first eight weeks of life result from umbilical tetanus contracted as a consequence of the mother's ignorance of hygienic practices; kwashiorkor (a protein-deficiency disease) is widespread among young children. Children who survive infancy and early childhood suffer nutritional and hygienic deficiencies so weakening the constitution that as adults they have relatively little resistance to disease in general.

Malaria is the cause of few cases of hospitalization and death, but its debilitating effect on the population has been enormous. It is conjectured that malaria has been suffered at one time or another by nearly all of the three-quarters of the population living in malarial areas, which originally included all of the territory below elevations of 1,650 feet.

Malaria eradication is the responsibility of the National Malaria Eradication Service, which was founded by an agreement between the Haitian government, the WHO, and the PAHO with financial help from the United States aid program and the United Nations Children's Fund (UNICEF). A limited number of control measures were initiated in 1954, but full-scale activity did not commence until 1961. Initial activities, confined to house spraying, were supplemented during the late 1960s by distribution of antimalarial tablets throughout the malarial area. About 90 percent of the rural population appears to have taken the pills, a remarkably high acceptance ratio, and the government reported that the incidence of malaria had declined from 14 percent of the population in the affected areas in 1961 to 0.5 percent in 1969.

Tuberculosis ranks with malaria and malnutrition as the most serious of the health hazards. In the mid-1960s it was estimated that between 300 and 350 people per 100,000 of the population died annually as a consequence of the disease. Crowded and unsanitary housing combined with malnutrition and inadequate medical care have contributed to the severity of its effect. Between 1964 and 1969 the number of cases reported rose irregularly from 89.6 to 102.8 per 100,000 of the population. The apparent increase, however, probably reflected a more complete diagnosis and reporting of new cases. A vaccination program was initiated in 1951 for newborn babies in hospitals and for schoolchildren in major urban centers. The 1972 target for children aged five and under called for 250,000 vaccinations.

Yaws once rivaled or exceeded malaria in its severity as a health hazard, but it has virtually been eliminated. A conspicuous role in control of the disease was played by the late President Duvalier during his service in charge of the country's public health program immediately before his assumption of the presidency. The eradication program, which resulted in a decline in incidence from 1.7 million cases of yaws in 1950 to fewer than 100 reported in 1969, involved a house-to-house search for cases and the administration of penicillin to those found to be infected. It was estimated that 97 percent of the population was reached, and in 1970 it was possible for the government to report that some 100,000 disabled farmers had been able to return to their fields.

Parasitic infections plague children and adults alike. Roundworms and pinworms are common. Roundworm infection reaches a peak during the mango season when country people frequently eat unwashed fruit that has fallen to the ground. Hookworm is extremely widespread in the countryside where people walk barefoot over ground polluted by human excreta.

Typhoid fever is endemic, and epidemics occur frequently during the dry months. Between 1961 and 1968 the incidence of typhoid per 100,000 of the population increased from 6.2 to 33.1. The government, however, reported its hopes that improvement of the water supply, scheduled for the early 1970s, would reduce the death toll of typhoid by 60 percent and the toll of diarrhetic ailments by 40 percent.

Influenza-like infections occur in epidemic form, and bronchopneumonia, lobar pneumonia, and bronchitis cases are frequent and severe.

Reported cases of leprosy are few—only two new cases were reported in 1968—but the actual incidence is believed to be much higher. In 1968 there were 177 known active cases; of these, 157 were under control. Reported cases of syphilis declined from 5,201 in 1962 to 1,455 in 1969. An apparent sharp rise in incidence during the 1950s was probably the consequence of the decline in yaws, a disease with symptoms often so similar that many venereal cases were probably misdiagnosed as yaws.

Whooping cough and measles are common ailments among the young, and the former is a major cause for child mortality. Diphtheria and scarlet fever are apparently rare, possibly as a result of under-reporting. Jaundice and hepatitis are present, but their degree of incidence is unknown.

Neither heart disease nor cancer has been reported as a significant cause of death. They are of major importance in other Latin American countries, however, and they are believed to be responsible for many deaths in Haiti that go undiagnosed or are attributed to other causes, particularly in rural areas.

Although neither yellow fever nor smallpox has been reported since the 1930s, a campaign against smallpox has continued. Between 1962 and 1969 some 2.6 million persons were inoculated against smallpox, partly in conjunction with the activities of the mobile control teams engaged in the campaign against yaws. In 1970 it was predicted that 80 percent of the population would be inoculated by 1972. Dengue fever appears frequently, particularly in the vicinity of Cap-Haïtien, although eradication of the mosquito vector commenced in the early 1950s. North Americans residing in Haiti are reported to be particularly susceptible to the disease.

Medical Personnel and Facilities

Medical personnel and facilities of all kinds are relatively plentiful in Port-au-Prince and almost nonexistent in the countryside, where three-fourths or more of the population resides; their availability in provincial towns (*villes de province*) is between these two extremes. In the country as a whole, however, in all categories of personnel and facilities, the supply in relation to the size of the population is among the lowest in Latin America.

In 1969 some 361 physicians were practicing in Haiti, a ratio of about 0.7 per 10,000 of the population. Other data, for 1967, showed that 43 percent were engaged in general practice and that 13 percent were specialists in gynecology and obstetrics; 13 percent, in pediatrics; 11 percent, in internal medicine; and 7 percent, in surgery. The remainder specialized in psychiatry, radiology, pathology, and anesthesiology.

In 1969 there were ninety-six practicing dentists, a ratio of about 0.2 per 10,000 population. The figure is considerably lower than ones cited for earlier years but probably represents only more accurate reporting; of 144 dentists registered in 1960, for example, some 44 were found to have ceased practice or to have left the country. The 415 graduate nurses and 806 nursing auxiliaries reported in 1967 represented 0.9 and 1.7, respectively, per 1,000 population.

In the mid-1960s nearly two-thirds of the physicians and one-third of the dentists were employed by the public health service. Because of low public pay schedules, however, all or most worked in the public service only part time in order to reserve a portion of their time for private practice. Because a majority of the large hospitals and outpatient facilities were operated by the government, it is probable that a high proportion of both graduate and auxiliary nurses were also publicly employed.

In 1968 about 60 percent of the country's physicians practiced in Port-au-Prince and in nearby Pétionville, and most of the remainder were in the larger provincial towns. A majority of the dentists and nurses also practiced in the capital city.

Physicians are trained in a six-year course at the Faculty of Medicine and Pharmacy of the University of Haiti. The sixth year consists of an internship, and graduates are required to spend two years in rural practice or in residency in a hospital. In addition, many of the leading physicians and surgeons have received graduate training in France, the United States, or Canada. Dentists are also trained at the University of Haiti in the Faculty of Dentistry, which had operated as part of the Faculty of Medicine and Pharmacy before its establishment as a separate entity in 1950. Graduate nurses are trained in a three-year school maintained by the Secretariat of State for Public Health and Population in the Central Hospital of Port-au-Prince and in hospitals in Cap-Haïtien and Les Cayes. Nursing auxiliaries attend the National School of Nursing Auxiliaries, which was established by the secretariat in 1967.

The flight of trained medical personnel from Haiti had reached epidemic proportions in 1968, when a decree was issued prohibiting medical personnel from emigrating. The movement was motivated in considerable measure by the prospect of far better working conditions and salaries offered abroad. There was also a political motivation, which at least in part involved resentment over President Duvalier's imposition of an oath of loyalty to his government as a condition for obtaining a license to practice medicine.

During the 1950s it was estimated that the 200-plus graduates of the University of Haiti's medical faculty had been equaled by the number departing the country to practice in the United States, Canada, France, and the African nations. In the late 1960s it was estimated that as many as 500 Haitian doctors were living abroad, about 200 of them in the United States, and that there were more Haitian nurses in Canada than in Port-au-Prince. A 1960 survey had found that the 100 dentists practicing in Haiti were offset by twenty-three who had gone to other countries.

PAHO statistics indicate that in 1967 there were forty-four hospitals in the country. Some thirty-six of these were general hospitals; three were institutions for the care of those with tuberculosis; two were for mental cases; and two were for other special purposes. There were 3,329 beds in all, averaging about 0.7 per 1,000 of the population—the lowest rate among the nations of the Western Hemisphere. The ratio was 4.7 in Port-au-Prince and 0.5 in the remainder of the country. Only about half of the hospitals were state owned, but these included most of the larger institutions and had nearly three-fourths of the beds. In addition, a number of church-operated units receive public assistance.

The General Hospital of Port-au-Prince is the country's largest, having 500 beds and 100 bassinets. There is also a 200-bed tuberculosis sanitarium in Port-au-Prince, and there are general hospitals with 100 or more beds in Cap-Haïtien, Jacmel, Les Cayes, Gonaïves, and Jérémie. Many of the smaller units are hospital-dispensaries with ten to twenty beds. Church-owned facilities, most with fifty or fewer beds, are operated by Roman Catholic orders and by several Protestant denominations. The largest and most prestigious of the private institutions is the seventy-bed Albert Schweitzer Hospital at Deschappeles on the Artibonite Plain. The remainder, referred to as clinics, are small establishments with fifty or fewer beds.

In addition, in 1968 some thirty-six health centers and 217 outpatient clinics and dispensaries attended about 400,000 outpatients, who paid an average of a little less than two visits per patient. These units ranged in size from centers and some dispensaries with regular staffs to rural units occasionally visited by a physician. Reporting on the number and status of these units is confused by irregular Haitian and international nomenclature identifying clinics and dispensaries that may or may not include some hospital beds and may be either permanent or mobile facilities.

Supplementing the public health system, there are various dispensaries operated by Roman Catholic orders and Protestant denominations and a scattering of dispensaries with a few hospital beds that are maintained by plantations and other commercial organizations. Business firms employing more than 100 workers are required to maintain a dispensary headed by a Haitian physician. In addition, during 1968 dental clinics treated 63,000 patients. The clinics were staffed by visiting dentists whose work was largely confined to extractions.

Public hospital and outpatient care is free, but bed patients must provide their own meals, and a shortage of drugs often makes it necessary for patients to supply their own. In practice, some payment for services is often made in money or in kind. The peasant seeking treatment may, for example, bring some vegetables or a chicken to the public or mission dispensary.

The concentration of medical personnel of all kinds in Port-au-Prince results in a supply that appears sufficient to meet the effective demand for them in that city. Even in Port-au-Prince, however, hospital beds and equipment are in short supply, and sanitary conditions tend to be poor. Elsewhere, except in urban centers where district hospitals are located, there are few personnel and facilities available. Medical care in the countryside consists principally of services provided in connection with the generally effective preventive programs, such as those directed against malaria and yaws. Services available at the mission and commercial-firm dispensaries in the countryside are generally among the best in the country, and peasants are fairly receptive to modern medical attention. They tend to seek it only when in acute need, however, and tend to regard it as a supplement to folk remedies administered by family members or by the voodoo priest.

The need for more and better medical personnel and facilities is acute, but it is of secondary importance. The most significant health needs are for better nutrition and environmental sanitation combined with better education in these needs and in health practices sufficient to make possible a more effective utilization of the personnel and facilities available.

Folk Medical Beliefs

Although there is little positive resistance to the limited amount of modern medical assistance available in the countryside, sickness and death are seldom attributed to natural causes. Amulets provide good preventive medicine, souls can be stolen and bottled, and illnesses of all kinds are believed to be transmitted by psychic rather than by physical vectors.

Both superstitious beliefs and herbal medicine are part of voodooism. The ministrations of the voodoo priesthood have at once been condemned as perpetuating the generally low level of peasant health and commended as of practical value.

Some writers contend that voodoo and disease have an interacting effect in the sense that the high incidence of ill health leads to a climate of anxiety in which voodoo flourishes most readily. Practitioners of the cult are said to prey on the anxiety of their clients, to the extent of deliberately prolonging their illnesses. For example, the general failure of people suffering from jaundice to appear at hospitals and outpatient facilities is attributed to the belief that the disease cannot be cured by modern medicine. In addition, it is believed that cow's milk is too strong for infants, that goat's milk is bad for all young children, and that meat of all kinds is bad for the young. The extent to which these beliefs can be attributed to voodoo is problematical, but in Haiti superstition and the cult are close to synonymous.

At the same time, the recreational value that is present in voodoo rites is important to the health of the peasants, and the pharmacopoeia available to its practitioners is formidable. The camomile flower is useful for reducing swellings and tumors; hogwood bark promotes urination; soursop is used as a sedative; the wild plum leaf reduces chills; and bastard cedar bark is steeped in boiling water to produce an astringent useful in the treatment of diarrhea.

Environmental Sanitation

In the early 1970s nearly half of the urban population had direct or easy-access connections with piped water (see Housing, this ch.). Piped water was available only to a negligible portion of the rural population, however; even in Port-au-Prince, where water is filtered and chlorine has been added, it was recommended that tap water be boiled before drinking. In 1970 the CAMEP completed the first phase of a program for expanding the water-supply system in metropolitan Port-au-Prince and commenced a second phase involving drilling of wells, building new storage facilities, and expanding the distribution system. It aimed at supplying an average of 160 liters (42.3 gallons) of water annually to the projected 1980 population of 1 million persons. The SHRH and COALEP were engaged in the improvement and extension of the systems of Cap-Haïtien, Gonaïves, Port-de-Paix, and several other provincial towns. Plans for another eleven projects included improvement of the system in Kenscoff, near Port-au-Prince, and its extension to neighboring communities.

Port-au-Prince has a small sewer system, but in the early 1970s it was unable to meet the needs of the population. It was necessary for residents of some of the better residential areas to rely on septic tanks, and in the poorer sections of the city sewerage often flowed in the gutters. Garbage and refuse in Port-au-Prince are collected by covered trucks at varying intervals, but in poorer sections garbage sometimes litters the streets. In the suburban areas and in the provincial towns there is usually some public collection; but in outlying areas householders dispose of garbage by burning it or by dumping it in nearby ravines. In rural areas, people customarily cook and eat out-of-doors, and trash is usually burned in the open fires.

Latrines are in general use in urban areas not having sewerage connections, but a substantial part of the urban population relies on public facilities, and the latrines are seldom fly-proofed. In rural Haiti, facilities for disposal of excreta are few, and soil contamination is general. To meet this deficiency, the government in the early 1970s was engaged in installing sanitary latrines in country hamlets. In 1970 an accord was signed with the WHO and the PAHO for installation of sanitary latrines in the vicinity of Mirebalais in the upper part of the Artibonite Plain. The program called for installation of 10,000 units in a four-year period, and a similar program was contemplated for the Health District of Les Cayes. The program was designed specifically to lower the rate of infant mortality and reduce such transmittable diseases as typhoid fever, dysentery, infant diarrhea, and intestinal parasites.

Haitians are clean people who bathe frequently, although the streams and ditches often used for this purpose are not always clean, and no epidemic (louse-borne) typhus is reported. In addition, an infusion made from boiling the bark of the mamey tree serves as a traditional deterrent to lice and flea infestation. A large number of rats are sustained by the often uncollected garbage, however, and the size of the rat population coupled with the fact that murine (flea-borne) typhus has been reported in the Dominican Republic makes this disease a potential hazard in Haiti.

Storage plants are lacking, and supervision of the slaughter of animals is inadequate. The presence of undulant fever and bovine tuberculosis in cattle and tapeworm infestation in pigs make thorough cooking of meat desirable. Pasteurized milk is available in Port-au-Prince, but even in this city the boiling of milk is recommended. Conditions in the open-air markets are crowded and often unsanitary; vegetables should be washed in treated water and cooked, and it is recommended that fruits be washed and peeled.

WELFARE

The Haitian community has traditionally looked after its own welfare considerations. Public assistance has been limited, and the peasant has tended to look with distrust on whatever public help has been proffered. The attitude of suspicion is slowly changing, and the initial steps toward establishment of a social security program have been taken; but welfare has remained in large part a concern of the family, the community, church and other private groups, and international organizations.

In 1972 the only persons receiving public pensions were a few retired public officials and members of the armed forces who were covered by special old-age insurance programs. A 1965 decree had established an old-age program for workers, and in 1970 about 35,000 employed persons were making payment into the fund. No retirement payment, however, has as yet been reported. The plan calls for compulsory coverage of all persons holding paid jobs, with the exception of aliens with diplomatic status or with special exemptions from taxation and members of religious communities. Unpaid family workers are exempted, and public officials and military personnel may participate on a voluntary basis.

Under the old-age pension program, eligible persons must have reached the age of sixty years and paid contributions over a period of at least twenty years. Eligibility is severely limited, however, by a requirement that the government determine the otherwise eligible person who has reached the age of sixty years to be no longer capable of performing any occupational activity.

Persons reaching the age of sixty who have contributed for at least fifteen years may make a lump-sum payment equal to the amount of contributions lacking on the basis of the highest wages paid. At any time, persons who have contributed during fewer than fifteen years are entitled to the reimbursement of contributions already paid plus annual interest at the rate of 6 percent.

Provision is made for survivor benefits. One half of the pension that a pensioner was receiving at the time of his death or the retirement benefits he might have claimed at that time are payable to the widow until she remarries, to minor children, or to children up to the age of twenty-five years who are continuing their educations. In addition to old-age pensions, the 1965 decree calls for medical care for the insured person, his spouse, and his minor children. It provides also for short-term loans, scholarships for children, and funeral expenses as advances on death benefits payable.

The program is funded by employer and worker contributions. The employer contribution consists of 1 percent of his total wage bill. The worker contribution ranges from 2 to 4 percent of wages, depending on the amount of wages earned. In establishing the scheme, the government contributed an initial G500,000 and donated a building to serve as the medical center for persons insured under the program. The Commercial Bank of Haiti—named to serve as trustee of the fund—was also to contribute an initial G500,000 and was to equip the medical center.

The government operates asylums, where cripples and mental patients are received, and almshouses for the poor. There are also several privately operated almshouses. A large proportion of the welfare-type activity in the country is devoted to the distribution of food. After the sharp cutback of United States economic assistance in 1963, the program was virtually reduced to food distribution and help in malaria control. In 1970 the bulk of the equivalent of US$8 million entering the country as foreign aid consisted of funds earmarked for food distribution; of this total, the United States donated the equivalent of US$1.5 million under Public Law 480 (Food for Peace Program) for foods to be distributed through private, voluntary welfare agencies. In the late 1960s and early 1970s the Cooperative for American Relief Everywhere (CARE) was engaged in a community health and development program in northwestern Haiti, and UNICEF as well as various domestic and foreign Roman Catholic and Protestant church organizations were active in the welfare field.

Mutual help remains of primary importance. Members of the work societies that hire out for peak work period assignments on the farms assist one another in time of need. The Congo Society of Cap Rouge in the 1950s was reported maintaining a health insurance program funded by small sums deducted from the earnings of members. Elderly persons of peasant families are cared for unquestioningly by their children. The family elder without sons is looked after by other members of the community, both because of a sense of moral obligation and because of superstitious apprehension that failure to provide care might later cause the spirit of the deceased elder to curse those who had neglected him.

CHAPTER 6

EDUCATION, CULTURAL LIFE, AND
PUBLIC INFORMATION

Haiti's dual culture, which has been a prominent feature of the society since the colonial period, has been perpetuated in part by an educational system geared primarily to the needs of the French-speaking elite. Few of the approximately 90 percent of the population who speak Creole (see Glossary) have achieved literacy. The low literacy rate, in combination with a political climate generally less than conducive to free expression, has retarded the development of the communications media. Despite these and other handicaps, however, literature, painting, and folk music have developed strong traditions.

In the early 1970s the predominantly urban secondary-school enrollment remained small but was growing at a rapid rate. The rate of growth of primary schools was lower than that of the school-age population, however, and the number of students in the country's one university, the University of Haiti, was lower than it had been a decade earlier. The country's literacy rate was among the lowest in Latin America; the rate of attrition at all levels of schooling was very high; most of the schools were located in the cities and towns, where only a small fraction of the population resided; and children often commenced school so late that the enrollment of teenagers in kindergarten was commonplace.

The high value that people place on education is illustrated by the fact that Port-au-Prince students from homes lacking electricity are frequently seen studying under street lamps and by the relatively large number who seek higher education abroad. Improvement of the educational system is, however, hindered by a variety of factors. Rural and urban schools are the responsibilities of different secretariats of state; the predominantly rural character of the population exacerbates the problem of providing an adequate number of schools; and the low level of national income severely limits the amount of money that can be devoted to development of the program. Of equal or greater significance, the curricula are for the most part based on the French cultural pattern, which has little relevance to the needs and interests of most of the population; and instruction is in the French language, which is spoken and understood by only a small minority of the people.

The nature of the abundant outpouring of folk expression has not changed much since the colonial period. What has changed, and in the process has introduced Haitian culture to the international community of patrons of the arts, has been the attitudes and interests of the country's intellectual elite.

Despite a national market severely limited by poverty and illiteracy and a political climate that has fluctuated between anarchy and tyranny, Haiti has always had a distinguished intelligentsia—one that has included many prolific writers. In fact, it has been estimated that on a per capita basis the country's writers are accredited with more book titles (many of them published in France) than any other country in the Western Hemisphere except the United States.

The cultural products of the elite of the nineteenth century were often of high quality, but they were essentially an extension of French culture. The recognition and cultivation by artists and scholars among the elites and the incipient middle class of a culture distinctively Haitian was catalyzed, ironically, by the humiliation of the United States occupation (1915-34). The experience gave rise not only to a search for a new national identity based on pride in the Negro race and the African heritage but also to the first powerful literary expressions of social consciousness and protest. The new trends in content were accompanied by increasing use of Creole and creolized French (see Glossary), although there is no standardized written version of the language and it has rarely been taught in Haitian schools.

The renaissance in literature that gathered momentum in the 1920s and 1930s was followed in the mid-1940s by the initiation of the primitive art movement, which in less than a decade had won international acclaim. Self-taught painters such as Hector Hyppolite and Wilson Bigaud—inspired by the voodoo religion's fusion of the natural and the supernatural and uninhibited by the academician's emphasis on linear perspective and other rules of naturalistic representation—introduced a truly innovative form of graphic storytelling. The noted critic of Latin American art, Leopoldo Castedo, commented: "The Haitian primitive painter is above all a narrator, less concerned with reproducing his vision of the world than with evoking an event by means of concrete symbols." Although the style of each painter has been highly individualistic, the movement as a whole has been characterized by inventive use of brilliant color and intriguing detail.

Music is the most nearly universal expression of the character and temperament—the pleasures, pains, and preoccupations—of the Haitian people. For the most part Haitian music is African in origin, and even secular and formal compositions are often adapted from, or inspired by, voodoo ritual music. Drums are the basic instrument, and dances tend to be uninhibited. The *méringue*, shared by all classes in the urban areas, is a typical musical form throughout the Caribbean region, but there are dozens of folk dances, popular in the rural areas, that are uniquely Haitian.

Because circulation of the principal newspapers is confined almost entirely to the Port-au-Prince area and because the country's single television station is received only in that area, the mass medium that reaches more people than any other is radio broadcasting. The government operates one station with several transmitters; a number of stations are operated by Protestant missionary groups; and the balance are commercially operated. Broadcasts are made in both French and Creole, and programs feature music and official releases.

Although the constitution guarantees freedom of expression and there is no precensorship, the press, radio, and television usually avoid publishing or broadcasting any material that might offend the government. Freedom of expression is thus limited by self-imposed censorship.

EDUCATION

Education in Haiti had a late start. During the colonial regime, schooling had been limited to the French elite to such an extent that the first chiefs of state in the independent country were illiterate. In the second decade of the nineteenth century, the country's first high school was established by President Alexandre Pétion; in the early 1970s it still existed as the Lycée Pétion in Port-au-Prince. A comprehensive system failed to develop, however, and the emerging elite who could afford the cost sent their children to school in Paris.

Educational development passed a milestone in 1860 when the signing of a concordat with the Vatican resulted in the assignment of additional teaching clergy to the young country. Education had already been largely an ecclesiastical function, but the arrival of additional priests further emphasized the influence of the Roman Catholic Church. The new priests were, for the most part, French, and they were motivated to further a rapprochement between Haiti and France.

In this atmosphere, the clerical teachers concentrated their efforts on the developing urban elite, particularly in the excellent new secondary schools, where Haitian students were made fully aware of the greatness of France, the backwardness of their own country, and its lack of capacity for self-rule. Virtually no schools of any sort were established in the countryside.

The effort to draw Haiti into the French sphere of influence was abandoned shortly before 1900, but it left a heritage in which education remained in large measure a system in which the clergy taught members of the upper class. Only a few went into the interior to teach the peasants.

During the 1920s, under the occupation by United States Marines, a considerable number of farm schools were established in which peasants could learn to read and write and could receive practical instruction in agriculture. These units were later absorbed into the regular primary system. The occupation authorities also were instrumental in establishing schools for vocational training in the larger urban areas, but the program was unpopular and collapsed even before the withdrawal of the marines in 1934.

During more recent years, the principal benchmark in educational progress has been the establishment in 1944 of the University of Haiti, which was formed from several preexisting academic faculties. A characteristic of the educational system during the years after World War II has been the plurality of its direction. No single government agency has had full charge of the public program, and at both primary and secondary levels religious and secular private schools have played an important role.

Most of the urban public educational program is under the direction of the Secretariat of State for National Education, but rural primary and secondary schools are functions of the Secretariat of State for Agriculture, Natural Resources and Rural Development, and other secretariats have responsibility for certain specialized forms of schooling. The country is divided into twenty-four school districts, but the geographical—if not the functional—centralization of the program is underlined by the fact that laws and regulations concerning national education make no reference to local boards.

Private education in the late 1960s and early 1970s continued to play an important role, but the extent to which the central government subsidized privately operated schools blurred the line of division between public and private education. At the primary level, for example, in 1967 a little less than half of the primary enrollment was in schools operated by the government and referred to as lay public institutions (*publiques laiques*). Most of the remainder was divided between church-operated but state-supported presbyterial schools and private institutions that were supported by tuition charges and contributions. The presbyterial schools, and some of the private ones, were operated by Roman Catholic orders and Protestant denominations. The Protestant groups were particularly important in rural areas where they maintained the mission primary schools, which in 1963 had an enrollment of an estimated 10,000 children. During the same year nearly 40 percent of the secondary students were in private institutions.

The small secondary school enrollment (about 10 percent of the primary school enrollment during the 1960s) does not include students in church-operated but publicly financed institutions in the public school sector comparable to the presbyterial primary units. During the 1960s, however, private education received public subsidies equivalent to about 10 percent of the funds allocated to public schools.

Some of the best private institutions are parts of conglomerates that offer a complete range of education from kindergarten through the secondary level; these schools draw their student bodies from the children of the elite. Others operate for profit, are of inferior quality, and function in rundown urban properties under the direction of teachers who are themselves barely literate.

Public schooling is free at all levels, but textbooks must usually be purchased. So few are available and they are so lacking in variety that, at both primary and secondary levels, rote learning is the rule. Text-books from France are used fairly extensively, and the Christian Brothers of Canada have published some texts designed for Haitian use; but there are few history or geography books written by and for Haitians. Haitian history and literature were not taught extensively before the regime of President François Duvalier, who produced the book *Oeuvres Essentielles* (Essential Works), which is used as a text at all levels.

Primary Schools

The primary school enrollment was officially estimated at 300,000 in 1970. Incomplete but more detailed data for 1967 quoted a figure of 255,152, including 112,291 girls (see table 1). In 1971 the Inter-American

Table 1. School Enrollment in Haiti, 1967

School	Enrollment		
	Male	Female	Total
Primary:			
Urban:			
Public	37,585	35,254	72,839
Presbyterial	17,866	23,736	41,602
Higher Primary	n.a.	n.a.	n.a.
Private	21,061	21,450	42,511
Subtotal	76,512	80,440	156,952[1]
Rural:			
Public	43,119	21,560	64,679
Private	23,230	10,291	33,521
Subtotal	66,349	31,851	98,200
Total	142,861	112,291	255,152[2]
Secondary:			
General			
Public	8,912	2,798	11,710
Private	4,351	4,945	9,296
Subtotal	13,263	7,743	21,006
Vocational			
Public	3,753	519	4,272
Private	458	1,215	1,673
Subtotal	4,211	1,734	5,945
Normal			
Urban	64	60	124
Rural	72	26	98
Subtotal	136	86	222
Total	17,610	9,563	27,173
Special	125	128	253

See footnotes at end of table.

Cont'd.

Table 1. School Enrollment in Haiti, 1967—Continued

School	Enrollment		
	Male	Female	Total
Adult	n.a.	n.a.	62,998
Higher:			
Faculty			
Agronomy	37	3	40
Arts and Sciences...............................	97	3	100
Medicine and Pharmacy	317	68	385
Dentistry	63	1	64
Education and Letters	190	41	231
Law and Administration	506	43	549
Ethnology	68	14	82
Subtotal	1,278	173	1,451
School of Higher International Studies	42	13	55
Private Schools of Higher Studies[3]	48	0	48
Total	1,368	186	1,554
GRAND TOTAL	n.a.	n.a.	347,130[4]

n.a.—not available.
[1]Does not include students in night schools.
[2]Does not include students in higher primary schools and night schools.
[3]Enrollment in School of Theology. Does not include enrollments in private law schools.
[4]Incomplete data.

Source: Adapted from Haiti, Département des Finances et des Affaires Economiques, Institut Haïtien de Statistique, *Bulletin de Statistique, Supplément Annuel,* Nos. I-II-III, Années 1967, 1968, 1969, Port-au-Prince, n.d., p. 9.

Development Bank cited 23 percent as the most recent estimate of the proportion of children in the five- to fourteen-year-old age bracket enrolled in primary classes and noted that the annual increase in numbers enrolled was at a rate lower than that of the population growth. Other data indicate that the rate had been somewhat higher—24.5 percent—in 1961 but that the rate during the census year of 1950 had been much lower—15.5 percent.

Primary education is compulsory by law, but exemptions may be granted for a variety of reasons; and the lack of a nearby school precludes attendance in many rural localities. The regular primary course consists of six grades, but it is preceded by two years of kindergarten (*enfantin*), which is heavily attended. Kindergarten is ordinarily offered in the primary schools and are counted statistically in the primary enrollment. Primary school proper consists of preparatory, elementary and intermediate cycles, each of which lasts two years. Promotion between grades is based on final examination marks combined with class marks recorded in trimesters; and at the end of the sixth year a graduation certificate (*certificat d'études primaires*) is awarded.

Students receiving this award may take examinations for entry in secondary school or may continue for three years of higher primary school leading to an elementary certificate (*brevet élémentaire*). Accordingly, it is possible for the student to take two years of kindergarten, six years of primary school, and three years of higher primary studies for a total of eleven primary years.

The rate of attrition is severe. In 1967 almost half of the primary students were enrolled in the two kindergarten grades, 18 percent were in the first grade of primary studies, and approximately 2 percent were in the sixth and final grade. The official statistics from which these percentages were derived did not include enrollment in the higher primary grades, but data for 1963 show about 1 percent of the primary students to have been in the higher cycle. Accordingly, it appears that a considerable proportion of those completing the regular primary school choose to enter upper primary grades rather than to go on to secondary school.

The school year commences in October and continues into July, with two-week vacations during the Christmas and Easter seasons. Slightly less than half of the days of the year are attendance days. In rural areas the school hours are from 9:00 A.M. to 11:30 A.M. and from 1:00 P.M. to 4:00 P.M. The urban school hours are from 8:00 A.M. to 11:00 A.M. and from 2:00 P.M. to 4:00 P.M.

Urban schools are modeled on the French pattern and provide the groundwork for classical studies at the secondary level. In theory, the rural system reflects the influence of the United States and endeavors to adapt schooling to the needs of rural life. In practice, however, its curriculum is similar to that of the urban schools, except that practical courses in agriculture and home economics are included.

Enrollment is growing at a much faster rate in urban than in rural establishments. In 1950 the number of children attending rural schools somewhat exceeded the number in urban ones, but in 1967 the urban enrollment exceeded the rural by a proportion of more than three to two. In addition, urban expenditures per student have been higher; during the 1963–67 period they averaged G86 (5 gourdes equal US$1) as compared with G59 in rural localities. Although during the 1960s girls slightly outnumbered boys in the urban classrooms, in the countryside boys were in a majority of more than two to one.

Dropout rates, excessive throughout the system, tend to be much higher in the country than in town. In 1967 about 31 percent of the urban and 60 percent of the rural students were in kindergarten, and a little less than 5 percent of the urban and slightly more than 1 percent of the rural students were in the sixth grade. Many of the rural primary units, however, did not offer the full primary course. In addition, attendance is better in town than in the country. Recent data were not available in 1972, but in 1956 it was calculated that about 88 percent of the urban children enrolled regularly attended classes; in rural schools the regular attendance rate was about 76 percent.

Repetition rates are high in both urban and rural sectors; comparative data were not available in 1972, but in 1960 some 48.3 percent of all primary students were repeating grades, 26.2 percent were new entrants, and 25.5 percent had been promoted. In addition, many do not begin school until relatively advanced ages. In 1967 approximately 283 beginning pupils, or more than 3 percent of the urban public enrollment in the first year of kindergarten, were ten years of age, and four individuals had reached the age of nineteen.

The rural system is criticized because the schools are often poorly located in relation to the population to be served, a circumstance contributing to low attendance. In addition, the absence of local school districts and of parent organizations leave little opportunity for rural parents to learn that school is important. Probably the most significant deterrent to attendance, however, is language. An experiment in teaching in Creole, the rural language, was undertaken in the Mirebalais region of the Artibonite Plain, but it was discontinued; and in the early 1970s the rural as well as the urban classes were conducted in French, a language little understood in the countryside. As a consequence, school for many children was a bewildering and frustrating experience. The only institution not using French as the language of instruction in 1972 was the English-speaking Union School in Port-au-Prince.

It is the stated position of Haitian educational authorities that full educational opportunities must be extended as quickly as possible to the rural population, but there is probably a conscious or unconscious reluctance on the part of many to create too great an increase in rural schooling too quickly; it could result in a corresponding increase in migration by an articulate peasantry to urban localities unable to absorb the flow. It appears to be the consensus of informed observers that the relatively slow pace of urbanization in Haiti is at least in part attributable to the low level of rural education. Moreover, so few children remain in primary school for a period long enough for them to learn and retain much of value that some educators believe that, in town as well as in the country, the limited available resources should be focused on ways to extend primary retention rates rather than on increasing enrollment.

Secondary Schools

In 1967 about 27,173 students were enrolled in schools of all kinds at the secondary level, an increase of about one-third over 1960. About 78 percent were in schools offering general or academic studies leading to university entrance. Over 21 percent were in vocational classes, and less than 1 percent were in normal schools. About 35 percent were girls, and 40 percent were in private schools. Secondary schooling is almost entirely urban; in 1965 only two of 105 secondary units in Haiti were located in the countryside. Students who have completed rural primary courses and wish to matriculate at the secondary level must find lodging in urban places. The government, however, offers a considerable number of scholarships (180 in 1961) to assist promising rural children in this respect, and some vocational schools have boarding facilities. Most of the rural students who do go to cities and towns to continue their educations remain there and swell the urban population; an undated study of the backgrounds of graduates of one Port-au-Prince vocational school revealed that although these students had originally come from various parts of the country, nearly all had remained in the capital city.

The course of study in general secondary schools lasts seven years, divided into a three-year basic cycle and a four-year upper cycle leading to a baccalaureate (*baccalauréat*) and possible university matriculation. The upper cycle is divided into tracks: Latin-Greek; Latin-Science; and Science-Modern Languages. At the last level, the study of English is required.

Although the curriculum has been broadened somewhat, it continues to place such emphasis on classics and the arts that the course of study in medicine at the University of Haiti includes a preparatory year consisting of courses in such subjects as physics, chemistry, and biology, which may have been omitted or insufficiently covered at the secondary level. Within the limits of its curriculum, however, the general secondary education offered in many of the schools is of good quality. Students who graduate usually are able to qualify for admission to the University of Haiti or to institutions of higher learning abroad. Graduates seeking to continue their studies in the United States, if their command of English permits, sometimes qualify for admission as university sophomores.

Enrollment tends to be concentrated in the lower grades, although not so heavily as at the primary level. Attrition is most drastic in the last two years, when highly demanding final examinations exact heavy tolls. In 1967 at the end of the sixth or rhetoric year (*rhétorique*), 2,742 took the examinations and 786 passed. At the end of the seventh or philosophy year (*philosophie*), 532 of the 625 students who took the graduation examinations were successful. The size of the class in the philosophy grade was about one-tenth that of the entering class in the same year.

The largest part of the enrollment in the vocational institutions is in the professional schools (*écoles professionelles*), which teach industrial skills. They admit students who have completed the primary cycle and offer three-year courses leading to an industrial skills certificate (*certificat d'aptitude professionelle*). The courses can be described as corresponding either to the three-year basic cycle of general secondary education or to the three years of higher primary school. They therefore are sometimes considered part of the primary system.

In 1967 the fourteen specialized skills taught included such fields as masonry, ceramics, and general mechanics. With the exception of a domestic-science school for girls, all of the institutions in this category are for males. Graduates of the domestic-science school can qualify for a primary teaching certificate after a year's advanced study.

Students who have completed the basic cycle of general secondary schooling may enroll in four-year vocational courses in commercial subjects, hotel work, or catering leading to certification. In addition, a two-year course in surveying is open to students who have completed five years of general secondary school.

The professional schools are all in the public sector. Their teachers are fairly well trained and compare favorably with those of the general secondary system. A large percentage of those trained in one craft, however, are reported to have found jobs only in another, or they have been unable to find employment because of a lack of available positions in their field of specializations or because employers prefer to train their own workers.

Most of the enrollment in commercial courses is in private schools of varying quality. In many of them the teachers are poorly paid, and the instruction tends to suffer as a consequence. A large majority of the students are girls. The instruction consists principally of the teaching of office skills, and the increasing number of young women seeking to become bilingual secretaries who go abroad to Jamaica or elsewhere for their training has been reflected in a generally downward trend in commercial enrollments.

The rudiments of gardening and agriculture are taught in rural primary schools, and the Secretariat of State for Agriculture, Natural Resources and Rural Development offers some agricultural courses at the lower secondary level. These latter courses are not considered part of the regular school system, however, and enrollments in them are not included in the school enrollment statistics.

Two normal schools at the secondary level train urban primary teachers; two others prepare teachers for rural employment. Their modest collective enrollment of 222 in 1967 included a small majority in the urban schools; women constituted a small majority in the urban units, and males were in a better than two-to-one majority in the rural units.

The general rule is that normal-school admission is limited to those who have successfully completed the general secondary cycle and that the regular course has a duration of three years leading to a teacher's certificate. A fourth year of practical teacher training is offered those who apply for it and carries with it a higher opening salary. Performance records are few, but in 1961 it was calculated that about one-third of the original matriculants obtained their teaching diplomas and that about one-fifth went on to obtain diplomas after the fourth year.

Higher Education

The University of Haiti (officially, but rarely in practice, denominated the State University of Haiti) was founded in 1944 by the merger of several faculties that had functioned previously as independent entities. Its oldest component is the Faculty of Medicine and Pharmacy, founded in 1830 as the National School of Medicine. The university was originally autonomous, but in the 1960s it was made the responsibility of the Secretariat of State for National Education. A baccalaureate from a secondary school is required for admission, and some of the faculties require the successful completion of entrance examinations.

University enrollments have declined in recent years, from 1,904 in 1956 to 1,227 in 1969. During the 1960s some 10 to 15 percent of the students were women. Dropout rates are high. The 140 students who took graduation examinations in 1967 (120 passed) represented about 9 percent of the enrollment.

The university is made up of seven faculties in addition to the School of Higher International Studies. In 1967 more than 36 percent of the students were engaged in the study of law and business administration, 26 percent studied medicine and pharmacy, and nearly 17 percent studied education and letters. The remaining faculties had far smaller enrollments; less than 3 percent, for example, were engaged in the study of agronomy. Social sciences, engineering, and architecture are studied in the Faculty of Arts and Sciences. The Faculty of Education and Letters (previously called the Higher Normal School) provides both teacher training and courses of study in the fields of philosophy, modern languages, mathematics, and natural sciences.

Curricula vary in length from six years in medicine (including one preparatory year and one year of internship) to five years in dentistry, four years in humanities and engineering, and three years in education, in pharmacy and in international studies. The several degrees offered in law require three years of study or longer. There is no university graduate studies program.

The University of Haiti is the country's only postsecondary institution having university status. At the postsecondary level there are also several small private institutions, including a school of theology and law schools at Cap-Haïtien, Gonaïves, Les Cayes, and Jérémie. Degrees conferred by the law schools are recognized by the University of Haiti.

The education offered at the postsecondary level is generally considered to be inferior in quality to that offered by the best secondary schools. As a consequence, children of the elite tend to seek undergraduate as well as graduate-level higher education in the United States, France, Canada, or Belgium. Educational authorities believe the principal problems of higher education that have been reflected in declining enrollments during the 1960s consist of a shortage of adequate facilities and a lack of qualified teachers. In terms of the interest of the economy, a still more important factor may be the continued overemphasis on the production of lawyers and the insufficient production of professionals in such needed fields of specialization as engineering and agronomy. Incomplete data available indicate that between 1945 and 1967 the proportion of students engaged in legal studies had not changed materially but that the already small proportion studying engineering and agronomy had undergone a sharp decline.

The Teaching Profession

Data with respect to the teachers are fragmentary, but in 1967 about 70 percent of the instructional staffs in the urban primary schools (other than higher primary and night classes) were women. In rural primary schools a little more than half of the public school teachers were men. Data were not available for rural private primary teachers. In secondary-level general classes nearly 90 percent of the public and about 70 percent of the private school teachers were men. In the vocational system, men were slightly in the majority in both public and private sectors.

A large proportion of the teachers at both primary and secondary levels are members of Roman Catholic orders or Protestant denominations. Lay teachers, both public and private, tend to come from working-class backgrounds, particularly at the primary level. Upper-class men are reluctant to accept employment in rural areas, and upper class women seldom are employed in any gainful capacity. Teaching is a respected occupation, however, and represents at least a limited access to upward social mobility in a socioeconomic environment where few such opportunities are available. The lack of other employment opportunities for educated persons—some with university backgrounds—has resulted in a proliferation of small private schools of various kinds in Port-au-Prince. Teacher attrition, however, is severe. Salaries are low, and personnel, on the primary level in particular, find it stultifying to attempt to impart elements of a classical education in the French language that some of the urban and most of the rural students can neither speak nor read.

During the early 1960s general secondary-level teachers in the public schools received an average of about G1,500 annually. The primary-level teacher received 10 to 20 percent less, and vocational school personnel received pay varying between the other two amounts. Private school personnel pay rates varied widely, both above and below the public school average: Secondary-level teachers in public schools frequently supplement their salaries by part-time employment in private establishments. Public school teachers receive small seniority wage increases at five-year intervals, and rural primary-level personnel receive wages slightly lower than those paid urban teaching personnel. Instructors in the adult education program are part-time personnel paid hourly at a rate equivalent to the national minimum wage of G5 per day.

92

Primary teachers are drawn from graduates of the urban and rural normal schools. Secondary personnel should be graduates of the education program of the University of Haiti but may be appointed after successful completion of competitive examinations if they are graduates of general secondary schools. Most of the secondary teachers are reported to meet the requirements, and a few have additional qualifications, usually acquired abroad. Primary personnel may be less qualified. Comprehensive data are lacking, but in 1961 less than 10 percent of the rural staff were reported to be qualified, and the number of new teachers graduated annually from the urban normal schools was barely sufficient to make up for natural attrition in the urban primary teachers' corps. More recent data on normal-school graduation are not available, but between 1961 and 1967 enrollments declined by nearly one-third.

In 1967 all but twelve of the 207 persons engaged in teaching at the University of Haiti were men. The student-teacher ratio was nominally less than eight to one, but many of the teaching staff were professional people teaching on a part-time basis. A considerable number held advanced degrees from European and North American institutions of higher education. Professors are appointed by the president of Haiti, and lecturers are appointed by the secretary of state for education; such appointments must receive presidential approval.

Literacy and Adult Education

In the early 1970s the adult literacy rate (persons fifteen years or older are considered adult) was estimated at a maximum of 20 percent and a minimum of 10 percent. The 1950 census had found it to be 10.5 percent; it had been estimated at 8 percent in 1914.

The consensus of the estimates for literacy in the late 1960s and early 1970s was closer to 10 than to 20 percent, and, even at the highest estimate, literacy in Haiti was lower than in any other country of Latin America. The low proportion derived in considerable measure from a level of national income that made it impossible to devote massive sums of money to the literacy program and from the fact that Haiti was among the hemisphere's least urbanized countries. Basically, however, it was a reflection of the fact that the rural majority spoke Creole but had access to formal schooling only in French. In the early 1970s some adult education in Creole had commenced, but an alphabet for Creole had been approved only during the François Duvalier administration, and very little reading matter in it was available.

As a consequence of the low rate of literacy, adult education has largely been a matter of teaching people to read and write. The earliest phase of the country's adult program took place between the early 1940s and 1951; about 13,000 persons received literacy certificates, and an additional 40,000 learned to read and write Creole according to the Laubach method, largely under guidance of Protestant mission teachers. The Creole students did not receive certificates because the government did not wish to encourage the Laubach method, which was not conducive to the learning of French.

During the remainder of the 1950s an estimated 14,000 persons were made literate as a result of several small government programs. An orthography that would aid Creole speakers in learning and becoming literate in French was accepted by the government, and in 1961 the National Office for Literacy and Community Action (Office National d'Alphabétisation et d'Action Communitaire—ONAAC) was established as the principal public adult education agency, operated jointly by the secretariats of state for education and for agriculture but funded by the former. It received about 3 percent of the secretariat's budgetary allocations for the 1961/62 fiscal year. Early in 1972 it had an enrollment estimated at 120,000.

The ONAAC receives assistance from voluntary associations, such as the Christian Service and the Haitian-American Community Help Organization. The continued low level of literacy makes it necessary that ONAAC devote most of its efforts to teaching people to read and write. ONAAC also, however, provides guidance in rural home improvement, in nutrition, and in the training of community leaders to give instruction in modern agricultural practices.

ARTISTIC AND INTELLECTUAL EXPRESSION

Literature

Critics have generally discerned four stages in the evolution of Haitian literature. The first, spanning the period from independence in 1804 to about 1820, was characterized by chauvinism and the pioneering spirit. The second, influenced by romanticism, began slowly and reached full maturity only after the fall of President Jean-Pierre Boyer in 1860 led to greater freedom of expression. Although the histories and biographies that predominated during the first period and the poetry and fiction that gained popularity during the second often dealt with Haitian subject matter, they were indistinguishable in style from the French works of corresponding time periods. Many of the Haitian literary figures were educated in France, had their books published there, and received recognition from the French Academy (l'Académie Française).

Jacques C. Antoine, founder of two literary journals in the 1930s and 1940s, maintains that Haitian literature was born of anger directed against the white masters of the colonial period. He suggests that the obsession, throughout much of the nineteenth century, to prove that the Negro was not intellectually inferior resulted in a "servile imitation of French models"—French not only in style but in mode of thinking as well. Antoine concedes, however, that there were exceptions, such as Oswald Durand, whose lyric poetry in both French and Creole conveyed something of the national mystique.

A third stage, generally described as one of the most brilliant epochs of Haitian letters, began toward the end of the nineteenth century and continued beyond the centennial of national independence in 1904. The so-called Centennial Generation was distinguished by the dedication of its members to a rejuvenation of society through literature. It was composed in part of former pupils of the Lycée Pétion, who had studied under teachers imported from France. They were stimulated by the need to compete with—and at the same time distinguish themselves from—their comrades who had studied in Paris. In 1894 they grouped themselves around the magazine *La Jeune Haïti*, whose founder, Justin Lhérisson, was noted for his portrayal of Haitian family life.

Massillon Coicou, poet and playwright of the Centennial Generation, was one of the first writers to introduce Creole into the national literature. In 1898 Coicou and other members of the club known as Les Emulateurs (The Emulators) founded the literary journal *La Ronde*. The second director of that journal, Dantes Bellegarde (1877–1966), distinguished himself as diplomat and educator as well as philosopher and social historian. Author of some twenty-four books, he was the last influential figure in a long line of francophile traditionalists.

Another member of that generation, Jean Price-Mars, was a precursor of the fourth and contemporary stage of Haitian literary development. Early in the twentieth century, Price-Mars and his fellow ethnologist J.-C. Dorsainvil focused attention on Haitian folklore and paid tribute to its literary values. It was not until the United States occupation, however, that the nationalism and social consciousness that have characterized the contemporary period pervaded the intellectual community. The transition in both style and content constituted the literary expression of *négritude*. This upsurge of pride in blackness and in the African heritage, reflected since the 1940s in virtually all aspects of national life, has been viewed as an attempt by the culturally ambivalent middle and upper classes, especially those of the intelligentsia who had been educated in Paris, to establish their identity. The peasants, of course, had no need of it; they knew who they were.

Resentment against foreign occupation was translated into wide-ranging literary efforts, including novels, poetry, drama, essays, and scholarly works. The anguish of occupation and the shock of the rediscovery that mulattoes, long the favored race in Haiti, were still treated as racially inferior by many whites was perhaps best expressed by Leon Laleau in his book *Le Choc* (The Shock).

Driven by curiosity about voodoo and folkways, educated young people, such as those who founded *La Revue Indigène* (The Indigenous Review) in 1927, left their comfortable homes to live in slums and rural villages. Their experiences generated social protest as well as literary nationalism. These trends reach a high point in the poems, novels, and ethnological studies of Jacques Romain. His *Gouverneurs de la Rosée* (Masters of the Dew), a powerful and realistic portrayal in creolized

French of life in a peasant community, has been translated into some seventeen languages. It was published four months after his untimely death in 1944.

Three novels of Haitian peasant life, *Le Crayon de Dieu* (The Pencil of God), *Canapé-Vert* (The Green Couch), and *La Bête de Musseau* (The Beast of the Haitian Hills), written by the brothers Pierre Marcelin and Philippe Thoby-Marcelin, also received widespread acclaim at home and abroad. They were written with greater detachment than were the works of Romain.

Efforts by Frank Fouché and F. Morisseau-Leroy to nationalize the dramatic arts included the rendering of Sophocles' *Oedipus Rex* and *Antigone* into their own version of Creole. Several poets, including Carl Brouard, Magloire St. Aude, and Emile Roumer, have been noted for works that, although linguistically French, are Creole in expression and sentiment. In 1935 Louis Diaquoi, a leading poet and journalist, fostered a group called *The Sorcerers* (Les Griots), who derived their inspiration from voodoo. François Duvalier, a member of this group, later used his intimate knowledge of the religion to great advantage in concentrating power in the presidency.

One of the most prominent of the younger poets is René Depestre. His *Minerai Noir* (Black Ore) and *Traduit du Grand Large* (Crossing of the Open Sea), written in exile, denounce the white world and express nostalgia for Africa and belief in human brotherhood.

Haitian literary activity more or less coasted on the momentum of the renaissance of the 1940s until the mid-1960s. As Duvalier had himself been a participant in the black nationalist literary movement, he did not move initially to supress it in systematic fashion. In fact, he introduced national literature into the schools for the first time. By the mid-1960s, however, the pervasiveness of political repression was such that most members of the intelligentsia had been rendered silent or driven into exile, and national literary development was suspended.

The Graphic Arts

The renaissance in literature had been underway for about fifteen years before the rich potential in painting and sculpture flowered into a national movement. Until the Art Center was opened in Port-au-Prince in 1944, those who painted for the love of it did so in isolation, without encouragement, instruction, or recognition. There were no art schools, museums, or commercial galleries.

The movement was sparked by a United States artist, DeWitt Peters, who was teaching English in a Haitian government school. Peters felt frustrated because there was no colony of artists with whom to spend his leisure hours. He rented a building and spread the word that artists were invited to meet there, work together, and exhibit their work; self-taught painters began to appear and timidly offer their work in exchange for a few dollars and painting materials.

When Rigaud Benoit first appeared at the center in 1945, for example, he was so unsure of the value of his work that he attributed most of it to "friends."

The most famous of the Haitian primitive painters, the voodoo *houngan* (priest) Hector Hyppolite, was discovered when Peters passed his house and was captivated by the decorative painting on his door. In 1946 Hyppolite brought Wilson Bigaud, then a boy of fifteen, to the center. Philomé Obin, whose talent had already been recognized in Cap-Haïtien, continued to work in his hometown, where he later established his own school, but he sent many of his paintings to the center.

Selden Rodman, North American poet and anthologist, became associated with the Art Center in 1946, and in 1948 he directed the Haitian Art Center in New York, through which many Haitian paintings made their way into United States collections. Meanwhile, in 1947 a small selection of Haitian paintings, especially those of Hyppolite, had aroused great excitement at the international exhibit of the United Nations Educational, Scientific and Cultural Organization (UNESCO) in Paris. Episcopal Bishop Alfred Voegeli gave the primitive art movement a boost when he commissioned the center to decorate the walls of the Holy Trinity Cathedral (Cathédrale Sainte Trinité) in Port-au-Prince. Benoit, Obin, Castera Bazile, and several others participated in the effort. The most highly acclaimed of the several now-famous murals is Bigaud's *Miracle at Cana*, in which the New Testament feast is placed in a Haitian setting and embellished with such details as a policeman chasing a thief.

The voodoo influence has been most notable in the paintings of Hyppolite, whose creative skills had been devoted for many years to such ceremonial designs as the *vèvè*, which are drawn in the dust and later stamped out by the dancers (see ch. 4). Although he painted, often with a house-painting brush, in bold strokes of bright color, the mystic quality of his personality is evident in his work. He died of a heart attack in 1948 while painting his own portrait.

Next to Hyppolite, Bigaud is probably the most famous of the Haitian painters. His canvases, among which *Earthly Paradise* and *Cock Fight* are particularly well known, are filled with great detail. The jungles of Enguerrand Gourgue, like those of Bigaud, are noted for their baroque lushness. René Vincent is noted for his psychological expressiveness; and Toussaint Auguste, for the balanced symmetry of his work.

By 1950 the primitive art movement had grown enough to develop rival groups, one of which established its own gallery, the Center for Plastic Arts (Foyer des Arts Plastiques), in Port-au-Prince and had achieved international fame. Primitive art has continued to flourish, but in recent years artists have also experimented with modern trends emanating from Europe and the United States.

Early Haitian sculpture, such as the portrait busts by Louis Edmond

Laforesteris and the monument to Toussaint Louverture by Norman Ulysse Charles, was stylistically French. The movement launched by the Art Center, however, gave rise to innovation in sculpture and wood-carving and called attention to the African artistic heritage. The sculpture of Valentin bears striking resemblance to that of West Africa, although he was not known to have been familiar with it. Odilon Duperier, once a carpenter's assistant, gained fame for the excellence of his carved masks. Jasmin Joseph is noted for his imaginative terra cotta sculptures; and Georges Liataud, for his work in sheet iron.

Haitian architecture, scarcely affected by the renaissance in painting and sculpture, reflects the country's colonial past and its dual culture. The thatched huts (cailles), modeled by the first Negro slaves after those they had known in Africa, are still the characteristic dwellings in the rural areas, although many have been embellished with brightly painted doors, shutters and woodwork. Architecture resembling that of French châteaus predominates in the urban areas. Some of the more outstanding examples of French-inspired architecture are the eighteenth-century cathedral at Port-au-Prince, the Sans-Souci palace (built for King Henry I in the early nineteenth century), the Iron Market, the National Palace, and several elegant mansions in the French style of the late nineteenth century. The country's most impressive architectural monument is the Citadelle near Cap-Haïtien, begun in 1804 under the direction of Henri Besse, a Haitian engineer. According to legend, the construction of this massive mountaintop fortress cost the lives of some 20,000 to 25,000 slaves.

In recent decades there has been a transition from gingerbread detail and high-peaked structures inspired by French architecture toward the simpler lines and functionalism of modern international architecture; several Haitian architects, especially Robert Baussan and Albert Mangones, are noted for their contributions to this development. The transfer of political control over the past few decades from the French-oriented mulatto elite to the black middle class is reflected in the capital in a more general way by the abandonment of uniformity or style coordination in architecture and in the trend toward greater use of bright colors rather than white.

Music and Dance

Music is an integral part of the lives of all Haitians. Playing the piano is a common pastime for the women of the elite, and drawing room recitals featuring local or visiting performers are often arranged. Music and dance have served as emotional catharses since the days of slavery. The street vendor chants the merits of her wares, and the farmer sings in the fields. Voodoo dances are performed by peasants of all ages, from toddlers to the old and infirm, and fathers teach the art of drumming to their young sons. In *Ainsi Parla l'Oncle* (Thus Spoke the Uncle), Price-Mars writes that, "A Haitian could accurately be described as one who sings and suffers, who toils and laughs, who dances and resigns himself to his fate. With joy in his heart or tears in his eyes he sings."

Most Haitian music is of African origin and has its national roots in voodoo. In the voodoo rituals there are songs to every god or *loa*. Possession by the *loa* is induced mainly by the drummers, although the *houngan's* female chorus is also important to the ceremony. Some of the ceremonial songs have been adapted, with little change in rhythm or melody, for secular usage. Gossip, anecdotes, affection, patriotism, and even political satire are among the secular themes that spice the work songs of the *combite* and the party songs of the *bamboche* (see ch. 5).

Most of the country's dances—and there are dozens of them—were born of voodoo also. The peasants dance individually rather than in couples; their uninhibited bodily motions respond to the rhythm of the drums. One of the dances most commonly seen at a *bamboche* is known as the *danse pinyique*. The dance that the elite has shared with the urban lower classes, as well as with most of the other Caribbean countries, is the *méringue*. The lyrics of the *méringue* are often full of innuendo concerning love or politics.

In addition to drums of all sizes and descriptions, Haitian musical instruments include the bamboo flute, the tambourine, the African *marimba*, the conch shell *lambi*, the papaya-stem piston, and the bamboo *base-vaccine*.

Haitian folk music was transmitted orally from generation to generation with no other means of dissemination for many years; however, during the 1930s a North American, Harold Courlander, and two Haitians, Werner Jaegerhuber and Lina Mathon-Blanchet, began collecting, printing, describing, recording, and arranging public performances of Haitian songs and dances for folklore enthusiasts beyond the nation's borders. In 1939 Madame Blanchet organized a group of young people to perform the traditional songs and dances. Since then several such groups have performed in Haiti and abroad. Jean Léon Destiné, after making a name for himself on the New York stage with his solo interpretations of Haitian dances, has returned periodically to Port-au-Prince to direct the Folkore Troupe of Haiti, a government sponsored entity, in its regular seasons at the Verdure Theater (Théâtre de Verdure). Emerante de Pradines and Odette Wiener also organized troupes that have performed at home and abroad; Katherine Dunham, a United States citizen who spent several years in Haiti, has incorporated Haitian rhythms into her internationally renowned modern dance routines.

The most successful of the contemporary Haitian composers of formal music have been those who have looked to the folklore for their inspiration. Jaegerhuber incorporated folksongs into an impressive operatic rendition of Romain's novel *Masters of the Dew* and wrote a complete mass in which he used African rhythms. Justin Elie, Théramène Manès, Occide Joanty, and Ludovic Lamothe are also noted for their use of folk rhythms, melodies, and legends in their formal compositions.

PUBLIC INFORMATION

In 1972 freedom of the press was guaranteed by the constitution, and formal censorship was not in effect, but most editors and publishers were careful not to print material that might be offensive to the government. Throughout the history of the country there have been many instances of rigorous press censorship and suppression of publications, and editorial immunity has rarely been a reality. Even during the United States occupation (1915–34), through which the United States government hoped to introduce democratic practices, the occupying forces considered it necessary to alter provisions of the American-sponsored Constitution of 1918 guaranteeing freedom of the press. This action was taken to bring under control the opposition press, which had persisted in publishing propaganda against the governments of Haiti and the United States. The press was censored, and editors were jailed.

President Sténio Vincent (1930–41) imprisoned editors without trial and suppressed their publications. President Elie Lescot (1941–46) arrested and jailed critical journalists. President Dumarsais Estimé (1946–50) closed a number of newspapers. President Paul Magloire (1950–56) arrested editors and banned partisan radio broadcasts; in 1953 the presses of *Haiti Démocratique*, an opposition newspaper, were smashed.

President François Duvalier's control of mass media was virtually complete. Shortly after Duvalier took office in 1957 the publisher and the leading columnist of the *Haiti-Miroir* were arrested; the editor of the *Indépendance* was detained; and the plants of these opposition papers and *Le Matin* were destroyed. Another opposition paper—*Le Patriote*—ceased publication after its offices were bombed and members of its staff were injured. In 1961 Duvalier closed *La Phalange*, a Roman Catholic daily that, as of 1972, had not resumed publication.

Duvalier forced surviving newspapers to do his bidding by granting subsidies, by compelling newspapers to publish—as their own—previously prepared progovernment editorials, and by assigning to regular editorial staffs writers directly controlled by the government. These controls were in effect at the time of his death in 1971.

Newspapers, Periodicals, and Books

During the third quarter of the eighteenth century the colony of Saint-Domingue supported an estimated fifty newspapers and other journals. Because of the high cost of production subscriptions to these publications were limited almost entirely to members of the upper class. The first newspaper was the *Gazette de Saint-Domingue*, a

100

weekly that in the late 1780s had about 1,500 subscribers. The monthly *Journal de Saint-Domingue* ran to sixty-four pages of articles on belles lettres and such subjects as commerce, agriculture, health, natural history, and science; but, for lack of subscribers, it lasted less than two years. An official newspaper, the *Gazette Politique et Commerciale d'Haiti*, appeared in 1804—the year in which the republic was founded. It was followed by hundreds of short-lived journals published during the nineteenth century and the first half of the twentieth century.

In 1972 the principal daily newspapers, all published in Port-au-Prince, were *Le Nouveau Monde, Le Matin, Le Nouvelliste, Panorama*, and *Le Jour. Le Nouveau Monde*, a semiofficial daily, had an estimated circulation of 5,000 or more. *Le Matin*, founded in 1907, had an estimated circulation of 3,000 or more. *Le Nouvelliste*, established in 1896, was the oldest newspaper being published in 1972; its circulation was an estimated 5,000 or more. *Le Jour*, founded in 1950, had a circulation estimated at about 1,000. All of these dailies had general appeal. A newspaper that tended to take a relatively independent position was *Panorama*, founded in 1956. Its circulation was estimated at 1,500 or more.

The size of the dailies in 1972 ranged from four to eight pages; all of the newspapers carried advertising. Coverage of international news was small, and the only foreign news agency providing service to Haitian publications was the French Press Agency (Agence France Presse—AFP).

In addition to official statements and foreign news items considered to be of outstanding importance, the contents of the daily newspapers consisted largely of gossip, reports of cultural events, sports news, and articles on home economics. Little space was given to crime news, and political news was usually confined to official releases.

Periodicals played only a limited role in the field of public information. Several weeklies were published regularly, and a number of periodicals appeared sporadically. A scholarly journal, *Revue de la Société Haïtienne d'Histoire et de Géographie*, was published quarterly.

There were several printing firms in Port-au-Prince in 1972 but no publishing houses. A substantial proportion of Haitian writers had their works published outside of the country, and the latest statistics available in 1972 indicated that in 1965 a total of twenty-five books were printed in Haiti.

Radio, Television and Motion Pictures

Because newspaper circulation and television broadcasting are limited to the Port-au-Prince area, the nation's primary information and advertising medium is radio. In 1972 there were sixteen active broadcasting stations, most of which were privately operated and licensed to advertise. They broadcast in both French and Creole. The number of receivers in the country was estimated at 300,000. Large numbers of people did not hear radio broadcasts regularly.

In 1972 the three most powerful broadcasting stations (ten kilowatts each) were Radio Nouveau Monde, Radio Haiti Inter—both in Port-au-Prince—and Voix Evangélique, in Cap-Haïtien, operated by the Oriental Missionary Society, a Protestant-based organization that had a number of other transmitters in Cap-Haïtien and Port-au-Prince. The government station was La Voix de la Revolution, with several transmitters—all in Port-au-Prince—the most powerful of which broadcast on seven kilowatts. Radio Lumière was operated by the West Indies Bible Mission, a Protestant organization; it broadcast religious and cultural programs over transmitters in Aux Cayes, Cap-Haïtien, and Port-au-Prince, the most powerful of which utilized five kilowatts. Power used by other stations—most of them in Cap-Haïtien and Port-au-Prince—ranged from 1,000 watts down to 100 watts. In order to present special features or government-sponsored programs local stations made arrangements to rebroadcast programs emanating from the more powerful stations.

There was one television station, commercially operated and broadcasting on two channels in 1972. The two channels were receivable only in the Port-au-Prince area. One telecast was in French, and one was in English; both operated only during evening hours.

Motion picture theaters in 1972 numbered thirty, with a total of 17,000 seats. Eight of the theaters had wide screens. The number of admissions in 1972 may have run as high as 1 million. French films predominated, but a considerable number of films from the United States and other countries were being shown with French soundtracks.

Foreign Government Activity

In 1972 the French government was engaged in fairly extensive cultural activities in Haiti. The French Alliance (Alliance Française) conducted academic, language, and other cultural programs and carried out an exchange program in which French professors and teachers came to Haiti and Haitian students were sent to France. The French also distributed films and publications. The United States Information Agency provided material to the press and to radio and television stations. It also provided instruction in English in a binational center in Port-au-Prince, and operated a library.

Other countries engaging in cultural activities in Haiti were the Federal Republic of Germany (West Germany), Italy, Spain, Great Britain, Canada, and a number of Latin American countries.

Communist groups were small and ineffectual, owing to a lack of strong communist leaders, to a general lack of interest in political ideology, and to a strong anticommunist position maintained by the Haitian government. Radio Havana broadcast to Haiti in French and Creole—fourteen hours per week—endeavoring to incite Haitians to revolt, as did Radio Peace and Progress in Moscow, which broadcast thirty-minute programs daily.

SECTION II. POLITICAL

CHAPTER 7

GOVERNMENT AND POLITICAL DYNAMICS

The political system of Haiti in 1972 was a legacy of the thirteen-and-one-half-year authoritarian rule of President François Duvalier, popularly known at home and abroad as Papa Doc. Upon his death in April 1971, his title of president-for-life had been bestowed upon his nineteen-year-old son Jean-Claude, who was to be assisted in the responsibilities of government by a regency composed of his mother, the cabinet, and the leaders of the country's several military and paramilitary forces.

Formally, the governmental structure is modeled after that of the United States, with executive, legislative, and judicial branches; but in practice the executive has generally ruled without effective interference from the other branches. Local government, since 1957, has been under the direct control of the president; previously, effective authority had been shared between the army and the *houngans*, or voodoo priests.

The country's dual culture—generated by a French-oriented mulatto elite and a black African-oriented majority—is reflected in the broad outlines of political competition. The black nationalist movement that came to dominate political life after World War II developed largely as a reaction against the cooperation of the mulatto elites with the United States occupation forces. The movement was spearheaded by a small and insecure black middle class that sought the support of, and claimed to speak for, the neglected masses.

François Duvalier, an early participant in the movement, succeeded during the first years of his rule in eliminating his rivals and in gaining control over the army—the only institution that had served as an autonomous center of political power. Having established a network of armed bodies, each of which reported directly to him and served as a check on the others, and having convinced most of the believers in voodoo that he possessed supernatural powers, he achieved a measure of personal control over national life that was probably as extensive as the country's level of development permitted. Actively opposed throughout the period of his rule by the elites of his own country and at one time or another by the Vatican and the governments of Cuba, the Dominican Republic, and the United States, Duvalier outmaneuvered every enemy except death.

The power that was so tightly centralized in the person of Duvalier has become dispersed, since his death, among certain members of the regency. The most influential member of that informal body for the first nineteen months after Duvalier's death was reportedly Luckner Cambronne, minister of interior and national defense, who commanded the loyalty of several armed groups and had acquired control of some of the most important sectors of the economy. On November 15, 1972, President Jean-Claude Duvalier announced that Cambronne had been dismissed from the cabinet and had taken asylum in the Colombian Embassy. His replacement as minister of interior and national defense was Roger Lafontant, formerly Haitian consul general in New York.

The country has never aspired to playing an active role in international affairs. Culturally, the elites have looked to France, whereas those who have sought to speak for the masses have made symbolic gestures of unity with Africa. But only the intermittently tense relations with the Dominican Republic and the client relationship with the United States have been matters of more than ceremonial significance in the twentieth century. For the most part, Haiti has wanted only to be left alone.

CONSTITUTIONAL FRAMEWORK

With the exception of the nineteen years (1915-34) of United States intervention, chief executives of Haiti have usually ruled with virtually absolute authority. The provisions of the carefully drafted constitutions have sometimes been ignored because they reflected aspirations rather than political realities and were not in accord with the aims of the chief executive. In 1972 the Constitution of 1964, as amended on January 14, 1971, was in effect. The most significant changes in the amended constitution were the revision of Article 91, reducing the minimum age requirement for the office of the presidency from forty to eighteen, and the insertion of a new Article 100 giving President Duvalier the power to designate his successor. This legitimized the announcement made by President Duvalier that his son Jean-Claude was to succeed him as president-for-life.

The country has had more than twenty constitutions, sixteen of which were promulgated before the United States intervention. The first constitution, drawn up in 1801 by direction of Toussaint Louverture after the successful slave rebellion, made Toussaint governor of what was then a French colony and made the colony essentially self-governing (see ch. 3). Laws were to be made by a central assembly and promulgated by the governor without referring them to the French government. This constitution was not accepted by Napoleon, who stated that it contained provisions contrary to the dignity of the French people and to the sovereignty of the French Empire, of which Haiti (than Saint-Domingue) was only a part. Toussaint refused to accept French domination, whereupon Napoleon dispatched a military expedition that failed in its attempt to reestablish French control.

In 1804 Jean-Jacques Dessalines was appointed ruler of the country by his military followers, and a constitution promulgated the following year abolished slavery, forbade ownership of Haitian soil by any white man, and made the word *Negro* synonymous with the term *Haitian*. After the death of Dessalines in 1806, Henry Christophe became president of the northern half of the country and the next year promulgated a new constitution that made him the first president-for-life. Succeeding presidents revised constitutions to suit their own political aims.

The title of president-for-life was abolished by the liberal Constitution of 1843, which broadened the restricted franchise by giving the masses the vote, introduced trial by jury, and required that the military be subservient to the civil authorities. The title of president-for-life was reestablished in 1868 and again abolished in 1870. After this no chief executive attempted to rule as a constitutional president-for-life until President Duvalier changed his term to a life presidency in 1964.

One perennial clause in the constitutions provided that the president appoint virtually all government officials. Article 93 of the amended Constitution of 1964 states: "The President of the Republic appoints or can revoke the appointment of secretaries of state, undersecretaries of state, and government officials and employees." This is a clause that has regularly been observed and was used by President Duvalier during his presidency (1957-71) to maintain tight political and economic control.

All constitutions up to the time of United States intervention specifically prohibited alien landownership. After the intervention in 1915, United States officials believed it would be difficult to encourage United States businessmen to invest in agricultural enterprises in Haiti if they could not own the land on which their money was to be spent. In 1917, when the Constitution of 1889 was in effect, the National Assembly was convened to consider adoption of a constitution that omitted the prohibition of alien landownership. The assembly refused to pass the United States-sponsored draft and drew up an anti-American constitution of its own, but before it could be passed the assembly was dissolved by the gendarmerie, and the United States-sponsored constitution was adopted by plebiscite in 1918. The most important provisions of the 1918 constitution were: the legalization of alien landownership; indefinite suspension of the elected bicameral Haitian legislature; temporary suspension of the irremovability of judges; and a legalization of all acts of the United States military occupation. The elected legislature was replaced by the Council of State appointed by the occupation's client president. Subsequent revisions and amendments to the constitution were promulgated in 1935, 1944, 1946, 1950, 1957, and 1964.

The Constitution of 1964, as amended in 1971, consists of a preamble and fifteen titles containing 201 articles. The first four titles define the country's territory, civil and political rights, civic duties, and the exercise of national sovereignty. In its description of the national territory, the constitution includes the island of Navassa, thirty-five miles west of the southern Haitian peninsula, that has been claimed by the United States since the 1860s.

According to the constitution, the country is divided into nine departments: Northeast, North, Northwest, Artibonite, Center, West, South, Southeast, and Grande Anse. The boundaries were to be determined by law, but by 1972 this had not been accomplished and the whole country was divided into five departments: Northwest, North, Artibonite, West, and South. Each was divided into *arrondissements* (divisions), communes, and rural sections. Article 16 states that all Haitians are equal before the law, except for certain advantages reserved for Haitian-born citizens, who were defined as those born of a father who was himself Haitian-born, or any person born in Haiti of a foreign father and a Haitian-born mother. Advantages of being Haitian-born included eligibility for the offices of the presidency and certain other governmental positions. Members of the legislature had to be Haitian citizens but not necessarily Haitian-born.

Individual freedom is guaranteed by the constitution, and no one may be arrested, detained, or prosecuted except in cases expressly set forth in law; and no one may be kept in detention for more than forty-eight hours without being brought before a judge competent to rule on the legality of his arrest, unless the judge approves the detention based on properly presented evidence. During President Duvalier's incumbency, however, these provisions were hardly sacrosanct; instances of arrest and detention for lengthy periods without trial, presumably for commission of acts contrary to the policies of the president, were common.

Title IV is concerned with national sovereignty, which is delegated to the executive, legislative, and judicial powers. The president and members of the legislature are elected directly by the people, but in 1972 there had been no presidential elections since 1961 when Duvalier had been reelected (see Political Dynamics, this ch.). The Constitution of 1964 proclaimed him president-for-life, and an amendment in 1971 authorized him to select his successor. Title IV also contains the eligibility requirements and duties of the executive, the members of the legislature, the secretaries of state (as cabinet members are called), and the members of the judiciary. Provisions in the amended Constitution of 1964 have reduced to eighteen years the minimum required age for the president, for members of the legislature, and for the secretaries of state.

Titles V, VI, VII, and VIII deal with the administration of the departments, public finances, and the economic system; whereas the social system, education, and health and welfare are discussed in Titles IX, X, and XI. The remaining four titles outline the duties and responsibilities of the armed forces, the methods of revising the constitution, and general provisions, including a description of the country's national colors, coat of arms, motto, national anthem, and a list of national holidays.

The Executive

Until 1950 the legislature elected the president. Subsequently he was chosen by the electorate at large. According to Article 46 of the Constitution of 1964, as amended, the Haitian people exercise the prerogatives of sovereignty by electing the president of the republic (see Political Dynamics, this ch.).

In order to qualify for the office of president, a candidate must be a native-born Haitian citizen, at least eighteen years old, a resident of Haiti, and in full enjoyment of civil and political rights. The president appoints the members of his cabinet, the prefects who govern the *arrondissements*, the members of the judiciary, and several other categories of public officials. He must approve and promulgate new laws and is responsible for ensuring the execution of the articles in the constitution and the acts and decrees of the National Assembly. Article 62 of the constitution states that in case of grave conflict between the legislative and executive powers, the president has the power to dissolve the legislature. In 1972 the members of the National Assembly were adherents of former President Duvalier, and there was no clear evidence of any friction between the executive and legislative branches of government.

The Cabinet

The president is assisted by a cabinet made up of secretaries of state. The number of members cannot be fewer than five, and additional members may be added if the president deems necessary. In 1972 eleven secretaries of state headed the ministries of interior and national defense (including police); foreign affairs; finance and economic affairs; coordination and information; commerce and industry; social affairs; national education; public health and population; public works, transportation and communications; justice; and agriculture, natural resources and rural development.

In order to qualify as secretary or undersecretary of state, an individual must be nativeborn and must never have renounced citizenship; he must be at least eighteen years of age and in full enjoyment of civil and political rights. The secretaries of state are permitted to appear before the National Assembly to defend administration bills or to voice the objections of the executive branch to bills proposed by the assembly. They are responsible, each in his own field, both for acts of their own departments and acts of the president, which they countersign. They receive a monthly salary of G3,000 (5 gourdes equal US$1). All appointments to the position of secretary or undersecretary of state are made personally by the president.

109

The Legislature

The legislature has been both bicameral and unicameral. The constitutions of 1950 and 1957 provided that a legislature of two chambers—the Senate and the Chamber of Deputies—would become the National Assembly when meeting in joint session. The members of both houses served six-year terms. The twenty-one senators were elected by an assembly composed of prominent individuals in each department, and the thirty-seven deputies were elected by popular vote. In 1961 President Duvalier, believing that the Senate was becoming recalcitrant, dissolved the legislature and created a unicameral body also known as the National Assembly when in session. In 1972 there were fifty-eight legislators, and the number was to remain fixed until such time as the area and number of electoral districts could be determined on the basis of the economic and political importance and the population density of each of the twenth-seven *arrondissements* into which the departments were divided. During the regime of President Duvalier, free election of the legislators was superseded by direct presidential appointment.

In order to be a member of the legislature, a candidate had to be a Haitian citizen, at least eighteen years old, in full enjoyment of civil and political rights, and must have resided at least five years in the district to be represented. The term of office remained at six years, and the legislators could be reelected an indefinite number of times.

The attributes of the National Assembly as defined by the constitution were: to declare war on the recommendation of the executive power; to approve or disapprove peace treaties and other international treaties and conventions; to revise the constitution; and to act as a high court of justice. The meetings were to be public. They could be held in secret, however, at the request of five members. In case of emergency, when the legislature was not in session, the executive could call an extraordinary session. The legislature meets in April of each year, and the session lasts three months.

According to the constitution, members of the legislature enjoy immunity from the day they take the oath of office until the expiration of their mandate. They cannot be kept out of the assembly, nor may they be prosecuted for their opinions and votes in the exercise of their office. The constitution gives the National Assembly the power to initiate legislation, which is then sent to the chief executive for approval and promulgation. During the regime of President Duvalier, however, this process was reversed, and the handpicked body of legislators served primarily as a rubber stamp to approve the laws and decrees submitted to it by the president of the republic.

The Judiciary

The highest court is called the Court of Cassation. It is composed of a president, a vice president, and ten judges. It usually functions in two chambers with five judges each, but when it hears appeals and pleas of unconstitutionality of laws and decrees it must function as a whole. Judges of the Court of Cassation must be at least thirty years old, must have practiced law for at least ten years, and must have held the position of judge or public attorney for at least seven years.

Below the Court of Cassation are four courts of appeal located in Port-au-Prince, Les Cayes, Gonaïves, and Cap-Haïtien. The court at Port-au-Prince has a president and five judges, whereas the others have a president and four judges. These courts hear both civil and criminal cases, and in order to be appointed the judges must have been either judges of courts of first instance for three years or military advocates for at least ten years. These courts hear all appeals from courts of first instance and criminal appeals from justice of the peace courts when something more than a mere correctional matter is involved.

Courts of first instance are known as civil tribunals and criminal tribunals. Both are located in the thirteen cities of Port-au-Prince, Cap-Haïtien, Les Cayes, Gonaïves, Jacmel, Saint-Marc, Petit-Goâve, Port-de-Paix, Jérémie, Anse-à-Veau, Aquin, Fort-Liberté, and Hinche. Each court has one judge and various other officers. They hear first instance civil cases in which the amount involved is not greater than G5,000 and all criminal cases other than police matters. Judges must have practiced law for at least two years.

Justice of the peace courts are located in each of the country's 124 communes and in other places as determined by law. Each court has one judge and other officials. In order to be appointed an individual must have a law degree, be at least twenty-five years of age, be in full enjoyment of civil and political rights, and must have completed a probationary period of at least one year. These courts hear all cases where the amount involved does not exceed G500 and first instance cases where the amount does not exceed G1,000. They also handle landlord and tenant cases. Their jurisdiction in criminal matters extends only to cases where the penalty does not exceed six months in jail.

In addition, there are accounts courts that deal with administrative contracts, land courts that hear cases involving property rights, juvenile courts, military courts, and labor courts. The president of the republic appoints all judges. Those in the Court of Cassation and courts of appeal serve ten years, the others, seven years. The country's legal system stems basically from Roman law, as modified by French civil law of the Napoleonic period. According to the constitution the president may not direct the decisions of the courts, but his influence is very great since he appoints all the judges. In cases of crises if a state of emergency is declared, the usual rules of justice are suspended, and the president can convoke military tribunals responsible solely to him.

POLITICAL DYNAMICS

The Social Environment and Political Attitudes

Haiti was the first Latin American country to gain independence and the first state in the world to be established by a revolt of slaves, but since that upheaval the country has experienced little social change. A rigid social structure in which the approximately 10 percent of the population who are mulatto, French-speaking, literate, and Roman Catholic constitute a self-conscious elite, overlaps cleavages between city and country and between Port-au-Prince and the provinces. Haitian political competition has always pitted the mulatto elites against the poverty-stricken, illiterate, Creole-speaking, voodoo-practicing black masses (see ch. 4).

Except for the period of occupation by the United States Marines and the decade following their withdrawal, the presidential palace has generally been occupied by representatives of the black majority. Nevertheless, most nonelites have had to settle for vicarious rather than actual political participation, while their economic situation has worsened and social services have remained virtually nonexistent. Although the economic status and occupational roles of individual mulattoes have been no more secure over the last dozen years than those of blacks, the French-speaking elite as a class has maintained its grip on the economy and on such social institutions as the schools and the Roman Catholic Church; the colonizers' mentality they have exhibited toward the black majority has served to inhibit social integration and exacerbate racial tension.

Although most members of the elite can speak and understand Creole, and many actually practice voodoo as well as Catholicism, they cling to French culture as a means of distinguishing themselves from the masses. Some blacks have been able to attain elite status through the acquisition of wealth and adherence to French culture, but most educated blacks constitute a small, insecure, culturally isolated middle class. The rejection of the colonial past (of which the American occupation is seen as a more recent chapter) by the masses and the black middle class, who have served as their spokesmen, is reflected in antipathy toward the Haitian elites. Such antielite feelings can be and have been mobilized by political leaders; they have been, in fact, a major source of strength for the Duvaliers.

The attempts of François Duvalier to identify himself with the deeply rooted sentiments of *négritude* (glorification of the Afro-Haitian cultural legacy and rejection of all things European) even included redesigning the flag. Formerly it consisted of red and blue horizontal stripes, representing mulatto and black, participating in the state, which was symbolized by the staff. In 1964 the colors were changed to red and black and the stripes were placed vertically, so that only the black was in direct contact with the staff. Duvalier, in fact, contributed significantly to the enlargement of the black middle class, as he expanded the bureaucracy and moved in blacks at the expense of mulattoes. He also promoted blacks and demoted mulattoes in the military, the church, and other institutions.

Although racial and class antipathy, typically nourished by black heads-of-state, runs high among both elites and nonelites, the most notable characteristic of nonelite attitudes toward public affairs is apathy, bred on the one hand out of ignorance, on the other of experience. Even for the educated urbanites, the rumor mill has generally been the most reliable source of information. During the few brief periods in the country's history when the communications media have been relatively uncontrolled, illiteracy has shielded some 90 percent of the population from disruptive or unsettling ideas in print, and the country has only about one radio receiver per 6,000 persons, the lowest ratio in the hemisphere.

The experience of the Haitian peasant from earliest childhood teaches him that obedience and subservience, first to parents, and later to political and religious leaders, is a requisite of survival. Peasants in even the most isolated villages have witnessed or heard about the fate of individuals who failed to demonstrate the expected subservience to functionaries of the government. Most observers of Haitian society believe that the peasant generally fears the wrath of the voodoo gods even more than that of secular rulers. More than a dozen attempts to topple the Duvalier government, made by exiles from among the mulatto elites, were aborted in part as a result of the social distance between the insurgents and the peasants they had hoped to mobilize and, in part, because of the empirically well-founded pessimism of the peasants.

Violence and its corollaries, generalized fear and suspicion, have been enduring characteristics of the Haitian political culture. The country has had thirty-six chiefs-of-state since independence. Twenty-four were forced to resign; seven were killed in office. Sténio Vincent (1930–41), the last president installed during the United States occupation, was the only president in the twentieth century who finished his term of office peacefully and handed power over to an elected successor. The present National Palace is the fourth of its kind. All three of its predecessors were blown up by explosions of the munitions stored in the basement.

The tenor of the Duvalier era has not been totally out of keeping with the nation's past. But the calculated official use of violence and the degree of autocracy achieved by Duvalier reached an extreme that has been equaled in few countries in recent decades. The system became as nearly totalitarian as the technologically and economically underdeveloped conditions of the state permitted.

Unable to influence public affairs or to find personal security in their own country, a great many Haitians have gone into exile. It has been estimated that by the mid-1960s, 80 percent of the country's most highly qualified professionals—several thousand—had fled to the United States, Canada, or Africa and that about 30 percent of the Haitian people were living outside the country. The number of Haitian exiles in the Dominican Republic alone has been estimated to be as high as 300,000; and there were more Haitians in New York City, some 40,000 to 50,000, than in any Haitian city except Port-au-Prince (see ch. 2).

The Duvalier Era

The presidential election of September 1957, following a chaotic six-month period in which five governments rose and fell, took place under army supervision. More than 900,000 of the 1.6 million registered voters (which included women for the first time) cast their ballots. The official tally gave Duvalier 679,884 votes, and Senator Louis Déjoie, the only opponent who was able to remain in the race to the finish, received 266,993. Twenty-three of Duvalier's thirty-seven followers seeking seats in the Chamber of Deputies were elected.

Duvalier, a soft-spoken physician, had studied at the University of Michigan, participated in the national campaign for the eradication of yaws, and written extensively on the country's Afro-Haitian cultural heritage. His election was in keeping with the wishes of the army, but it was seen also as a victory for the incipient black middle class and, indirectly, for the black masses over the mulatto elites. Like his predecessor, President Paul Magloire, whose authoritarian rule he had vigorously opposed, Duvalier rode into office on a platform calling for political liberty and social reform.

Duvalier's first step toward the consolidation of his grip on the government was a systematic purge of Déjoie's political party, the Haitian Democratic Alliance (L'Alliance Démocratique d'Haiti) and of the personalist parties of other political figures. It was followed in short order by the banning of strikes and by other measures to incapacitate the struggling trade union movement and the intimidation of the communications media. The latter was accomplished through imprisonment and coercion of editors; bombing and raiding of offices; and control of access to electricity, labor, and other essentials.

The elimination of rivals and the suppression of nuclei of discontent and criticism were clearly within the national tradition, but Duvalier's innovations stemmed in part from his belief that supporters were potentially even more dangerous than antagonists. Thus, he insisted that not even his most loyal followers be allowed to develop or retain independent sources of political or economic strength. He even insisted on dealing individually with members of his own cabinet for fear that if they became accustomed to exchanging ideas among themselves, they might plot to overthrow him; and judges, upon their appointment by Duvalier himself, were required to sign an undated letter of resignation.

About five months after taking office Duvalier moved to gain complete control over the military. Although the loyalty of the army's commanding general was unquestioned, his closest allies were removed to remote rural posts, and he was subsequently replaced. The officers' ranks were purged of those whose loyalty to Duvalier was unproved or who demonstrated leadership potential. The function of nominating the rural administrators (*chefs de section*), formerly exercised by the army chief-of-staff, was assumed by Duvalier personally. The chief of the Dessalines Batallion, the central garrison of the capital, was instructed to report to the president rather than to the chief-of-staff; and the practice of concentrating the national arsenal in the basement of the presidential palace was revived.

By mid-1958, nighttime raids, arbitrary imprisonment, torture, and mysterious disappearance and death had become commonplace, and the National Assembly had been rendered sufficiently subservient to declare a state of seige and vote the president extraordinary powers. After the first of several invasion attempts by exiles, which punctuated Duvalier's rule, it was decreed that anyone found to be spreading rumors would be shot, and the application of the decree was made retroactive to mid-1957. Like most other decrees, it was enforced inefficiently, but the arbitrariness and capriciousness of the enforcement of such repressive measures contributed to the general climate of terror.

The elaborate so-called security apparatus that made such repression possible was drawn from Duvalier's fervent supporters among the black middle class and among the urban and rural masses. The term *tonton macoute* (Creole for bagmen or bogeymen) actually applies to all of the activists of the Duvalier regime, a nationwide network that has been described as a resurrection of the early twentieth-century phenomenon known as cacoism (see ch. 3). The term is more commonly used, however, by foreign observers to refer to the loosely organized gangs of men drawn largely from the slums of Port-au-Prince, who were licensed to snuff out opposition to the regime by whatever means they saw fit and to support themselves through extortion. They were generally identifiable by their costume—blue serge suits, open-neck shirts, dark glasses, and sidearms—and their obtrusive manner in a population characteristically subservient. Clement Barbot, Duvalier's closest adviser during the 1958–59 period, claimed to have 25,000 such men under arms. The hardcore element of these gangs, located in the capital, has been estimated to number about 2,000. All were enrolled directly by the president, and many reported directly to him. Although all of the *tontons macoutes* from the simple licensed thugs to those who occupied high positions in government and private enterprise, served as semisecret police, Duvalier also established the Secret Police Force (Police Secrète), which was engaged more systematically in intelligence and undercover work.

115

The Civil Militia (Milice Civile) was one of the first of the paramilitary groups created as a counterforce to the military. Since 1962 it has been known as the National Security Volunteers (Volontaries de la Sécurité Nationale). Its units, found in virtually every village, are highly visible in their blue denim uniforms. About half of its approximately 15,000 members, mostly rural peasants, are armed.

The Presidential Guard (Garde Présidentiel), an elite unit of several hundred members, was removed from the control of the General Staff in 1959 and ordered to report directly to Duvalier. In 1972 its members continued to be barracked on the grounds of the National Palace and to have access to the basement arsenal. Their power is in turn countered by the Dessalines Battalion, of about equal numbers, also barracked near the palace; it likewise reports directly to the president.

In addition to these very tangible sources of power, Duvalier derived immeasurable strength from an intangible one. Like most middle class blacks striving to acquire elite status, Duvalier professed Catholicism and, although he carried on a running battle with the church throughout most of his presidency, he did not hesitate to use its trappings whenever he deemed it appropriate to confer legitimacy on his government in the eyes of Haitian elites and the outside world. But Duvalier had devoted many years to the study of the voodoo religion. His somber dress—black suits, hats, ties, and horn-rimmed glasses—and unsmiling countenance gave him a striking resemblance to the usual renderings of the Baron Samedi, in voodoo iconology the keeper of the tombs. It has been estimated that a large percentage, probably the majority, of the Haitian people believed that he was the earthly manifestation of this most feared of all the voodoo gods.

Sources differ as to whether Duvalier was a true believer in voodoo, but he kept at least one *bocor*, or sorcerer, with him at all times and often personally assumed the role of *houngan*. Furthermore, he took advantage of the political potential in the organizational structure of the religion in a manner that none of his predecessors had attempted. The very loose countrywide network of voodoo priests was brought under the direct centralized control of the president. Through a combination of cooption and intimidation all *houngans* and *bocors* after 1958, were forced to acknowledge the existence of a superior authority within their own sphere of influence. The powers that they continued to exercise over their communities were delegated to them by the state.

Despite such safeguards, Duvalier took no chances with the electorate. Several previous heads of state had been overthrown when it became apparent, as the end of their constitutional term approached, that they did not intend to relinquish power. So Duvalier did not wait for the end of his six-year term in 1963 to make his move. On the occasion of elections for the legislature in 1961, ballots were printed in the usual manner. At the top of each one were the words "François Duvalier, Président de la République," but there was no indication that an election for the presidency was being held. Armed military and para-military personnel rounded up the voters. Although it was estimated that only about 100,000 voted, few were surprised to hear that 1,320,748 ballots had been cast and that all of the deputies nominated by Duvalier had been elected by overwhelming margins; but no one expected to hear Duvalier express his pleasure at having been elected to another six-year term.

In 1964 Duvalier devised a means of dispensing once and for all with the electoral charades. Responding to "popular demand," he allowed the legislature, in May, to adopt a new constitution declaring him to be president-for-life. The new constitution was ratified by a plebiscite the following month. The official tally showed 3,234 votes against and 2,800,000 for; voters had been encouraged to cast as many ballots—already marked "oui"—as they wished.

By 1964 it had become apparent that neither social reform nor economic development was to be seriously pursued. The need for cash remained a problem throughout the 1960s, however, and citizens and foreigners alike were required to purchase "economic liberation" bonds, participate in the national lottery and various insurance programs, and contribute to such extrabudgetary organizations as the Movement of National Renovation (Mouvement de Rénovation Nationale). Contributions were collected frequently from businessmen, and funds were deducted from the salaries of government employees, who during some months simply were not paid. An additional source of revenue was a maze of toll booths erected throughout the urban areas and on rural roads and bridges.

Ostensibly the revenue was to be used for building schools, hospitals, roads, and the like, but few new public facilities came into being. At least 65 percent of the budget was generally diverted to the upkeep of the various security forces. Many of the government projects that were actually carried out were designed to perpetuate the personality cult. Among them were Duvalierville, a new town partially constructed on the outskirts of Port-au-Prince, and a series of enormous neon signs scattered about Port-au-Prince containing messages from Duvalier, such as "I am the Haitian flag, one and indivisible," and "I have no enemies save the enemies of the country."

There was no lack of opposition to Duvalier during his last half-dozen years in office, but by the mid-1960s the consolidation of power in his person was such that none of his enemies, internal or external, was able to mount a credible threat. Nevertheless, even minor challenges to his rule generally resulted in a further tightening of personal control. After the execution of six teenagers who had painted a "Down with Duvalier" sign on a Port-au-Prince wall, he ordered that all youth organizations—even the Boy Scouts—be disbanded.

In the late 1960s, despite the occasional bombings, mutinies, abortive invasions, and the like, the most serious threat to Duvalier's control appeared to be found in the intrigues of palace politics. Cabinet posts and other positions of responsibility were constantly reshuffled, and many of Duvalier's former confidants were imprisoned or executed; the more fortunate fled into exile. His suspicions that those about him were plotting his demise extended to his own family. In 1967, just after the marriage of Duvalier's strong-willed eldest daughter, Marie-Denise, to Lieutenant Colonel Max Dominique, military commander of Port-au-Prince, Duvalier personally directed the execution of nineteen of Dominique's closest colleagues in the army. Dominique was exiled as titular ambassador to Spain and a month later was dismissed from the army and ordered to stand trial for treason. The charges against Dominique were eventually dropped, and he was reinstated in the army and reassigned as ambassador to France. Marie-Denise served as her father's private secretary during the year before his death.

In January 1971 Duvalier, in failing health, persuaded the national assembly to revise the constitution to allow him to name his successor and to lower the age qualifications for the office from forty to eighteen. Passing over a number of experienced advisers and the politically talented Marie-Denise, Duvalier announced that the successor was to be his son, Jean-Claude. The official results of the referendum on the amendment conferring legitimacy on the succession were about 2.5 million votes in favor and one vote against.

Three months later the sixty-four-year-old ruler died, and the pre-ordained succession took place in an atmosphere of order but great uneasiness. Like his father, the nineteen-year-old Jean-Claude assumed the title of president-for-life. Real power, however, was dispersed in what has been described as a collegium or regency, composed of the elder Duvalier's widow, Simone Ovide, and several individuals who were among Duvalier's most trusted advisers just before his death.

First among equals in this informal and rather fluid collective leadership until November 1972 was reportedly Luckner Cambronne, formerly a public works minister and a private secretary to Duvalier. Officially he held the portfolios of interior and national defense (including police). Unofficially, he was often referred to as the "minister of everything," and he signed documents as "Acting Prime Minister." Upon the elder Duvalier's death, Cambronne removed several leaders of the Civil Militia—including Rosalie Adolphe—who presided over the dreaded Fort Dimanche prison and took control of that institution. With foreign assistance, he also armed and trained a new counter-insurgency force of about 560 men. The force, known as the Leopards, was theoretically an elite unit of the army, although it answered directly to Cambronne rather than to the army chief of staff; it was reportedly made up largely of *tontons macoutes*.

Duvalier, just before his death, had released the names of his designees for a new cabinet; and its members, as well as Antonio André,

118

head of the national bank, were generally considered to be members of the regency. Adrien Raymond, minister of foreign relations and brother of the army chief of staff, was said to be the most influential civilian in this group. But the regents with the greatest influence were those who commanded the loyalty of armed bodies. In addition to Cambronne, these included: General Claude Raymond, army chief of staff; General Gracia Jacques, head of the Presidential Guard and, at least on some occasions, personal bodyguard to Jean-Claude; General Breton Claude, commander of the Dessalines Battalion and Frank Roman, head of the Port-au-Prince police force.

Patterns of Political Competition

In the broad sociological sense, political competition in Haiti has always been between the mulatto elites and the black masses; but in the more narrow and immediate sense of the active quest for decision-making roles and for influence over policy, competition has generally been among individuals and their personal followings rather than among groups defined by interest or ideology. With the exception of the communist party, which has never been strong, the country has never had full-fledged political parties with organizational structures and continuity independent of their leaders.

Duvalier had his own party, which he dubbed the Sole Party of Revolutionary and Governmental Action (Parti Unique de l'Action Révolutionaire et Gouvernementale), but it had none of the usual functions of a party, since holders of both "elective" and appointive office were handpicked by Duvalier. His base of power, which passed to his son and the regency upon his death, was the nonorganized body of activists—encompassing all of the security forces, as well as many cabinet members, chauffeur-guides, and other persons scattered throughout the critical public and private entities—known as the *tontons macoutes*.

Several individuals who were active in the political arena at the time of the 1957 elections had attached party labels to their followings, but such groups were among the first casualties of Duvalier's campaign to eliminate opposition. Many of the political personalities and their loyal supporters who managed to escape into exile have organized "liberation" groups. Some of these groups have staged invasions, dropped bombs on Port-au-Prince, beamed in radio programs in Creole, and in other ways attempted to spark a rebellion, but the consequences of such initiatives have always been new waves of arrests and a tightening of autocratic control. The most effective exile group in the mid-1960s was the Haitian Coalition, led by Paul Magloire and Raymond Joseph, but by 1972 it was moribund. The Haitian Resistance, a New York-based coalition of about a dozen organizations, emerged after the death of Duvalier in 1971. Its spokesman, former Army Lieutenant François Benoit, urged the United States to withdraw support from the government of President Jean-Claude Duvalier.

Organizations representing economic interest groups have rarely been effective in influencing policy or the outcome of struggles for power. The fact that the country was overwhelmingly rural militated against the early organization of unions, although several had been established by the late 1940s. The Haitian Workers' Federation (Fédération Haïtienne des Travaillers—FHT), under the leadership of Daniel Fignole, joined some thirty unaffiliated unions in a general strike in 1956 that was instrumental in toppling Magloire. Both of the federations—the National Workers' Union (Union National des Travaillers—UNT) and the Haitian National Laborers' Union (Union National Ouvriers d'Haiti—UNOH)—which together absorbed most of the individual unions after Magloire's departure, had opposed François Duvalier. They were disbanded immediately after he took office, and the leaders that escaped execution or imprisonment fled into exile. Strikes have occasionally occurred since, but they have been quickly suppressed, and labor has virtually ceased to have a political role.

Businessmen as a group have had no independent role either, as there has occasionally been something to be gained from supporting the regime and there has always been much to lose in opposing it. University students have traditionally been active in politics. A student strike in 1929, for example, was instrumental in forcing the resignation of President Louis Borno. Students were among the boldest and most persistent opponents of the Duvalier government in its first few years. They struck as late as November 1960 because one of the officers of the National Union of Haitian Students (Union National Etudiants Haïtiens) had been imprisoned. But the use of reprisals, including imprisonment, against parents and other relatives of dissident students has generally been effective in suppressing student activity.

Haiti severed all ties with the Vatican in 1805, and Roman Catholic priests were not allowed into the country again until 1860. In the interim voodoo had become deeply entrenched as the explicator and organizer of life, especially in the rural areas. Nevertheless, the Roman Catholic Church, for more than a century, has been an important factor in political competition. Roman Catholicism has been an integral part of the heritage of the French-oriented elite, and the church has been regarded as an enemy of the Haitian masses by the nationalists who gained prominence after the American occupation. François Duvalier and his supporters resented the church because it attempted to suppress voodoo practices, because most of the priests were of French or French-Canadian derivation, and because it managed to retain more independence than most institutions in the society. Furthermore, it was considered capable of serving as a rallying point for urban discontent. Duvalier began expelling priests and bishops critical of his regime and filling the vacancies with his supporters before the end of his first year in office. In 1960 he deported the archbishop, François Poirier, on the charge that he had been financing communist activities. That action resulted in his excommunication. The excommunication was lifted in 1966, however, and Duvalier participated in the inauguration of the country's first native Haitian archbishop and four new Haitian bishops.

Voodoo, the people's religion, has always had some influence on the country's political life, because not even the most sophisticated leaders from among the elites have been certain that they were beyond the reach of its sorcerers. A few past presidents had been practitioners of voodoo, but none before Duvalier had succeeded in controlling its priests and using it as a pillar of political strength.

The country's dominant political institution from the end of the United States occupation until the Duvalier assumption of power was the army, called the Garde d'Haiti during the occupation; in 1949 it was renamed the Forces Armées d'Haiti. Trained by the United States Marines to keep order in the country after their withdrawal, it served as a praetorian guard, supervising elections, overthrowing presidents it deemed to be exceeding their proper role, and often providing presidents from its own ranks.

Duvalier used purges and selective promotions to bring the army, on which his power initially rested, under his control. He removed career officers, ended professional training, and took away most of their weapons. But his most effective means of weakening the institution as an autonomous center of political power was the creation of countervailing centers of paramilitary and police power. The army has reportedly gained in cohesiveness and in influence vis-à-vis the other security forces since the death of Duvalier. It numbered about 7,000 in 1972.

In 1972 the most significant struggle for power appeared to be within the realm of palace politics. Marie-Denise Dominique, having served as private secretary to her father, stayed on initially to assist—and to influence—her brother. In August 1971, however, she clashed with her mother and brother as a result of their failure to oppose the arrest, on Cambronne's orders, of her husband's cousin. Having lost that battle, she left to join her husband Lieutenant Colonel Max Dominique, in his ambassadorial exile. In early 1972 Dominique, accused by Cambronne of having plotted a coup, was removed from his diplomatic post.

Cambronne proceeded in the ensuing months to order several waves of arrests, but such actions failed to intimidate his enemies. Cambronne's business ventures, particularly the export of blood plasma to the United States, had generated widespread resentment.

FOREIGN RELATIONS

A major recurrent tendency in Haiti's relations with the outside world has been isolationism, a consequence in large measure of its experiences with colonialism and foreign occupation and of its consciousness of being a black republic in a predominantly white hemisphere. Although the elites still look to France for cultural inspiration and although François Duvalier made a point of establishing relations with several African countries in order to emphasize his commitment to *négritude*, the only relations that have been a source of constant preoccupation have been those with the Dominican Republic and with the United States.

Relations with Cuba might best be seen as an aspect of United States-Haitian relations, as the presence of a socialist government in the Caribbean has been used by Haiti as a bargaining chip; François Duvalier alternately charged that the communist menace, emanating from Cuba, threatened the security of his country and intimated sympathy with the Castro regime in his attempts to secure United States assistance.

Haiti's initiatives in international organizations, primarily the Organization of American States (OAS), have resulted from its clashes with the Dominican Republic. The country has generally followed the lead of the United States in casting its votes in the OAS and the United Nations, but when it has found itself in the position of casting the decisive vote, as on the expulsion of Cuba from the OAS in 1962 and the dispatching of an Inter-American Peace Force to the Dominican Republic in 1965, it has bargained its vote for economic assistance.

Relations with the Dominican Republic

Tension has generally run high between Haiti and the Dominican Republic since the Dominicans gained their independence in 1844, having experienced twenty-two years of Haitian occupation. Legends growing out of the occupation have kept fears and racial animosity alive in the Dominican Republic. The most serious incident between the two countries in the twentieth century was the massacre in 1937 by the Dominican army, under the government of Rafael Leónidas Trujillo Molina, of an unknown number (Haiti claimed 12,000; the Dominican Republic claimed 18,000) of Haitians, mostly seasonal agricultural workers, in the Dominican Republic.

Leaders in each country have habitually attempted to influence internal political struggles in the other, and political exiles and refugees, with or without the complicity of sympathetic governments, have kept the island seething with plots and rumors of plots. Since World War II, however, disputes between the two countries have been mitigated by the intercession of the OAS. The second application of the Inter-American Treaty of Reciprocal Assistance (commonly known as the 1947 Rio Treaty) took place in response to charges of aggression brought by Haiti against the Dominican Republic, together with countercharges by the latter against Haiti, Cuba, and Guatemala. Haiti first appealed to the OAS in 1949, claiming that the activities of a former Haitian army officer, who had taken asylum in the Dominican Republic, endangered the peace, but the OAS Council determined that the circumstances did not warrant recourse to the collective security treaty. Haiti then turned to the Inter-American Peace Committee, which was able to smooth over the immediate crisis.

Within a year, however, the situation had deteriorated again, and the charges and countercharges indicated to the OAS Council a clear threat to the peace. An investigating committee, dispatched by the council, discovered the complicity of the Dominican government in a plot against Haiti, as well as of the governments of Cuba and Guatemala in plots against the Dominican Republic. Because of the complexity of the situation a continuing special committee was appointed to try to defuse crises as they arose. It was assumed that the exposure of extralegal activities on the part of several governments had the effect of deflating the whole movement of political subversion.

Trujillo, who had governed the Dominican Republic since 1930, had generally attempted to eliminate Haitian presidents who were neither fearful of him nor dependent on him, and during Duvalier's first year as Haitian president the two men were bitter rivals. They soon realized, however, that antiauthoritarian forces throughout the Caribbean were seeking to overthrow both of them, so in 1958 they signed a mutual assistance pact, the Agreement of Malpasse.

Relations became tense again after the assassination of Trujillo in 1961, and especially after the election of Juan Bosch to the presidency of the Dominican Republic in 1962. In 1963 Bosch's government appealed to the OAS alleging the forcible entrance and occupation of the Dominican Embassy in Port-au-Prince as one of many acts by the Haitian government that endangered the peace. The machinery of the Rio Treaty was set into motion, and a committee authorized to carry out conciliatory, as well as investigative, functions was sent to the island. Charges and countercharges mounted, and the Haitian government rejected the recommendations of the committee. Although no clashes took place between the armed forces of the two countries, disturbing incidents continued, and the OAS Council left the case open until August 1966.

Haiti resumed diplomatic relations with the Dominican Republic after the election of Joaquín Balaguer to the Dominican presidency in 1966. Since that time relations between the two countries have generally been correct, although disparaging or threatening remarks have occasionally been exchanged and the border between the two countries has been closed part of the time.

Agreements signed in 1972 with the Dominican Republic were expected to result in a significant expansion of trade between the two countries. They provided for the establishment of a joint free zone, for tariff reductions on foreign products, and for simplified trade transactions and also called for improvements in transportation.

Relations with the United States

Attitudes in both countries about race have always been a factor in Haitian-United States relations. The United States did not recognize the government of Haiti until its own slaves had been emancipated. The fact that the United States occupation forces (1915–34) returned power to the mulatto minority also influenced subsequent relations, especially after the black nationalist revolution of 1946 (see ch. 3).

All Haitian presidents since World War II have sought United States assistance, although those who have sought the support of the black masses as well often exploited resentment against the former occupying power by being strongly critical of the United States and attempting to display their independence from it. From 1946 through 1971 Haiti received a total of US$126.5 million in economic and military assistance. Haiti also received a portion of what had been the Cuban sugar quota in the United States market when it was abolished and redistributed. Despite aid and the country's proximity to the United States, however, the United States has had little influence, since the withdrawal of its troops, on internal affairs in Haiti; and relations have not always been cordial.

Relations were close during World War II, when the United States had access to Haitian bases, but began to deteriorate in the immediate postwar years as the black nationalist movement gained strength. The restoration in Haiti of the traditional ban on foreign ownership of property, which had been removed during the United States occupation, was a particular source of friction. Nevertheless, the United States continued to supply economic aid in various forms and, in 1955, entered into a bilaterial military assistance agreement.

François Duvalier had been the candidate favored by the United States in 1957, and when, in 1958, he requested a Marine mission to undertake the training of the Haitian army, his request was favorably received. The mission arrived in early 1959. Its director soon found, however, that Duvalier was not interested in a well-trained army but rather in using the United States mission as evidence of that country's support for his regime.

After the inauguration of President John F. Kennedy there was a change in United States policy toward extraconstitutional regimes in Latin America. The United States threatened to cut off aid when Duvalier staged his ingenious reelection in 1961 but changed its position in January 1962 when Haiti held the swing vote in the OAS on the expulsion of Cuba. Most aid was suspended in July 1962, but during the Cuban missile crisis in October of that year the United States needed access to Haitian airfields and ports, and some aid was renewed. In particular, the United States assisted in the construction of a jet airport, one of Duvalier's pet projects. When Duvalier resisted United States pressure to step down at the end of his original six-year term in May 1963, the United States cut off economic aid and suspended diplomatic relations for a month in protest. Military assistance was suspended as well, as the mission chief was declared persona non grata, and United States missions were withdrawn.

Duvalier escalated his verbal attacks on the United States and claimed that he did not need or want its assistance. For about two years relations were exceedingly cool, and the only forms of United States assistance Haiti received were participation in a malaria eradication program and the Food for Peace program. With the advent of the Dominican crisis in April 1965, however, the United States once again found Haiti's vote in the OAS to be crucial; aid was renewed at that time and was increased in 1966. Radio jamming equipment was provided, for example, to counter the broadcasts of anti-Duvalier exiles. Governor Nelson Rockefeller, as special envoy of President Richard Nixon was well received in 1969.

Nevertheless, Duvalier, in his later years, generally stressed his indifference to, and lack of dependence on, the United States and his country's orientation toward Africa. He arranged an extravagant reception for Ethiopian Emperor Haile Selassie and in 1969, during the Nigerian civil war, he recognized Biafra. On the occasion of the last OAS vote during his lifetime, on measures for dealing with diplomatic kidnappings and other forms of terrorism, Haiti joined the other "hardliners"—Brazil, Argentina, Paraguay, Ecuador, and Guatemala—in staging a walkout. Whereas the majority adopted a resolution providing that persons accused of kidnapping or otherwise assaulting diplomats must be extradited or brought to trial by the country in which they were apprehended, the hardliners had demanded multilateral action against all forms of political terrorism.

The government of Jean-Claude Duvalier and the regency that assumed power after the death of François Duvalier in April 1971 placed a high priority on improving the country's image abroad and its relations with the United States in order to attract tourists and foreign investors and to increase Haiti's share of United States assistance. In all of these endeavors it appeared to be having considerable success.

It was reported that 83,000 tourists visited the country in 1971, some drawn by the bargain prices, others by the liberal divorce laws. United States private investment increased sharply in 1971, as did economic assistance, which was up to US$4.3 million as opposed to US$3.8 million in 1970. The Nixon administration late in 1970 had lifted the ban imposed by President Kennedy on the sale of arms to Haiti, and the Department of State had authorized more than US$1 million in private arms sales in 1971. One company, based in Miami, had also been engaged to train the Leopards, Haiti's new counterinsurgency force. In March of 1972 a Haitian delegation was cordially received in Washington, D.C., and in July a seven-man United States survey team spent a week in Haiti assessing that country's request for military assistance.

SECTION III. ECONOMIC

CHAPTER 8

THE ECONOMY

In 1972 Haiti's economy had completed its fourth straight year of growth after more than two decades of stagnation. The United Nations had noted that Haiti was the only country in the world experiencing almost no growth during most of the 1950s and 1960s; and the expanding birth rate had caused the per capita gross national product (GNP) to fall by an annual average of 2.3 percent between 1961 and 1967. The prolonged slump was finally broken during fiscal year 1968/69 when the GNP grew by 3.3 percent, and this was followed by growth rates of 4.7 percent in 1969/70 and 5.7 percent in 1970/71. The improvement was attributable to a more favorable government fiscal position; renewed business confidence; increased private, domestic, and foreign investment; and a rising flow of tourists. Construction was up, new banks were being established in the country, and foreign reserves had increased to record levels.

The total GNP reached G1,900 million (5 gourdes equal US$1) in 1970/71, and per capita GNP grew to G370. The balance-of-payments situation also improved because of increased exports, tourism, and remittances from Haitians working abroad. During the five-year period from 1966 to 1970 there was a small accumulated surplus of US$2 million in the balance of payments. Despite the improvement Haiti, in terms of per capita income, was the poorest country in the Western Hemisphere in 1972.

All economic statements and data concerning Haiti are informal and based mainly upon estimates and must therefore be treated with caution. The Haitian Statistical Institute can provide only partial data on most subjects. Because there has not been an accurate recent population count, the accuracy of per capita growth rates and income figures is open to question. Foreign trade statistics are usually not true values, and budget figures are arbitrarily made to balance.

Agriculture is the pillar of the economy. Until 1968 it had always contributed more than half of the gross domestic product (GDP). Subsequently the relative percentage fell slightly but was still more than 48 percent in 1970/71 (see table 2). More than 87 percent of the estimated 1.9 million person labor force was working in agriculture in the late 1960s. During the first half of the nineteenth century the land

Table 2. Haitian Gross Domestic Product, Fiscal Years 1967/71*
(by percentages)

Economic Sector	1966/67	1967/68	1968/69	1969/70	1970/71
Agriculture	51.1	50.3	50.0	47.9	48.2
Manufacturing	9.5	9.7	9.9	11.3	11.3
Commerce	10.1	10.3	9.9	10.0	9.9
Housing (rentals)	9.9	9.7	9.6	9.6	9.4
Services	6.4	6.4	6.0	6.3	6.2
Government	4.9	4.2	4.4	4.8	4.6
Construction	2.7	2.9	3.1	3.4	3.6
Transportation	2.5	3.7	3.5	3.4	3.3
Mining	1.2	1.4	2.0	1.7	1.9
Utilities	0.9	0.7	0.9	0.8	0.8
Banking and insurance	0.8	0.7	0.7	0.8	0.8
Total	100.0	100.0	100.0	100.0	100.0

*Fiscal year is October 1 through September 30.
Source: Adapted from Haiti, Presses Nationales d'Haiti, *Priorités de la Planification et Projections Quinquennales*, I, Port-au-Prince, 1972, p. 14a.

tenure pattern was transformed from one of large estates producing export crops to one of basically small holdings producing primarily for the domestic market and only secondarily for the export market. As of 1972 agriculture was characterized by the existence of a large number of small subsistence plots worked by traditional methods and suffering from soil exhaustion and erosion, frequent droughts, and the isolation of most producers from the market.

Manufacturing, including artisanry, accounted for the next leading component of GDP—over 11 percent in 1970/71. Commerce, once the second leading sector, dropped to third place with less than 10 percent of GDP. These two sectors together accounted for only about 4 percent of the labor force. House rentals, services, government, construction, transportation, mining, utilities, and banking and insurance, in that order, accounted for the balance of GDP. About 2.9 percent of the labor force was employed in construction; 1.5 percent, in government; and the balance, in the other sectors.

GOVERNMENT ROLE

Haitian government policy is to intervene in the economy only to the extent necessary to take up any slack left by private investment in certain sectors, to meet certain unmet needs, and to stimulate the economy. The maximum effort of the government during the late 1960s and efforts planned for the 1970s were to be in the fields of energy, communications, and irrigation. In addition, the government has occasionally helped save domestic companies from failure by becoming a partner and financing the company's capital needs.

Overall economic planning is carried out by the National Development and Planning Council (Conseil National de Développement et de Planification—CONADEP), which was created in 1963 as a result of tripartite assistance from the Organization of American States (OAS), the United Nations Economic Commission for Latin America, and the Inter-American Development Bank (IDB). Before the establishment of CONADEP, the only guidance was a five-year plan announced by the government of President Paul Magloire, which called for a total expenditure of G200 million in several fields. Not having any priorities, the plan was merely a list of projects, and there never was a final accounting of the few projects started.

CONADEP is headed by the president of the republic and is composed of the secretaries of state for finance and economic affairs; public works, transportation, and communication; commerce and industry; agriculture, natural resources, and rural development; and the president of the National Bank of the Republic of Haiti (Banque Nationale de la République d'Haiti—BNRH). The council decides upon general economic policy and priorities, and a technical secretariat is charged with carrying out the policy as well as overseeing the execution of the development budget. The personnel of the technical secretariat are reported to be highly competent, but their activities are not well coordinated with the various ministries. Also, technical personnel in the ministries are unevenly distributed so that activities of some departments are not carried out as well as those of others. In addition, the lack of adequate data restricts the planning activities of the technicians.

CONADEP's first project was a short-range plan covering the 1963–65 period and calling for total investment of G978 million. This figure proved highly unrealistic, and less than G40 million was invested during the period of the plan. CONADEP then issued only general annual plans until it released a medium-range five-year plan to cover the 1972–76 period. This plan, called Priorities of National Planning and Five-Year Projections, was more realistic and adequately prepared. It projected an average annual GDP growth of 7.7 percent and per capita income of G475 by 1976. It anticipated total public investment of about G730 million, of which about half would have to come from external financing. Some of the priorities in the plan were for the expansion of coffee and sugar exports; increased government investment in roads, harbors, and irrigation; the expansion of tourism; an expansion of social services; and improvement of the taxation system.

AGRICULTURE

Land Use, Tenure, and Practices

Because no cadastral survey had ever been made as of 1972 and because most farmers planted more than one crop in the same plot, land use statistics were difficult to assess. The latest statistics available in 1972 indicated that of the 6.8 million acres of total land in the country, about 2.2 million acres, or 32 percent, were cropland. About 1.4 million acres of the cropland were located on steep mountain slopes. Rough pastures accounted for 18 percent of the total land, or about 1.2 million acres, of which amount 518,000 acres were located on the Central Plateau. Forests and wooded areas covered about 622,000 acres, and the large balance of the land was idle or unproductive, mainly because of the mountainous terrain. About 300,000 acres of the idle land was believed to be potentially arable, but only if it were intensively irrigated.

Before independence there were over 8,500 plantations in the country producing sugar, cotton, indigo, and coffee, and they occupied one-half of the total land area. After independence in 1804 the government first attempted to maintain the plantation system. Some plantations were given to government officials, others were leased to private persons, and the state retained ownership of the majority of them. Former slaves worked for wages or for a share of the profits. The workers perceived no difference in their status, however, and became recalcitrant. When the country was divided into northern and southern portions in 1806, Henry Christophe in the north forced the reluctant workers to work on the plantations until his death in 1819 (see ch. 3). Alexandre Pétion in the south and his successor, Jean Pierre Boyer, broke up the plantations, however, and either gave or sold small plots of land to former slaves and soldiers. Ex-soldiers customarily received their plots gratis. Squatters appropriated much of the remaining estates in both north and south after Christophe's death. Under the administration of President Louis Félicité Salomon (1879–88) the squatters could receive title to their land if they cultivated certain crops. The Law for Rural Family Welfare of January 1934 provided for government grants of up to 12½ acres of state lands for farmers who worked the land effectively for a five-year period.

The exact number of farms in the country is unknown but was estimated at over 560,000 in the late 1960s. The majority of the farms, estimated at 70 percent, were operated by their owners and their families. Others were operated by sharecroppers and renters, and a few were operated by managers (called *gérants*) who lived and worked someone else's land either for a salary or for the usufruct of a portion of the land. Many of the renters leased state land because the state retained large holdings, although some of the land was parceled out over the years. Little of the state-owned land was idle; most was occupied by renters and squatters.

The owners of most farms have not legally established their titles. Even those few persons having valid deeds may not know the exact location of their boundaries. The only title for most farmers is actual occupation and use of the land and the general recognition of this by the farmers' neighbors. Even land that is sold often is not accompanied by a deed. When a son marries, the father usually gives him a portion of the farm. If the plot is too small for further allotment, then the younger sons try to obtain their own land. Some families do not divide the land but work it together until the father dies.

Most farms are very small. It has been estimated that 90 percent of the farms are smaller than fifteen acres; 8 percent are between fifteen and sixty-five acres in size; and 2 percent are larger than sixty-five acres. Several local surveys during the 1960s in various parts of the country tend to confirm these estimates. In one section of the country in the north the largest farm was ninety acres; on the Beaumont plateau on the southern peninsula, the largest farm was fifty acres, and only twelve farms in six villages located there exceeded twelve acres; in the commune of Archaie, 60 percent of 900 farms surveyed were under nine acres in size. Many farms consist of noncontiguous plots situated far apart. A farmer may own one plot, sharecrop a second, and rent out a third. The noncontiguity of the plots permits the farmer to raise diverse crops.

Agricultural practices on small farms are traditional, and modern methods are practiced only on some of the larger farms. Tools are basic: machete, hoe, digging stick, pruning knife, ax, and serpette (a machete-like tool with a wider blade and a crescent-shaped tip). There were fewer than 100 tractors in the entire country in the early 1960s; these were, for the most part, found on the few plantations or on the government experimental farms. Although many farms have livestock, few farmers use them to pull plows. Occasionally neighbors will purchase a plow jointly.

Most farmers cut the ground cover with a machete and burn it before planting. Some farmers stack it on hillsides to retard erosion, but burning is preferred because rats tend to nest in the piled cuttings. The soil is usually turned with a hoe. If the ground is hard or stony, machetes and serpettes are used instead of the hoe. Trees on the plot may or may not be felled. If felled, the wood is sold, made into charcoal, or used for cooking fuel. Trees are felled with machetes and axes; very few saws are found in rural areas.

Because most farmers are reluctant to try new varieties, seed selection is usually poor. Only the sugarcane and rice farmers try new varieties. Planting more than one crop in the same field is common; usually a long-season crop is planted with a short-season crop. Most farmers are faced with the problem of insufficient time in which to perform the various phases of cultivation. If the ground is cleared too early, weeds return before planting; if cleared too late, rains may prevent seeding; if rains come early, then planting continues into summer. After planting, fields may be weeded once, twice, or not at all—depending upon the estimated maturity date of the crop.

Given crops are planted in the same field until the yield falls drastically; then other crops are planted in their place unless the land is obviously exhausted, in which case the field is left fallow and used for pasturage for three to five years. Few farmers restore the fertility of the soil by the application of fertilizer. Because fallowing is so widely practiced as a soil conservation method, a farmer may have as little as 50 percent of his farmland under cultivation.

Many farmers plant hedges around their fields in an attempt to exclude thieves and livestock that get loose from their tethers. The hedges are usually fruit trees or plants having medicinal use. Small boys of the family ward off birds with the use of slingshots. Furthermore, to protect the crops from thieves, the farmer may dig pitfalls with cacti in the bottom, or he may hire a *bocor* (sorcerer) to place curses on uninvited guests entering the fields. He may then post white flags or painted calabashes, which indicate that the property is protected by spirits (see ch. 4).

When a farmer requires help, he may hire other farmers as day wage laborers if his economic circumstances permit. For major projects that require several persons, the farmer is more likely to obtain the services of one of several types of mutual work associations. These associations may range from three to five persons to much larger groups and may vary in the time the members work and the form of compensation required by them. From fifteen to thirty neighbors usually form associations, which help one another on a reciprocal basis. The measure of reciprocity is the amount of work performed in a half-day; this is called a *ronde*. Depending upon the section of the country, these work groups are called either *corvées* or *combites* and are considered to be a form of rural recreation because of the food and drink expected to be served by the farmer at the end of the work period (see ch. 5; ch. 4).

Crops

Despite the small size of the majority of the farms, most farmers plant more than three crops; at least one is destined for cash sales, and the others are used by the family. A very wide range of crops is grown throughout the country. Most are consumed domestically, although some are raised primarily for export (see table 3).

Coffee is the major money crop and is produced on farms as small as one to two acres in size. The largest coffee plantation is about 175 acres. Coffee was first introduced in 1726 from Martinique; the fact that the colonial plantations were of modest size in contrast to the large sugar plantations and at the same time could be profitable influenced the ex-slaves to plant coffee trees on their small plots. Coffee is widely cultivated at altitudes between 900 feet and 5,000 feet on mountain slopes, and the center of production is located in the southern peninsula. The total area planted in coffee trees is estimated at 345,000 acres.

Annual coffee production during the twentieth century generally has been less than that of the nineteenth century. Trees are planted too closely together, and little attention is given them. Unripe berries are harvested indiscriminately together with ripe berries, and processing

Item	1966	1969	1970	1971
Corn	233.7	242.0	240.0	252.0
Millet	187.3	209.0	210.0	211.0
Plantains	222.1	188.8	188.8	190.0
Manioc	111.2	121.2	130.0	134.0
Rice	76.0	83.0	80.0	81.0
Sugar, refined	60.0[1]	65.0[1]	75.0[1]	70.0
Peas and legumes	41.1	39.5	40.0	42.0
Coffee	28.0	24.8	27.8	24.8
Meat[2]	22.0	21.0	22.0	n.a.
Sisal	27.0[1]	17.0[1]	17.0[1]	18.0[1]
Sweet potatoes	6.4	7.4	n.a	n.a
White potatoes	6.4	7.4	6.6	7.0
Cacao	2.2	2.7	2.9	3.1
Tobacco	1.0	2.2	2.2	2.2

n.a.—not available.
[1] Short tons.
[2] Commercial production of beef, veal, and pork products.

procedures cause damage to a goodly portion of the crop, although an increasing number of farmers are bringing their berries to processing plants rather than doing the processing themselves.

The government issued a coffee code in 1942 detailing the procedures to be followed for cultivation, transportation, storage, processing, and marketing of coffee. The code has been ineffectively enforced, and Haitian coffee does not maintain a high international standard. Many smaller coffee farmers started to turn to other cash crops during the late 1960s because of lower export prices. In the early 1970s the government announced plans to distribute new seeds and fertilizer to coffee farmers and to teach modern techniques in hope of stimulating production.

Sugarcane is the second leading export crop. It was brought to Haiti by Christopher Colombus on his second voyage and quickly became the leading crop before independence because of high European prices for sugar. Large sugarcane plantations existed as early as 1680. Efficiently managed, they had first priority for water use, were intensively irrigated, and were fertilized with manure and ashes. Canefields whose yields decreased were left fallow or were rotated with another crop. After the sugar plantations were broken up and the land was distributed to peasants, production declined and never again reached its preindependence level. In 1972 sugarcane was raised on four plantations, each having its own mill; it was also raised by several thousand small growers who either sell their production to the plantation mills or make crude sugar and alcohol themselves. The total production of the small growers exceeds that of the plantations.

133

The largest sugarcane producer since 1918 has been the Haitian-American Sugar Company, which operates about 20,000 acres of owned and leased land, all of which is irrigated. Total land in sugarcane in the country was estimated at over 217,000 acres in the late 1960s. In 1972 the government created the National Sugar Institute to help sugarcane producers introduce higher yielding varieties, modernize their equipment, and increase the use of fertilizer.

Sisal, a relatively new crop first planted in 1927, is another important cash crop. Sisal grows well on poor, arid soil and does not require irrigation. Its fiber is extracted from the leaves of the plant, which can be cut twice yearly. The fibers are exported in crude form or in the form of binder twine and rope. Sisal is used domestically to make hats, shoes, handbags, curtains, and carpets. Sisal was once grown both by large estates and by smaller producers, but since 1970 all production has been in the hands of the small growers—the larger farms shifted to sugarcane during the 1960s in reaction to lower world demand for sisal. Despite its importance as a cash crop to many small farmers, the government does not provide any type of technical assistance, fiscal incentive, or price support to sisal producers.

Rice is the most important domestic food crop grown. Consumption is higher in the moneyed urban areas than in the rural areas. The rice grown is principally paddy varieties, but some dry rice is also raised. The main growing zones are the Estère Valley and the areas around Liancourt, Dessalines, Desdunes, and Verrettes, all on the Artibonite Plain. There is sufficient production to meet domestic needs and occasionally export some of it.

Corn occupies a sizable percentage of the cropland but is almost always interplanted with other crops. It is grown from sea level up to high mountain slopes. Many varieties are raised, and there is enough production to satisfy local demand and also permit small exports. Corn is boiled, roasted, mashed into meal, or used to make a syrupy drink called *akassa*.

Several types of tubers are produced. The most prolific is manioc, also called cassava, which can yield between three and four tons per acre in Haitian soil. It cannot be cultivated for many successive years in the same plot as it depletes the soil. Cassava flour is used to make bread and starch. Sweet potatoes are another of the food staples. Many varieties are grown; all are rich in starch. Sweet potatoes are usually planted in ridge-shaped rows on flat lands with another crop planted between rows. Taro, a tropical Pacific plant, also is grown in Haiti, where it is called *malangá*.

A great many varieties of bananas and plantains are found in Haiti. Plantains, which are starchy cooking bananas originally brought from Africa with the slaves, are an important part of the rural diet. The plant matures in one year and bears fruit for five years before requiring replanting. Its leaves are used for sleeping mats, food wrappings, pot covers, and cattlefeed and as protection against rain. The stalks of the plant are used in house construction. Bananas are grown in most parts of the country and at altitudes up to 4,000 feet. Careless handling of the fruit by farmers causes much wastage.

Cacao has been grown since it was introduced into the country in 1666. The chief zone of production is the Grande Anse region of the southern peninsula. Most cacao farms are poorly managed; the trees are old, crowded together, and unpruned, and parasites grow on the branches and fruit. Farmers frequently damage the fruit during picking and processing. As a result, lower prices prevail for Haitian cacao than for cacao from other countries.

Cotton was once one of the small peasants' main cash crops, but in the middle of the 1930s the Mexican boll weevil appeared in the country, and yields have been small ever since. Imports are required in some years to meet domestic demand for cotton. Most of the cotton is grown on the Central Plateau and the Artibonite Plain. In the late 1960s the government was stimulating the adoption of modern production techniques by cotton farmers, and some improvement was being noted.

Sorghum and millet, two popular grains because they withstand drought, are grown mainly on dry plains and on stony slopes, and both are consumed on a wide scale. Beans are a vital source of protein and are found everywhere except in the dry areas of the country. Some bean varieties have a short growing season and permit two or three plantings annually. The most popular bean is the red kidney bean, but several other types are also produced.

Coconut seedlings have been distributed to farmers over the years by the government, and there are several small plantations on the Cayes Plain in addition to scattered palms on small holdings. Coconut meat is eaten fresh, dried into copra, and fed to animals, and coconut leaves and wood are used for thatching and building materials. Peanuts are a popular food and are consumed in several ways: roasted, as peanut butter, or boiled and made into little cakes. Almond trees are found on many farms; the nuts are used to make a type of nut brittle, the tree is used as shade for livestock, and its wood is used for tool handles. Several thousand acres of rubber trees growing in the Port Margot valley in the Department of the North produce a few hundred tons of rubber annually.

Export crops since the late 1930s have been grasses and plants from which essential oils are obtained for use in making perfumes, soaps, flavoring extracts, and medicinal products. These include vetiver (moth repellent extract), lemon-grass, amyris (rose scent), petit-grain (orange flavoring), neroli (perfumes), sweet basil, and citronella. Exports of these products are controlled by the government in order to maintain quality.

The climate permits the growth of numerous fruits and vegetables that constitute an important part of the diet. Okra, of African origin, is widely raised and used as an ingredient in soups, stews, and sauces. Tomatoes are seldom eaten raw because of their strong tangy flavor; they are cooked for stews and soups. Breadfruit is the chief starchy food of the humid lowlands. The fruit is baked or boiled and made into a sticky dough. Mangoes are the most common fruit, followed by avocados. Because of their abundance the fruit of these trees is also fed to livestock. Another widely distributed fruit tree is the mamey or mammee. Its fruit is eaten raw, made into preserves, and used for livestock. There are eight species of citrus fruit; oranges and limes are the most abundant. Eggplants and cabbages are grown primarily for sale in urban areas. Pineapples, cherries, and watermelons are also raised.

Tobacco, once an important cash crop and used in lieu of currency during the early colonial era, is now a minor crop. Guinea grass is a crop grown by many farmers for animal fodder. It is cut rather than foraged and taken to where the livestock are tethered. A variety of herbs and spices are grown for rural home use and for sale in urban markets. The most common are marjoram, absinthe, anise, thyme, oregano, black pepper, cinnamon, cloves, nutmeg, garlic, horseradish, and asafetida. Gathering is also done. Many farmers gather wild herbs and leaves for medicinal use, Spanish moss for mattress stuffing, mangrove bark for tanning, plant fibers for weaving, and tree saps for glues.

Livestock

Only a few farmers derive their livelihood exclusively from livestock. There are very few ranches in the country, and stockraising is a supplemental activity for most farmers; farmers view their animals as a type of savings account because they are convertible into cash when funds are needed. Many tenant farmers receive young animals from their landlords to care for and share the profits when the stock is sold.

Cattle are mainly breeds derived from Spanish criollo stock of colonial times that over the years have interbred with Holsteins, Jerseys, Guernseys, Ayrshires, and Brown Swiss. Upgrading has proved difficult because most cattle are bred at random, and the peasant usually sells his best animals first. No adequate animal census has been taken, but there were an estimated 800,000 head of cattle in 1971, all of which are used for beef, milk, and work. Cows seldom give more than one-half quart of milk daily. Most cattle are kept tethered until after the harvest, and then they are free to forage in the harvested fields. When tethered they are usually kept in the part of the field that is fallow. Farm children are occupied with bringing water and feed supplies to the tethered animals.

More goats than cattle are believed to exist on farms, but they are of less importance because their milk is of poorer quality and their meat is tougher. Sheep have difficulty thriving in Haiti because of the semi-arid conditions of most of the farms. Hogs and pigs are the favorite kind of peasant livestock because they are easy to feed. Horses and other equines are used in rural areas mainly for locomotion and secondarily as draft animals. Donkeys, the most numerous of the equines, are also used as pack animals to transport merchandise to town. Chickens are raised unpenned by almost every peasant family. Because they constitute a cash product, they are seldom eaten by the farm family. There is a significant flow of poultry and eggs to urban areas. In addition to chickens, turkeys, ducks, geese, and guinea hens are also raised. Many farmers also maintain beehives, and honey and beeswax are minor export products.

Fishing and Forestry

Haitian waters are in the path of major fish migrations, but the commercial fishing industry is undeveloped. The country has no trained marine scientists, and no study or exploration of the offshore waters has ever been made. The Fisheries Section of the Ministry of Agriculture, Natural Resources and Rural Development attempts to coordinate fishing activities; it reported annual catches of between 5,000 and 7,000 tons during most of the 1960s. The most valuable catch is spiny lobsters, which are exported.

About 15,000 persons, largely working independently, are estimated to be engaged in fishing. Most fishermen remain close to shore, and few venture into deeper waters. Nets are commonly used, but some fishermen rely entirely upon rod and line. Because the supply does not seem to satisfy demand, there is no difficulty in selling the daily catch, and it is believed that the industry could be expanded easily.

In addition to ocean fishing, goodly quantities of fresh-water fish are caught. The government operates a modest fresh-water fish-stocking project and distributes fingerlings to rivers, ponds, lakes, and flooded rice paddies. The most popular fresh-water fish is carp, introduced into Haiti by an Israeli technical assistance mission.

The forestry industry, once important, has declined because of excessive cutting of trees for both commercial use and for fuel by peasants. The stands of mahogany, once extensive, were heavily depleted, and since 1944 all exports of mahogany lumber have been prohibited. Only processed items made of mahogany can be exported. The government distributes mahogany seedlings, and a partially enforced law requires ten seedlings to be planted for each mahogany tree cut.

Some lignum vitae logs are exported, but most are used domestically. Other major varieties exploited are pine, oak, cedar, and rosewood. The Haitian pine has a particularly high turpentine content, and a minor industry has developed around this. The logging industry consists of individual full-time loggers who travel around the country buying and felling trees and then transporting them to the few sawyards.

INDUSTRY

No comprehensive survey of the industrial history of the country has ever been made, and industrial data are scattered. A 1960 survey listed over 400 industrial establishments, but almost 160 of them were neighborhood bakeries, and 130 were small distilleries. Over half the industrial labor force in that survey was employed in seventeen sisal fiber-processing plants. Industrial growth before 1959 had been hindered by the customs tariff, which levied lower duties on imported manufactured products than on their component parts. This made it cheaper to import the finished product than to assemble it in Haiti. A 1959 decree provided for customs duties exemptions on most raw materials, machinery, and equipment and granted certain fiscal benefits to companies manufacturing for export; lesser benefits were granted to domestic market manufacturers.

Since the 1959 customs modification, and particularly since 1968, a large number of small assembly plants have begun operation and have made the light assembly industry field one of the more promising economic sectors. Almost all of these new firms, many of which are Haitian owned, are processing United States components into finished goods for reexport back to the United States. The products are those requiring considerable hand labor and include such items as baseballs, beaded articles, belts, boots, brassieres, cotton gloves, electrical parts, fishing lures, handbags, denim jeans, hairpieces, neckties, uniforms, ornaments, toys, sandals, screwdrivers, shirts, and wallets.

The exact number of such assembling plants is unknown but was estimated at 150 in 1972. They are believed to have created at least 10,000 new jobs. Women employees predominate in these assembling plants.

The actual growth of firms manufacturing for the domestic market has been less rapid than the growth of the assembling plants because of the narrow consumer market. Although the value of production is small, there is a fairly large range of products: cigarettes, soap, dentifrices, shoes, soft drinks, leathergoods, fabrics, clothing, furniture, carpets, rugs, stoves, cooking utensils, edible oils, lard, flour, textiles, and plastics products. Three large sugar mills produce sugar, molasses, and sugar byproducts for both the domestic and export markets. In addition, there are numerous small sugar mills (whose motive power is draft animals) producing crude sugar for the local rural areas.

A small dynamic sector since 1968 has been the construction industry, spearheaded by the demand for building of the new processing plants and by increased government spending on infrastructure projects. There was only one cement plant in the country in 1972; and it was operating close to its capacity of 90,000 tons annually. The company had plans to increase capacity eventually to 300,000 tons. A semiautonomous company, Haiti Steel (Acero de Haiti), was created in

1971, with joint state and private participation, to regulate the production of all metallic products for construction and consumer use. It was not clear in 1972 whether this company would manufacture its own products or regulate the production of other firms' products.

Small shop and artisan craftwork account for a large percentage of total manufacturing production. A 1960 study by the United Nations indicated that nearly half of all manufacturing by value was done in shops employing fewer than four persons. Many of the individual artificers and small shops are located in rural areas so peasants need not travel to towns to obtain their services; these include shoemakers, tanners, bakers, potters, butchers, and brick and tile makers. Urban furniture is almost always custom made by craftsmen. Tailors and dressmakers set up shop on their front porches with handcrank sewing machines. Traveling tinsmiths make utensils from used containers. Blacksmiths make most of the simple tools for farmers. The major occupation of carpenters in rural areas is coffin making. Most rural persons can build their own homes and implements, but a coffin is a prestige item and must be properly made by an expert. Basket making is perhaps the most widespread handicraft and frequently is the most lucrative craft. In several localities of the country the entire population engages in the same artisan activity, and the artisans work in groups, each one in turn taking the entire day's production as his own. Some farmers engage in artisan activities as a secondary occupation.

There is a small mining industry, with a total employment of perhaps 2,000 persons. Petroleum prospecting has been carried out unsuccessfully. The most important mineral mined is bauxite, which has been produced since 1957 by one company, Reynolds Haitian Mines. The reserves are not large, but the aluminum content is high. The main deposits are located at the town of Miragoâne. Copper from deposits near Gonaïves is also mined, but production was falling during the 1960s because of declining copper content of the ore and recurring landslides, which continually damaged the facilities. Salt is the only other mineral produced in any quantity—about 10,000 tons annually. The salt is made by an evaporation process from ponds at Grande Saline in the Artibonite delta. The process is not very efficient, and the salt is not pure.

Until 1972 the country suffered from frequent power shortages, and further industrial growth was threatened. In that year the Péligre hydroelectric complex at Lake Péligre went into operation and brought the total capacity in the country up to 60,000 kilowatts; an additional 16,000 kilowatts was scheduled for 1973. In 1968 the OAS estimated Haiti's total hydroelectric potential to be about 140,000 kilowatts.

In 1971 the government took over the privately owned company, which used to generate almost all of the country's electricity, and turned the company and the Péligre complex over to the state power board. The power board hopes to be able to bring electricity to small towns and rural areas, as less than 1 percent of the rural population had access to electricity in 1972. In some towns small privately owned and operated generators supply power to the owner and his neighbors. Other small towns may operate a generator only to illuminate the town square, and the townspeople resort to oil lamps for their own illumination.

DOMESTIC TRADE AND TRANSPORTATION

Commerce and Marketing

Port-au-Prince is the commercial center of the country, followed by Cap-Haïtien. There are some supermarkets in the capital but no department stores. Most shops are speciality stores retailing a few related articles, mainly imported. Some of the coffee export houses are also importers and wholesalers of manufactured articles. In the smaller towns and villages most retail stores sell general merchandise and are operated by the owner and his family, who usually live above the store. Some of the smalltown merchants are also middlemen who buy produce from peasants and pass it on to larger centers. Most of the smalltown merchants are mulattoes. Merchants in the capital city are generally white and of German, Syrian, or Lebanese extraction. Many of the importers and exporters are foreign nationals.

Most commercial transactions, however, do not occur in stores but in the urban, smalltown, and rural markets. A large central market in the capital called the Iron Market has indoor and outdoor stalls where food, miscellaneous articles, and even such services as sewing and dressmaking can be obtained. In smaller urban areas and in towns and villages the marketplace may have no permanent fixtures except, perhaps, stone platforms or rough tables where merchandise can be displayed. Only a few markets outside the capital are roofed.

Almost every town has a market at least once weekly; some markets are held daily. A few are centers of interregional trade, but most are of a local nature. From 1936 to 1952 a law prohibited rural markets; all markets had to be located in urban areas. Although many rural markets closed during that period, the law was not fully enforced, and many markets could be found at road crossings where no towns existed.

Most of the sellers in the markets are women. Some farm wives may travel up to 100 days yearly to nearby markets; they may carry up to sixty pounds of merchandise on their shoulders. In the larger markets commodities are separated by variety, but in smaller markets the wares are mixed together and present a confused appearance to outsiders. Many retailers of the same commodity are friends or relatives and tend to cooperate with one another by exchanging merchandise or tending one another's stand.

In addition to the markets, housewives in the capital and other urban areas have the services of ambulatory vendors who hawk their wares in the street. In some residential neighborhoods of Port-au-Prince the vendors are so numerous and sell such diverse products that the housewife seldom has to travel to the marketplace to shop.

Price quotations are almost meaningless except in the urban specialty shops. In Port-au-Prince prices vary by type of customer; for example, higher prices are quoted to a foreigner than to a Haitian. In smaller towns the same prices usually are quoted to all customers. There is almost no grading of merchandise, and there is no widely accepted system of weights and measures. The same commodity may be quoted on a value basis, by weight, or by unit. Poultry and livestock are sold on the basis of their appearance rather than on weight, but butchered meat is sold by weight. Sometimes no scales are used even when an item is sold by weight; both buyer and seller judge the weight by lifting the article. Certain commodities are quoted in units of cooking pots, mess tins, or lard cans. The most popular such item is the *marmite*, a four- to five-pound cooking pot, which is further divided into *godets* (bowls). The volume of the *marmites* and *godets* vary by locality and are not uniform. Some old French measures are still in use, the most popular being the *aune*, equivalent to forty-seven inches. The most common land measure is the *carreau*, about 3.33 acres. There are twelve measures for coffee, varying from 2.3 pounds up to 2,133 pounds, and there are seventeen measures in the cacao trade.

Communication and Transportation

The transportation system, inadequate for the needs of the country, hinders the movement of agricultural produce from rural areas to urban centers. Many small interior towns are connected to each other only by foot or animal trails. There were 2,000 miles of roads in the country in 1969, of which only about 300 miles were paved. The lack of maintenance slowed travel on the paved sections; for example, the 170-mile road between Port-au-Prince and Cap Haïtien, the main highway in the country, took eight hours to travel in 1972. In that year the government created a permanent agency to maintain highways, the financing to come from earmarked gasoline taxes.

Most of the unpaved roads are impassable in rainy weather. There are almost no bridges, and most of the roads have only fords to cross rivers and streams; some roads follow the streambed and are completely submerged when it rains. One main road transversing the southern peninsula has 100 fords, and heavy rains prevent crossing until the water subsides. In dry weather the condition of most roads prevents speeds of more than twenty miles per hour.

As of 1969 there were about 16,500 vehicles in the country, of which almost 13,000 were automobiles. The remainder was mainly trucks and jeeps. Most trucks have benches and carry interurban passengers who wait at truck depots until the driver has a full load of cargo and passengers. Smaller trucks, or jitneys, carry up to seven passengers and provide a slightly more luxurious means of travel between cities and outlying areas. There are some interurban buses, but they maintain no fixed schedules. Within cities the primary means of public transportation is taxis or jitneys.

The state owns a short-line railroad called the National Railroad Company, but most of its system was inoperative in 1972 because of a lack of maintenance of the track and rolling stock. Only portions of its main line between Port-au-Prince and Verettes were in use. One of the sugar companies has a railroad subsidiary called the Cul-de-Sac Railroad Company, but it carries only freight and sugar.

There is one domestic airline, Haitian Air Transport Company (Compagnie Haïtienne de Transports Aeriens—COHATA), organized in 1943 by the Haitian military to provide service between major towns. Only Port-au-Prince and Cap-Haïtien have adequate airports; the Port-au-Prince International Airport can accommodate large jet aircraft. The other airports in the country have unpaved and unlit runways limiting traffic to daylight hours and good weather. Another Haitian-owned airline, Air Haiti, began offering international cargo service in late 1970 between Haiti, Puerto Rico, and Miami but did not provide domestic service. International passenger service is provided by several foreign airlines.

There are about fourteen seaports open to international commerce, only a few of which are important. Port-au-Prince is the principal seaport, handling about 90 percent of all imports and 60 percent of all exports by volume. In 1972 the facilities of Port-au-Prince were being enlarged so that handling capacity could be increased from 235,000 tons annually in 1972 to 510,000 tons by 1977. Most of the balance of the foreign trade, mainly coffee exports, is handled by Cap-Haïtien, Gonaïves, Jacmel, Les Cayes, Petit-Goâve, and Jérémie. About ten foreign shipping companies operated out of Haitian ports in 1972, and there were five domestically owned merchant vessels totaling 31,250 gross registered tons.

Coastal shipping is of great importance for many communities. Because of the inadequate overland transportation system, small sailboats and motor vessels provide the only communication between many towns and the capital. In the late 1960s there were over 300 such small craft, none of which registered more than sixty tons. The crews frequently acted as intermediaries for local residents, buying and selling merchandise in Port-au-Prince on a commission basis. The only river that can be used for inland transportation is the Grande Anse, navigable up to about forty miles.

Four firms provided telecommunications services. There were fewer than 5,000 telephones in the country in 1972. Port-au-Prince had a small dial system and was connected with Cap-Haïtien, Jérémie, Les Cayes, Jacmel, Saint-Marc, and Gonaïves. About twenty-eight localities had manual exchanges. There was local and international telegraph service, as well as international telephone service. Postal Service was provided between eighteen large post offices and 114 small postal agencies.

Tourism

The government views the tourist industry as a promising way of earning foreign exchange. The number of tourists visiting the country had fallen off during the 1960s because of an adverse image abroad of the internal political situation, but since 1968 Haiti has started to become popular once again. Tourists are attracted by the low prices, interesting folklore, French-style cuisine, and the colorfulness of the country. In 1971 over 87,000 persons visited Haiti; some came to take advantage of the country's liberal divorce laws, which have no residence requirements.

Many of the tourists come on cruise ships and stay only a few days, sleeping on board their ships. More rapid growth of tourism faces the obstacles of travel away from the capital, the shortage of adequately trained tourist personnel, and a lack of overseas promotion. The government maintains one tourist office in New York City. A free port was opened in 1972 on Tortue Island in an effort to stimulate tourism there, and a French tourist club acquired facilities near the capital to cater to European tourists. In addition, in 1972 the government offered to help finance up to 40 percent of the construction cost of new hotel facilities.

FOREIGN ECONOMIC RELATIONS

Trade

In 1972 Haiti's foreign trade policy was designed to increase the export of processed manufactured goods and to protect the new industries by means of high import duties, licenses, quotas, and prohibition of importation of certain items. In most years imports exceeded exports (see table 4). All exports except coffee require prior authorization from the Ministry of Commerce and Industry in order to ensure an adequate domestic supply of the product. Exporters of certain agricultural products must also be producers of that product or be a member of a producers cooperative.

Coffee has been the leading export since 1810 when it surpassed sugar. In some years it accounted for more than half of all exports. Haiti is a member of the International Coffee Organization, which sets annual export quotas for members. In most years Haiti has not been able to meet its basic quota because of inadequate production (see Agriculture, this ch.). In addition, because of poorer processing and lower quality, the price paid for Haitian coffee is lower than for coffee from other countries.

The category called light manufactures, including all assembly and

143

Table 4. Foreign Trade of Haiti, Fiscal Years 1966-70*
(in million U.S. dollars)

Commodity	1965/66	1966/67	1967/68	1968/69	1969/70
Imports:					
Manufactures	10.1	10.9	12.1	11.8	14.9
Machinery and					
transportation equipment	5.1	5.3	4.6	6.2	10.4
Food products	7.4	7.4	5.7	8.1	5.8
Chemicals	3.9	4.3	4.2	4.4	5.6
Fats and oils	2.7	2.5	2.3	2.7	3.5
Combustibles	2.2	2.0	2.3	3.6	2.9
Wood and tobacco	1.0	1.4	1.1	1.4	1.4
Raw materials	0.5	0.8	0.6	0.8	0.9
Miscellaneous	3.1	3.4	3.5	4.7	6.3
Total	36.0	38.0	36.4	43.7	51.7
Exports:					
Coffee	20.7	13.7	14.6	13.7	15.2
Light manufactures	1.2	2.5	4.9	4.4	7.0
Bauxite	3.6	3.3	4.1	6.5	5.6
Sugar	2.8	3.8	3.1	2.1	2.8
Essential oils	2.0	2.7	2.7	3.1	2.7
Sisal	2.8	1.4	1.6	2.5	1.8
Copper	1.9	1.8	1.2	1.5	1.2
Cacao	0.1	0.1	0.2	0.5	1.1
Miscellaneous	3.3	3.0	3.3	2.8	3.1
Total	38.4	32.3	35.7	37.1	40.5

*Fiscal year is October 1 through September 30.

Source: Adapted from Haiti, Administration Générale des Douanes, *Rapport Annuel de l'Administration Générale des Douanes pour l'Exercise, Octobre 1969-Septembre 1970*, Port-au-Prince, n.d., tables 14, 15.

transformation products, became the second leading export component during the 1967/68 fiscal year. Almost all of the production and exports go to the United States. Haiti has become the world's largest exporter of baseballs. Until it was surpassed by the category of light manufactures, bauxite was the second leading export. Sugar exports follow bauxite. Haiti has a small quota of 31,000 short tons under the United States Sugar Import Act of 1971, the same amount it had held previously.

Essential oils, sisal, copper, cacao, and miscellaneous products follow, in that order. Sisal exports have been declining because of lower world prices and increased domestic use of sisal for twine and bags. One important export before the 1960s was bananas, but mismanagement of the banana export trade and the failure to abide by contract terms caused buyers to turn to other suppliers. Haitian banana exports therefore fell to minimal amounts.

The percentage composition of imports has been fairly stable. The leading component has been manufactured consumer durables. Food

144

products and machinery usually follow in importance. The major food products imported are wheat, fish, vegetable oils, and lard. Other important imports are petroleum products, paper, glass, and pharmaceuticals.

Trade is carried on with about seventy countries annually, but significant trade relations are maintained with only about ten countries. The leading trading partner is the United States. Although it took a steadily increasing share of Haitian exports, from 42.6 percent in 1965/66 to over 58 percent in 1969/70, its share of the Haitian import market in the same period fell from over 56 percent to about 46 percent. Japan has been providing a steadily increasing share of the imports and moved into second place in 1966/67; its share was over 9 percent in 1969/70. France's share of the import market has also been increasing and was over 5 percent of the total in 1969/70. Other major suppliers during the 1960s were: the Federal Republic of Germany (West Germany), with about 5 percent annually; Belgium, 2 to 3 percent; Italy, 2 to 5 percent; the Netherlands, 2.5 to 3.5 percent; the United Kingdom, around 4 percent; Canada, 2.5 to 6 percent; and Curaçao, 3 to 5 percent. Curaçao provides all the fuels and lubricants.

Belgium was the second leading export market for Haitian exports, with 8 to 12 percent of the total. Most of the coffee exports went to Belgium. France followed with 7 to 10 percent of the total; Italy, 6 to 11 percent; the Netherlands, 5 to 8 percent; and Japan, 3 to 5 percent.

Foreign Aid and Investment

From available statistics it appeared that Haiti was the recipient of about US$160 million in foreign aid and assistance from 1946 through late 1972. From 1962 until about 1970 Haiti was almost without any assistance because most foreign governments and international institutions were reluctant to grant any. The reluctance stemmed from conflicting political views and Haiti's history of mismanagement of funds. Loans have been made only when there seemed to be some assurance of the funds going for the intended project.

The United States was the largest source of foreign aid, providing about US$120 million during the 1946–72 period, of which amount about US$85 million was in the form of grants. The Agency for International Development (AID) and its predecessor agencies provided about US$66 million (US$60 million in grants); the Export-Import Bank lent about US$28 million; the Food for Peace program provided about US$18 million; and miscellaneous agencies and projects, including military assistance, provided the rest.

The Inter-American Development Bank (IDB) supplied about US$25 million for port facilities, agriculture, industry, and water supplies. The IDB US$10-million loan for the expansion of the Port-au-Prince port facilities was the largest single loan the country had ever received.

The International Bank for Reconstruction and Development (IBRD, known as the World Bank) lent about US$3 million, the United Nations provided about US$10 million under various programs, and European countries and Israel provided the balance. The International Monetary Fund (IMF) negotiated twelve agreements, called standby arrangements, with Haiti from 1958 through 1972 in order to protect the country's low foreign exchange reserves. These agreements made available a stipulated amount of foreign exchange if needed. Haiti was an extensive user of the standby arrangements.

The exact amount of foreign investment in Haiti was unknown in 1972 but had been variously estimated at between US$50 million and US$60 million during the mid-1960s and between US$70 million and US$80 million in the late 1960s. Because of the large number of new assembling firms establishing themselves since 1968 this figure should be considerably higher. There were indications that two-thirds of all investments in industry during the 1960s came from foreign sources, mainly from the United States and France. In mid-1972 the government issued a decree prohibiting the granting of any further concessions for foreign exploitation of natural resources, including subsoil rights, and tourism.

FINANCE

Government Revenue and Expenditures

A draft budget for the central government is submitted by the finance minister to the cabinet in January and forwarded to the legislature in April for its approval for the next fiscal year, which begins on October 1 and terminates September 30. Because of the timelag between submission of the budget and beginning of the fiscal year, many items are frequently overlooked or underestimated, and a supplemental budget may have to be approved after the start of the fiscal year. The budget is not a true measure of public-sector finances because numerous accounts are not included. These are the accounts of many of the autonomous agencies, tax revenues that have been earmarked for a specific purpose, and the service on the public debt. None of these accounts are ever published.

The published budget of the central government is composed of two parts—the operating and development budgets. The 1969/70 operating budget was G138 million, and the development budget was G61 million. The 1970/71 operating budget dropped slightly to G137 million, whereas the development budget rose to G104 million. In 1971/72 the operating budget jumped to G148 million, but the development budget rose only to G107 million. The development budget relies heavily on foreign financing and presupposes that a certain percentage will come from abroad; it is seldom met as sufficient external financing is rarely forthcoming.

The largest share of the operating budget is applied to general government administration. This amounted to 38 percent in 1969/70 but was down to 32 percent in 1970/71. Defense and security accounted for 17 percent total expenditures in 1969/70 but only 14 percent in 1970/71. Education claimed 14 percent of the budget in 1969/70 and 12 percent in 1970/71. Health and sanitation accounted for 11 percent and 10 percent, respectively, in the two fiscal years. All of the other functions accounted for the balance of expenditures. The Ministry of Interior and National Defense received 31 percent of the budget in both fiscal years.

Although the total public debt is unknown, the known foreign component was about US$9.5 million in 1969. The equivalent of about 5 percent of the budget was estimated to be needed to amortize the public debt in 1969/70 and 1970/71. Some of the foreign debt had fallen into arrears during the 1960s, but an improved economic situation after 1968 helped the government once again to service its debts on schedule.

Taxes bring in the major percentage of government revenue—about 90 percent. Nontax sources, such as profits of the National Bank of the Republic of Haiti and the forced sale of government savings certificates to wage earners, bring in the balance. Despite the reliance on taxation as the major revenue source, the tax burden on the population is the lowest in the Western Hemisphere; it was about 7 to 8 percent of the GNP in the late 1960s.

The early leaders of the republic raised revenues by means of a territorial tax of one-fourth in kind on all produce. Henry Christophe added a tax on the titles of the nobility he created, but Pétion initiated the first customs duties on both imports and exports, which have remained the major revenue source. Additional varieties of taxes were added in the twentieth century. Import duties accounted for 38 percent of total revenue in 1970/71, and export taxes accounted for an additional 12 percent. Income taxes accounted for only 11 percent, special sugar taxes made up about 4 percent, and miscellaneous sales taxes accounted for the remainder.

Banking and Currency

The name of the currency is the gourde, believed to have been derived from the short name for the piastre-gourde, the most common French coin utilized during the colonial period. Other sources, however, contend that the name of the currency stems from the gourd, or calabash, which has multiple household uses and is a voodoo symbol for a high priest or priestess. The symbol for the gourde is G. The gourde is divided into 100 centimes and comes in banknotes in denominations of one, two, five, ten, twenty, and fifty.

The United States dollar is also legal tender in Haiti, based upon an agreement between the two countries made in 1919. The official rate of exchange in 1972 between the two currencies was 5 gourdes equal US$1, a rate that had been in effect since 1934. The par value for purposes of the IMF, however, was changed in April 1972 from 5 gourdes equal US$1 to 4.54 gourdes equal US$1 to compensate for the depreciation of the dollar in world markets. No black market has ever existed in Haiti, but it is known that Haitian banknotes have been quoted at a discount by New York City banks since 1961.

In late 1972 the banking system consisted of three government banks and credit facilities and seven private banks. The oldest and largest was the government-owned National Bank of the Republic of Haiti (Banque Nationale de la République d'Haïti—BNRH). In 1880 a private bank, the National Bank of Haiti, was created and made the fiscal agent of the government and was also permitted to issue money. In 1910, after several years of fiscal scandals, the bank was liquidated and replaced by the newly formed BNRH. Until 1934, when the government acquired full control, the BNRH was a private bank.

The BNRH is both a central bank and a commercial bank. In addition to issuing money and acting as the state's fiscal agent, it also controls the banking system, rediscounts commercial paper for the private banks, and carries out all regular commercial banking functions plus some nonbanking services, such as operating the Port-au-Prince wharf. The BNRH is managed by a five-man board of directors appointed by the president of the republic; one of the five is named the bank's president and general director.

The Institute for Agricultural and Industrial Development (Institut de Développement Agricole et Industriel—IDAI) is a government agency offering long-term credit to agriculture and industry. The institute was officially created in 1951 as the Haitian Institute for Agricultural and Industrial Credit; its name was changed in 1961 when it was merged with another government lending agency. The Bureau of Agricultural Credit—a small credit facility that is part of the Ministry of Agriculture, Natural Resources and Rural Development—finances loans to small farmers and cooperatives.

The oldest private bank, the Royal Bank of Canada, has operated in the country since 1919 and is engaged mainly in short-term commercial transactions and exchange operations. A Colombian bank, the Popular Bank of Bogotá, opened a Haitian branch in 1955 called the Haitian-Colombian Popular Bank (Banque Popular Colombo-Haïtienne), and the Commercial Bank of Haiti (Banque Commerciale d'Haiti) started operations in 1961. The improvement in the economy after 1969 induced several other foreign banks to open branches. The First National City Bank opened in 1971, and the Haiti Union Bank, partially owned by Dominican Republic interests, opened in 1972, as did the Bank of Nova Scotia. The National Bank of Paris was in the process of opening a branch in late 1972.

There is no securities exchange system in Haiti that would permit domestic firms to raise capital from local sources. A few companies issue bonds and stocks but have them traded on the over-the-counter market in New York City. About thirty-five insurance firms operate in Haiti, but only two or three are Haitian owned.

As of 1972 private banks could not make loans for longer than one year, but in that year the government expressed its desire to remove this restriction shortly. At the end of 1971 total outstanding credit was only about G95 million. Most persons, particularly small farmers, do not have access to institutionalized credit because tangible property is usually required as collateral. Such persons obtain their credit needs from moneylenders, middlemen, or exporters. Repayment of such loans need not be in cash but may be in kind. Interest is high, but in some cases a social relationship exists between the lender and the borrower, and little or no interest is charged.

SECTION IV.

NATIONAL SECURITY

CHAPTER 9

NATIONAL DEFENSE AND PUBLIC ORDER

In 1972 Haiti's security forces consisted of the armed services, which numbered about 6,000 officers and men, and a militia organization called the National Security Volunteers (Volontaires de la Sécurité Nationale—VSN), estimated to number from 7,000 to 10,000. The armed forces had a unified system in which operational command over the small coast guard and aviation corps was exercised by an army officer who was also chief of the general staff.

Military service was on a volunteer basis, and there were usually more volunteers than vacancies. The small strength of the armed forces had no detrimental impact on the labor force, and military spending averaged only about 2 percent of the gross national product (GNP).

Military service was a respected career, and both officers and men were proud of Haiti's military heritage. During the wars for independence the Haitian army was at first outclassed by the French forces in every respect except in spirit and leadership. Although the Haitians lost thousands of men they never relinquished pressure against the French, who eventually withdrew.

President François Duvalier, shortly after his inauguration, created an additional armed force known as the *tontons macoutes*. The name was derived from Haitian mythology, in which the *tontons macoutes* were bogeymen who placed little children in bags and kidnapped them. The *tontons macoutes* served President Duvalier as a semisecret police.

The security forces had the capability of maintaining internal security and public order. The centralized control of both the armed forces and the police provided the government with a countrywide intelligence net and an ability to dispatch units of the armed forces to any area in the interior. Although the Haitian peasant is vitally concerned about matters that affect him or his family, he is usually uninformed about political conditions and has shown no interest in joining or even providing support for the armed bands of exiles who have landed clandestinely on Haitian shores in abortive attempts to topple the government.

NATIONAL DEFENSE

National Defense Budget

For five years—1964 through 1968—military expenditures in Haiti averaged the equivalent of US$7.8 million, or about 2.4 percent of the GNP. Military expenditures (including the allocation for the police as well as for the armed forces) averaged about 14 percent of the total budget. Between 1950 and 1963 the country received US$4.5 million in military aid from the United States, after which the program was discontinued.

Organization and Control of the Armed Forces

In the late 1950s the chain of command in the armed forces stemmed from the president of the republic to the secretary of state for interior and national defense, and from that official to the chief of the general staff. From the general staff the chain of command went directly to the operational and support units. President François Duvalier, however, realized fully the importance and power of the army by observing the ease with which Colonel Paul Magloire had forced out President Dumarsais Estimé in 1950 and, soon after his inauguration, Duvalier set about emasculating the power of the officer corps.

President Duvalier removed many high-ranking officers from the active list and periodically reshuffled unit commanders. He dismissed not only officers whom he suspected had supported his three opponents in the presidential election, but also those who had supported him. He weakened the power of the army chief of staff (who also served as chief of the general staff) by assuming direct operational control over two elite units stationed in the capital city: the Dessalines Battalion and the Presidential Guard. He also removed from the army chief of staff the prerogative of selecting the commanders of key posts in the military departments and appointed only trustworthy supporters. He then utilized the basement of the presidential palace and its surrounding grounds as an armory for the storage of the principal items of the army's ordnance matériel. In 1972 there was no indication that the personal control over the armed forces exercised by former President François Duvalier had been relinquished by his son Jean-Claude.

For the dual purposes of national defense and the maintenance of public order the country was divided into six military departments with army units stationed in each (see fig. 4). The headquarters of these were: Northwest Department, Port-de-Paix; North, Cap-Haïtien; Artibonite, Gonaïves; Center, Hinche; West, Port-au-Prince; and South, Les Cayes. Each military department was divided into military districts, and these in turn into military subdistricts. Below the subdistricts were the rural posts—each headed by a chief, an army enlisted man who was the intermediary between the residents of the local area and the urban seat of the next higher military authority.

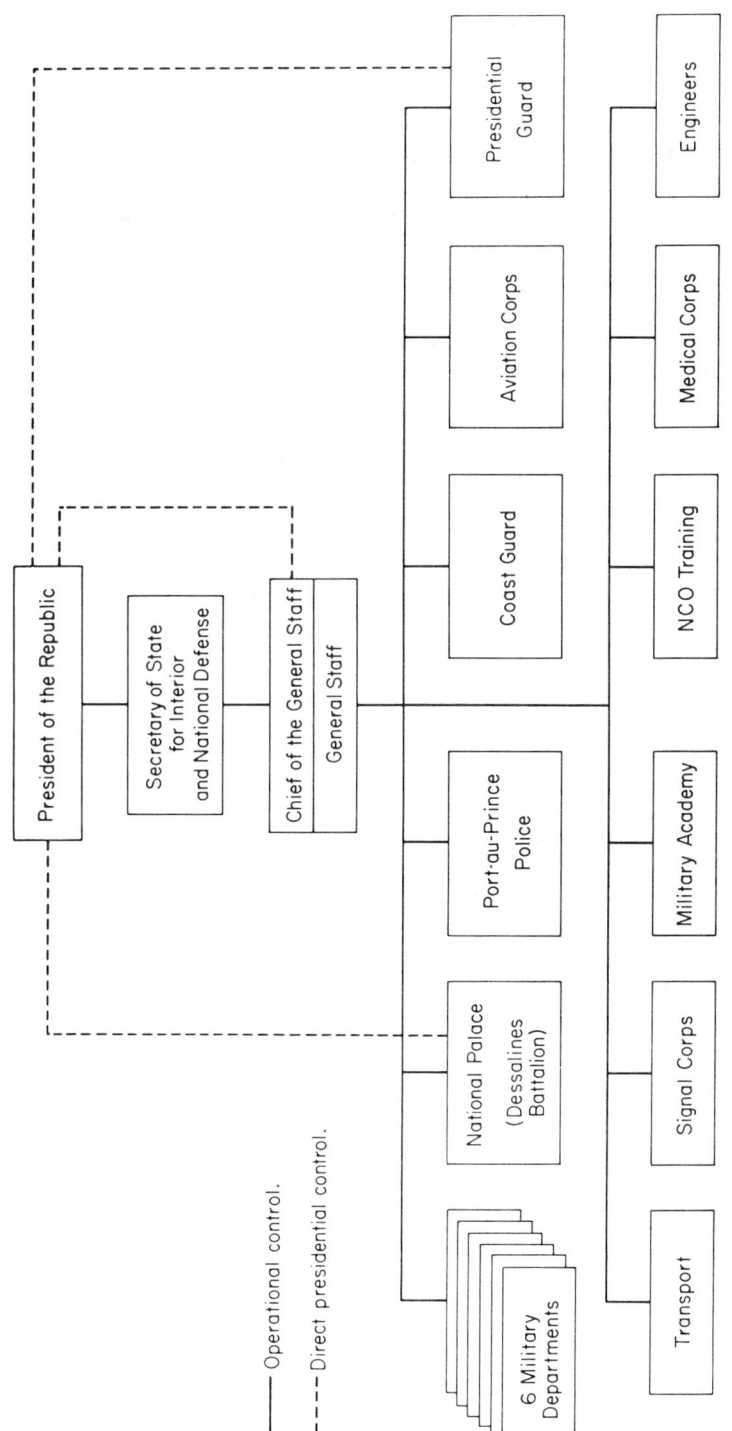

Figure 4. Organization of the Armed Forces of Haiti, 1973

——— Operational control.

- - - - Direct presidential control.

President of the Republic

Secretary of State for Interior and National Defense

Chief of the General Staff

General Staff

Presidential Guard

Aviation Corps

Coast Guard

Port-au-Prince Police

National Palace (Dessalines Battalion)

6 Military Departments

Engineers

Medical Corps

NCO Training

Military Academy

Signal Corps

Transport

The general staff consisted of four sections: personnel, intelligence, operations, and logistics. An army major general served as both chief of the general staff and commander of the armed forces. The two elite army units were the Dessalines Battalion, which consisted of about 500 men, and the Presidential Guard, which numbered about 700. The enlisted members of the Presidential Guard were housed on the ground floor and basement of the presidential palace, and those of the Dessalines Battalion were in the Caserne Dessalines, situated on the grounds in back of the palace.

Despite its name, the Port-au-Prince Police Force, with a total strength of about 400 men, was an army unit. There was a small coast guard of about 250 men whose main function was to prevent smuggling. The aviation corps, operating about twenty-five aircraft—both military and civilian—and having approximately 250 officers and men, operated the civilian airline. The airfield at Port-au-Prince could accommodate jet aircraft, and ten other cities had fields capable of accommodating C–47 type transport aircraft.

The military academy was established in 1941. It offered a three-year course for about sixty cadets. The Camp d'Application was a training school for noncommissioned officers. Within the army organization there were transportation, communications, medical, and engineer units. The communications section was of great importance to the government since it had voice radio and telegraph communication with the headquarters of the six military departments, and these in turn had at least telephone communication with the military districts, subdistricts, and rural sections. In many rural areas the only telephone was that controlled by the military, and orders could be transmitted immediately from the headquarters in Port-au-Prince to any outlying district. This made the police-army combination the most powerful unit in the governmental system.

Recruitment and Conditions of Service

Conditions of service in the armed forces are such that there has never been any need for conscription. A retirement and pension law has been in effect since 1935. Commissioned officers who have served twenty-five years may retire with a pension equal to one-half of their monthly pay at the time of retirement. The same provision applies to enlisted men with twenty-five years of service.

Officers and enlisted men who were disabled in the line of duty are obligated to appear before a board of medical officers. The board can decide to grant them one-half of their active duty pay at the time of retirement, regardless of the number of years they have served. The mandatory retirement age for officers is sixty, and that for enlisted men is fifty. One percent of the monthly salary for all members of the armed forces is withheld to create a pension fund. If a retired officer is a widower with legitimate minor children, at his death one-half of his pension goes to them until they are legally adults.

Both officers and enlisted men take pride in the military tradition of the republic. Each year on Army Day (November 18) the defeat of General Leclerc's forces is widely celebrated (see ch. 3). For commissioned personnel a military career offers both social and political mobility, since several of their number have attained the position of president of the republic.

Uniforms and Insignia

All three branches of the armed forces—the army, the air force, and the coast guard—have fatigue and garrison uniforms. Full dress white uniforms for officers are optional. Army officers on some occasions wear green blouses and beige slacks or riding britches and boots. Certain army units, especially the Dessalines Battalion and the Presidential Guard, have dress and parade uniforms of dark blue. The Port-au-Prince police wore army uniforms until 1972, when they were provided with light-blue uniforms to distinguish them from army units.

Army and aviation corps rank insignia are indicated on shoulder boards: one, two, or three chevrons for company grade officers; one, two, or three small gold stars for field grade officers; and one, two, or three larger silver stars for general officer rank. Coast guard rank insignia on dress uniforms consist of gold bands worn on the sleeve.

Awards and Decorations

The Haitian government has nine decorations, some of which are awarded only to military personnel and some to both military and civilian personnel, native and foreign. Two of these, the Military Medal and the Distinguished Service Medal, are awarded only to military personnel for heroism and exceptional courage during military or police action. Both officers and enlisted men receive awards for completing a specified number of years of active duty service with excellent records. The decorations are awarded only once, a silver star being worn on the ribbon for additional awards.

The Order of Pétion and Bolívar is awarded to the president, to foreign chiefs of state, and to foreign diplomatic personnel for service in the field of Pan Americanism. Other awards are made to civilian nationals for outstanding public services. The nine decorations were authorized by the Haitian government between the years of 1922 and 1958.

National Security Volunteers

The National Security Volunteers (Volontaires de la Sécurité Nationale—VSN) was organized by President François Duvalier as a counterpoise to the army. The members received the equivalent of military basic training and, although they were not officially paid salaries, some remuneration was received from the budgets of the communities in which the men served. The members were usually inhabitants of the outlying districts who went about their regular daily work unless called upon in case of an emergency, when they served as

155

an additional defense force. Since 1971 the importance of the organization as a security organ has declined significantly. It now more nearly resembles a political party than a military force.

The Tontons Macoutes

The *tontons macoutes* wore civilian clothes but carried side arms. They were integrated into government organizations as well as in important private enterprises. During the regime of President François Duvalier their strength was estimated to be between 1,500 and 5,000. The *tontons macoutes* were effective in providing the president with sufficient information on individuals and on government agencies to allow him to exercise autocratic control over the entire governmental structure, but their lack of restraint resulted in many atrocities. The president relieved several *tonton macoute* leaders of their positions and took measures to restrain their operations.

PUBLIC ORDER

Internal Security

In 1972 there was no substantial threat to the government of Haiti from either internal or external sources. Thousands of Haitians were living abroad, mostly émigrés from the regime of President François Duvalier. These groups were scattered throughout the Caribbean islands, the eastern United States, Canada, and West Africa. These émigré groups had no central organization, and frequently their leaders disagreed among themselves. Refugee Haitians were urged to return to their native land, but hesitated, realizing that control of both the government and the armed forces still rested with the Duvalier clan. During the regime of François Duvalier five invasion attempts had been made by small bands of armed men, including former military officers. The objectives in each case had been to recruit followers in numbers sufficient to challenge the armed forces and eventually to topple the government. In none of these incidents did the Haitian peasants rally to the invader cause, however, and in each case the invaders were killed or captured by army units.

The Haitian Communist Party was founded in 1930 and disintegrated the next year when its leaders were forced to flee the country. It has reappeared from time to time, and in 1969 a pro-Castro party and a pro-Soviet party merged to form the Unified Party of Haitian Communists (Parti Unifié des Communistes Haïtiens—PUCH). In 1970 the party was estimated to have only about 500 members. The party advocates the overthrow of the Duvalier-controlled government by armed struggle to be fought by an "army of liberation," but these sentiments are usually broadcast from abroad.

The Penal System

Data on the number of inmates in the country's penitentiaries and prisons were not available in 1972. There were two penitentiaries, Fort Dimanche and the National Penitentiary—both in Port-au-Prince—and prisons in the cities of Les Cayes, Hinche, Gonaïves, Cap- Haïtien, and Port-de-Paix. Prison labor was for state use only, and prison-made goods, such as license tags, furniture, and clothing, were made available for sale to public agencies.

The Penal Code and Code of Criminal Procedures

The Penal Code of Haiti was first promulgated in August 1835 and was amended nine times between 1846 and 1935. It recognized three categories of offenses—felonies, misdemeanors, and police contraventions—and defined the penalties imposed for them.

Punishments enumerated are: death; imprisonment for life with forced labor; imprisonment with forced labor for a specific number of years; and jail for a specific period. Punishments not requiring detention are banishment, loss of civil rights, and placement under special police surveillance.

Death sentences are executed by a firing squad, the execution taking place in a public area designated in the writ of condemnation. Men condemned to forced labor are employed on public projects; women are employed inside the penal institutions.

Accomplices receive the same punishment as the culprits. There is no punishment for offenses committed by persons acting under duress or under circumstances beyond their control, and mitigating circumstances may change punishments. The death penalty or imprisonment for life with forced labor may be changed to imprisonment for a period of ten to twenty years.

The death penalty is mandatory for taking up arms against Haiti; for giving military plans and intelligence to the enemy; for espionage; for attempts to assassinate the chief of state; and for murder and arson. Punishments for contraventions of minor police regulations range from small fines to jail sentences of from one day to six months.

The Code of Criminal Procedures was first promulgated in 1835 and last amended in February 1958. According to the code, urban and rural police are responsible for investigating felonies, misdemeanors, and police violations against persons or property. The justice of the peace or the judge investigates the act and determines whether or not a trial is to be held. In the case of a criminal trial, a jury is called for. All Haitians twenty-five years or older, who enjoy full civil and political rights and are not incapacitated, are eligible for jury duty.

The code reiterates certain articles in the constitution that guarantee civil rights and individual freedom. No one may be arrested, detained, or prosecuted except in those cases set forth in the laws. Arrest and detention may take place only on warrant from a legally competent official. No one may be kept in detention for more than forty-eight hours without being brought before a judge competent to rule on the legality of his arrest and unless the judge approves the detention in a decision based on the study of all the available evidence.

Although the Penal Code and the Code of Criminal Procedures were designed to ensure that justice was administered and that individual rights were fully protected, this has not been the case. For example, during the twenty-one years of the presidential regimes of Paul Magloire and François Duvalier, many individuals were summarily arrested and detained for months or years without benefit of trial. At the expense of the legislative and judicial branches, the executive branch has for many years controlled all aspects of governmental structure, and at the end of 1972 this was still the case.

Incidence of Crime

In 1972 official statistics on the incidence of crime were not available, but instances of urban and rural crime were reported in the Port-au-Prince newspapers. These usually concerned offenses such as robbery, assault, mugging, and street fighting. The continued annual increase in population, overcrowded and inadequate housing, and unemployment contributed to the growth of the crime rate in the capital city.

Crimes in rural areas, however, represented only a small percentage of the total, perhaps because the lack of variation in the economic status of the members of a small rural community minimizes temptation and because the Haitian peasant allegedly does not resort to violence unless he feels severely threatened. The fact that rural property owners tend to keep zealous guard over their possessions may also account for the relative absence of crime in rural areas. Anyone entering another's property at night without a light or without calling out to identify himself is liable to be shot. Also, the members of a rural community are continually under the watchful eye of the chief of the military rural post in their community.

Official government statistics published in 1969 indicate that 138,593 individuals were arrested for various offenses during the years 1966, 1967, and 1968. The leading categories of crime were: those against property; disturbing the peace; and those against persons. Of the total number of persons arrested in the three years mentioned, only 30,000 were proved guilty and sentenced. Over 600 juveniles were arrested during the same period, most for vagrancy, but seven juveniles averaging twelve years of age were arrested for murder.

BIBLIOGRAPHY

Section I. Social

Adams, Richard N. *Plantation Systems of the New World*. Washington: Pan American Union, 1959.

Alexander, Robert J. *Organized Labor in Latin America*. New York: Free Press, 1965.

————. *Today's Latin America*. (2d ed., rev.) Garden City: Doubleday, Anchor Books, 1968.

Alexis, Stephen. *Black Liberator: The Life of Toussaint Louverture*. (Trans., William Stirling.) New York: Macmillan, 1949.

Alleyne, Mervyn C. "Communication Between the Elite and Masses." Pages 12–19 in F. M. Andic and T. G. Mathews (eds.), *The Caribbean in Transition: Papers on Social, Political, and Economic Development*. Río Piedras, Puerto Rico: University of Puerto Rico, Instituto de Estudias del Caribe, 1965.

————. "Panorama de la lingüística y ensenanza de idiomas en el Caribe," *Caribbean Studies* [Río Piedras, Puerto Rico], XII, No. 1, April, 1972.

Arriaga, Eduardo E. *New Life Tables for Latin American Populations in the Nineteenth and Twentieth Centuries*. (Population Monograph Series, No. 3.) Berkeley: University of California, Institute of International Studies, 1968.

Bailey, Norman A. *Latin America in World Politics*. New York: Walker, 1967.

Bastien, Rémy. "Haitian Rural Family Organization," *Social and Economic Studies* [Kingston, Jamaica], X, 1961, 478–510.

Bellegarde, Dantes. *Ecrivains Haïtiens*. Port-au-Prince: Cheriqnit, 1948.

Bellegarde-Smith, Patrick. "Haiti: Notes on Socio-Cultural Development," The American University, 1972 (Unpublished manuscript.).

Blakemore, Harold. *Latin America*. London: Oxford University Press, 1966.

Bourguignon, Erika. "Class Structure and Acculturation in Haiti," *Ohio Journal of Science*, LII, No. 6, 1952, 317–320.

Brand, W. *Impressions of Haiti*. New York: Humanities Press, 1968.

————. *Impressions of Haiti*. The Hague: Mouton, 1965.

Butland, Gilbert J. *Latin America: A Regional Study*. New York: John Wiley and Sons, 1966.

Cabon, P. Adolphe. *Mgr. Alexis-Jean-Marie Guillox.* Port-au-Prince: Grand Séminaire d'Haïti Saint-Jacques and Archevêché de Port-au-Prince, 1929.

Casimir, Jean. "Aperçu sur la structure sociale d'Haïti," *América Latina* [Rio de Janeiro], VIII, No. 3, 1965, 40-61.

―――. *La República de Haití: Ensayo de interpretacíon sociológica.* Mexico, 1962.

Castedo, Leopoldo. *A History of Latin American Art and Architecture from Pre-Colombian Times to the Present.* (Trans. and ed., Phyllis Freeman.) New York: Praeger, 1969.

Cave, Hugh B. *Haiti: Highroad to Adventure.* New York: Henry Holt, 1952.

Comhaire, Jean. "The Haitian 'Chef de Section'," *American Anthropologist,* LVII, 1955, 620-624.

Comhaire-Sylvain, Jean. "Urban Stratification in Haiti," *Social and Economic Studies* [Kingston, Jamaica], VIII, No. 2, 1959, 179-189.

Comhaire-Sylvain, Suzanne. "Courtship, Marriage, and Plasaj at Kenscoff, Haiti," *Social and Economic Studies* [Kingston, Jamaica], VII, 1958, 210-233.

―――. "The Household at Kenscoff, Haiti," *Social and Economic Studies* [Kingston, Jamaica], X, 1961, 192-222.

Condí, Maryse. "Literature of the French Caribbean." Pages 786-788 in Claudio Véliz (ed.), *Latin America and the Caribbean: A Handbook.* New York: Praeger, 1968.

Cook, Mercer (ed.). *An Introduction to Haiti.* Washington: Pan American Union, 1951.

Coulthard, G. R. "Parallelisms and Divergencies Between 'Negritude' and 'Indigenismo'," *Caribbean Studies* [Río Piedras, Puerto Rico], VIII, 1968, 31-55.

Courlander, Harold. *The Drum and the Hoe: Life and Lore of the Haitian People.* Berkeley: University of California Press, 1960.

―――. *Haiti Singing.* Chapel Hill: University of North Carolina Press, 1939.

Courlander, Harold, and Bastien, Rémy. *Religion and Politics in Haiti* (Institute for Cross-Cultural Research Studies, I.) Washington: ICR, 1966.

Crassweller, Robert D. *The Caribbean Community: Changing Societies and U.S. Policy.* New York: Praeger, for the Council on Foreign Relations, 1972.

Dale, George A. *Education in Haiti.* (Bulletin 1959, No. 20.) Washington: GPO, U.S. Department of Health, Education, and Welfare, 1959.

Dame, Hartley F. *Latin America, 1970.* Washington: Stryker-Post Publications, 1970.

Davis, Harold E. *History of Latin America.* New York: Ronald Press, 1968.

Davis, H. P. *Black Democracy: The Story of Haiti.* (Rev. ed.) New York: Biblo and Tannen, 1967.

Davis, Kingsley. *World Urbanization, 1950–1970,* I: Basic Data for Cities, Countries and Regions. (Population Monograph Series, No. 4.) Berkeley: University of California, Institute of International Studies, 1969.

Demographic Yearbook, 1960. New York: United Nations, 1961.

Demographic Yearbook, 1970. New York: United Nations, 1971.

de Young, Maurice. "Class Parameters in Haitian Society," *Journal of Interamerican Studies,* I, No. 4, October 1959, 449–458.

Dorsainvil, J.-C. (Avec la collaboration des Frères de l'Instruction Chrétienne.) *Manuel d'Histoire d'Haiti.* Port-au-Prince: Procure des Frères de l'Instruction Chrétienne, 1926.

Editor and Publisher International Year Book. New York: Editor and Publisher, 1971.

Engber, Marjorie. *Caribbean Fiction and Poetry.* New York: Center for Inter-American Relations, 1970.

Fagg, John Edwin. *Cuba, Haiti and the Dominican Republic.* (The Modern Nations in Historical Perspective.) Englewood Cliffs: Prentice-Hall, 1965.

Foreign Broadcast Information Service. *Broadcasting Stations of the World,* Part I: Amplitude Modulation Broadcasting Stations According to Country and City. Washington: GPO, January 1971.

———. *Broadcasting Stations of the World,* Part IV: Television Stations. Washington: GPO, January 1971.

Gerassi, John. *The Great Fear in Latin America.* (Rev. ed.) New York: Collier Books, 1968.

Gingres, Jean-Pierre O. *Duvalier, Caribbean Cyclone: The History of Haiti and its Present Government.* New York: Exposition Press, 1967.

Gold, Herbert. "Progress in Haiti: Leopards in Sneakers Instead of Tontons Macoutes," *New York Times Magazine,* March 12, 1972, 34–35, 50–60.

González, Gustavo R. "The Migration of High-Level Manpower," *International Labour Review* [Geneva], XCVIII, No. 6, December 1968, 551–570.

Haidar, Walter, and Alvarez, Ray. U.S. Department of Commerce: Bureau of International Commerce. "Basic Data on the Economy of Haiti," *Overseas Business Reports* (OBR 70-13.) Washington: GPO, 1970.

Haiti. Conseil National de Devéloppement et de Planification. *Plan d'Action Economique et Sociale, 1970–1971.* Port-au-Prince: 1970.

Haiti. Département des Finances et des Affaires Economiques. *Recensement de la République d'Haïti, 1971.* Port-au-Prince: 1972.

Haiti. Embassy in Washington. *News About Haiti,* I, No. 2, June 1972, entire issue.

———. *News About Haiti,* I, No. 3, July 1972, entire issue.

Haiti. Service de la Population. *Enquête sur la Population de la Fossette* (Cap-Haïtien). Etudes Démographiques, Economiques, et Sociologiques, Publication No. 3.) Port-au-Prince: 1961.

161

Haiti. Département des Finances et des Affaires Economiques. Institut Haïtien de Statistique. *Bulletin de Statistique. Supplément Annuel.* Nos. I, II, III, Années 1967-1968-1969. Port-au-Prince: n.d.

―――. *Guide Economique de la République d'Haïti.* Port-au-Prince: 1964.

Haiti: A Selected and Partially Annotated Bibliography. New York: United Nations, Institute for Training and Research, 1972.

Hall, Robert, et al. *Haitian Creole: Grammar, Texts, Vocabulary.* (American Anthropological Association Memoir No. 74.) Chicago: American Anthropological Association, 1953.

Harmon, Carter. *The West Indies.* (Life World Library.) New York: Time, 1966.

Heinl, Robert Debs, Jr. "Haiti: A Case Study in Freedom," *New Republic,* CL, May 16, 1964, 15-21.

―――. "Haiti: Next Mess in the Caribbean?" *Atlantic Monthly,* CCXX, November 1967, 83-89.

Herskovits, Melville J. *Life in a Haitian Valley.* New York: Doubleday, Anchor Books, 1971.

Hoetink, Harry. "Over de sociaal-raciale structuur van Haiti," *Tijdschrift van het Koninklijk Nederlandsch Aardrijkskundig Genootschap* [Netherlands], LXXVIII, No. 2, 1961, 146-156.

Holly, Marc Aurele. *Agriculture in Haiti.* New York: Vantage Press, 1955.

Horowitz, Michael M. (ed.) *Peoples and Cultures of the Caribbean.* Garden City: Natural History Press, for the American Museum of Natural History, 1971.

Hyppolite, Michelson P. *Contes Dramatiques Haïtiens.* Port-au-Prince: Musée du Peuple Haïtiens, 1956.

Inter-American Development Bank. *Socio-Economic Progress in Latin America, Annual Report, 1971.* Washington: 1972.

―――. *Socio-Economic Progress in Latin America: Social Progress Trust Fund: Tenth Annual Report, 1970.* Washington: 1971.

International Labor Organization. International Labor Office. *Labour Force Projections 1965-1985, Latin America.* Geneva: 1971.

International Planned Parenthood Federation. *Family Planning in Five Continents.* London: 1969.

International Yearbook of Education, 1969, XXXI. Paris: United Nations Educational, Scientific and Cultural Organization, 1970.

James, Preston. *Latin America* (4th ed.) New York: Odyssey Press,1969.

Kantor, Harry. *Patterns of Politics and Political Systems in Latin America.* Chicago: Rand McNally, 1969.

Leyburn, James G. *The Haitian People* (Rev. ed.) New Haven: Yale University Press, 1966.

Lobb, John. "Caste and Class in Haiti," *American Journal of Sociology,* XLVI, 1940, 23-34.

Logan, Rayford W. *Haiti and the Dominican Republic.* (Under auspices

162

of Royal Institute of International Affairs.) New York: Oxford University Press, 1968.

Lubin, Maurice A. "Five Haitian Poets." Pages 70-80 in *Young Poetry of the Americas* (Cultural Themes, I.) Washington: General Secretariat of the Organization of American States, 1964.

Manigat, Leslie F. *Haiti of the Sixties, Object of International Concern.* Washington: Washington Center of Foreign Policy Research, 1964.

Matthews, Herbert L. *A World in Revolution: A Newspaperman's Memoir.* New York: Charles Scribners Sons, 1971.

Mecham, John Lloyd. *A Survey of United States-Latin American Relations.* Boston: Houghton Mifflin, 1965.

Mercado Villar, Olga, and de la Puente Lafoy, Patricio. *Características del Proceso Migratorio en América Latina, Estudios Preliminares.* Santiago: Centro Para el Desarrollo Ecónomico y Social de América Latina—DESAL, 1968 (mimeo.).

Métraux, Alfred. *Haiti: Black Peasants and Voodoo.* (Trans., Peter Lengyel.) New York: Universe Books, 1960.

———. *Voodoo in Haiti.* New York: Schocken Books, 1972.

Michel, Emilio Cordero. *La Revolución Haitiana y Santo Domingo.* Santo Domingo: Editora Nacional, 1968.

Milne, Jean. *Fiesta Time in Latin America.* Los Angeles: Ward Ritchie Press, 1965.

Minerals Yearbook, 1969, IV: Area Reports: International. Washington: GPO, for U.S. Department of the Interior, Bureau of Mines, 1971.

Mintz, Sidney W. "Pratik: Haitian Personal Economic Relationships." Pages 54-63 in *Proceedings of the Annual Spring Meetings of the American Ethnological Society.* New York: American Ethnological Society, 1961.

Mintz, Sidney W., and Wolf, Eric. "An Analysis of Ritual Coparenthood," *Southwestern Journal of Anthropology,* VI, 1950, 341-368.

Moore, O. Ernest. *Haiti: Its Stagnant Society and Shackled Economy.* (An Exposition-University Book.) New York: Exposition Press, 1972.

Morison, Samuel Eliot. *Admiral of the Ocean Sea: A Life of Christopher Columbus.* Boston: Little, Brown, 1942.

Needler, Martin C. *Political Systems of Latin America.* New York: Van Nostrand Reinhold, 1970.

Okezie, Joyce A. "Social Factors Influencing Choice of Language and Linguistic Form in Haiti," The American University, Department of Languages and Foreign Studies, 1972 (Unpublished manuscript.).

"Old-Age Insurance in Haiti," *International Labour Review* [Geneva], XCIII, No. 4, April 1966, 443-444.

Organización de los Estados Americanos. Instituto Interamericano de Estadística. *América en Cifras, 1965. Situación Cultural: Educación y Otros Aspectos Culturales.* Washington: 1967.

———. *América en Cifras, 1970. Situación Cultural: Educación y Otros Aspectos Culturales.* Washington: 1971.

Organización de los Estados Americanos. Instituto Interamericano de Estadística. *América en Cifras, 1970: Situacion Social: Hogar, Habitacion, Mejoramiento Urbano, Prevision Social, Asistencia Médica y de Salud, y Trabajo,* Washington: 1971.

―――. *América en Cifras, 1970: Situación Social: Hogar, Habitación, Mejoramiento Urbano, Prevision Social, Asistencia Médica y de Salud, y Trabajo.* Washington: 1971.

―――. *América en Cifras: Situación Física: Territorio y Clima.* Washington: 1972.

Organization of American States. *Statistical Compendium of the Americas.* Washington: 1971.

Organization of American States. General Secretariat. *Haiti.* (American Republics Series No. 12.) Washington: 1963 (reprint 1971.).

―――. *21 Latin American Meals* (641.5-#-7488.) Washington: n.d.

Pan American Health Organization. *Annual Report of the Director, 1969.* Washington: 1970.

―――. *Annual Report of the Director, 1970.* Washington: 1971.

―――. *Facts on Health Progress, 1971.* Washington: 1971.

―――. *Health Conditions in the Americas, 1961-1964.* Washington: 1966.

―――. *Health Conditions in the Americas, 1965-1968.* Washington: 1970.

Papers of the Conference on Research and Resources of Haiti. New York: Research Institute for the Study of Man, 1969.

Porter, Charles O., and Alexander, Robert J. *The Struggle for Democracy in Latin America.* New York: Macmillan, 1961.

Pressoir, Charles-Fernand. *Débats sur le Créole et le Folklore.* Port-au-Prince: Imprimérie de l'Etat, 1947.

Publishers' International Directory (3d ed.) Munich-Pullach: Verlag Dokumentation, 1967.

Ratliff, William E. (ed.) *Yearbook of Latin American Communist Affairs, 1971.* Stanford: Hoover Institution Press, 1971.

"Report on Haiti," *Latin American Report,* VI, No. 6, May/June 1967, 4-9.

Rippy, J. Fred. *Latin America: A Modern History.* Ann Arbor: University of Michigan Press, 1968.

Robertson, William S. *History of the Latin American Nations* (Rev. ed.) New York: D. Appleton, 1930.

Roberts, Thomas D., et al. *Area Handbook for the Dominican Republic.* Washington: GPO, for The American University, 1966.

Robinson, Harry. *Latin America: A Geographical Survey.* New York: Praeger, 1967.

Rodman, Selden. "Artistas de Haití," *Américas,* XX, No. 10, October 1968, 8-15.

―――. *Haiti: The Black Republic.* New York: Devin-Adair, 1954.

Rotberg, Robert I., and Clague, Christopher K. *Haiti: The Politics of Squalor.* Boston: Houghton Mifflin, 1971.

Schaedel, Richard P. *An Essay on the Human Resources of Haiti.* Port-au-Prince: U.S. Agency for International Development/Haiti, 1962.

Scofield, John. "Haiti: West Africa in the West Indies," *National Geographic Magazine,* CXIX, No. 2, February 1961, 227-260.

Simpson, George. "Haiti's Social Structure," *American Sociological Review,* VI, 1941, 640-649.

―――. "Sexual and Familial Institutions in Northern Haiti," *American Anthropologist,* XLIV, 1942, 655-674.

Stebbins, Richard P., and Amoia, Alba (eds.) *Political Handbook and Atlas of the World, 1970.* New York: Simon and Schuster, 1970.

Stewart, William A. "Creole Languages in the Caribbean." Pages 34-53 in Frank A. Rice (ed.), *Study of the Role of Second Languages in Asia, Africa, and Latin America.* Washington: Center for Applied Linguistics, 1962.

―――. "Functional Distribution of Creole and French in Haiti." Pages 149-159 in Elisabeth D. Woodward (ed.), *Report of the Thirteenth Annual Round Table Meeting on Linguistics and Language Studies.* (Georgetown University Monograph Series on Languages and Linguistics No. 15.) Washington: Georgetown University Press, 1963.

Stoddard, Theodore L. (ed.) *Religion and Politics in Haiti.* (Institute for Cross-Cultural Research Studies No. 1.) Washington: ICR, 1966.

Street, John M. "Problems of Health and Nutrition in Haiti," *Geographical Review,* LXI, October 1971, 599-600.

Stycos, J. Mayone. "Haitian Attitudes Toward Family Size," *Human Organization,* XXIII, No. 1, 1964, 42-47.

Taylor, Douglas. "New Languages for Old in the West Indies," *Comparative Studies in Society and History,* III, 1961, 277-288.

Turner, Frederick. *Catholicism and Political Development in Latin America.* Chapel Hill: University of North Carolina Press, 1971.

Underwood, Frances W. "Land and its Manipulation Among Haitian Peasantry." Pages 469-482 in Ward H. Goodenough (ed.), *Exploration in Cultural Anthropology.* New York: McGraw-Hill, 1964.

―――. *The Marketing System in Peasant Haiti.* (Yale University Publications in Anthropology No. 60.) New Haven: Yale University Press, 1960.

Unión Panamericana. *Datos Básicos de Población en América Latina, 1970.* Washington: 1970.

United Nations. *Statistics on Children and Youth in Latin America, Supplement to Statistical Bulletin for Latin America.* Santiago: 1970.

―――. *World Economic Survey, 1969-1970.* New York: 1971.

U.S. Agency for International Development. *Population Program Assistance.* Washington: 1970.

―――. *Summary of Economic and Social Indicators, 18 Latin American Countries: 1960-1969.* Washington: 1970 (mimeo.).

U.S. Department of State. *Foreign Relations of the United States, 1945: Diplomatic Papers: The American Republics,* IX. Washington: GPO, 1969.

———. *Republic of Haiti: Background Notes.* (Publication No. 8287.) Washington: November 1970.

U.S. Embassy in Port-au-Prince. *Haiti: Post Report.* Port-au-Prince: 1972.

U.S. Department of Agriculture. Economic Research Service. *Haiti's Agriculture and Trade.* (ERS-Foreign 283.) Washington: n.d.

U.S. Department of Labor. Bureau of Labor Statistics. *Labor Conditions in Haiti.* (Labor Digest No. 49.) Washington: 1964.

———. *Labor Law and Practice in Haiti.* (BLS Report No. 243.) Washington: GPO, 1963.

U.S. Department of the Army. Walter Reed Army Medical Center. Walter Reed Army Institute of Research. *Haiti, Health Publication No. 4.* Washington: 1960.

University of California at Los Angeles. Latin American Center. *Statistical Abstract of Latin America, 1970.* Los Angeles: 1971.

Valdman, Albert. "The Language Situation in Haiti." Pages 61–62 in Dell Hymes (ed.), *Pidginization and Creolization of Languages.* London: Cambridge University Press, 1971.

———. "Language Standardization in a Diglossia Situation: Haiti." Pages 365–379 in Joshua A. Fishman, Charles A. Ferguson, and Jyotirindra Das Gupta (eds.), *Language Problems in the Developing Nations.* New York: Wiley, 1968.

Viau, Alfred. *Negros, Mulattos, Blancos.* Ciudad Trujillo (Santo Domingo): Editora Montalvo, 1955.

Wechsler, Sally (ed.). *Publisher's World, 1968/69.* New York: R. R. Bowker, 1968.

Wilgus, A. Curtis. *The Development of Hispanic America.* New York: Farrar and Rinehart, 1941.

———. *Historical Atlas of Latin America.* New York: Cooper Square Publishers, 1967.

Wilgus, A. Curtis (ed.). *The Caribbean: Contemporary Trends.* (School of Inter-American Studies, Series I, III.) Gainesville: University of Florida Press, 1953.

Wilgus, A. Curtis, and D'Eca, Raul. *Latin American History: A Summary of Political, Economic, Social, and Cultural Events from 1492 to the Present.* New York: Barnes and Noble, 1967 (5th printing).

Williams, Eric. *From Columbus to Castro: The History of the Caribbean, 1492–1969.* New York: Harper and Row, 1970.

Williams, Mary Wilhelmine; Bartlett, Ruhl J.; and Miller, Russell E. *The People and Politics of Latin America* (4th ed.). Boston: Ginn, 1958.

Wilson, Ruth Danenhower. *Here is Haiti.* New York: Philosophical Library, 1957.

Wingfield, Roland, and Parenton, Vernon. "Class Structure and Class Conflict in Haitian Society," *Social Forces*, XLIII, No. 3, 1965, 338–347.

Wood, Harold A. *Northern Haiti: Land, Land Use, and Settlement.* Toronto: University of Toronto Press, 1963.

The World and its Peoples: The Caribbean Region and Central America. New York: Greystone Press, 1969.

World Health Organization. *Third Report on the World Health Situation, 1961–64.* Geneva: 1967.

Worldmark Encyclopedia of the Nations, III: Americas. (Ed., Louis Barron.) New York: Worldmark Press, Harper and Row, 1967.

World Survey of Education, III: Secondary Education. New York: Columbia University Press, International Documents Service, 1961.

World Survey of Education, IV: Higher Education. New York: United Nations Educational, Scientific and Cultural Organization Publications Center, 1966.

World Survey of Education, V: Educational Policy, Legislation, and Administration. Paris: UNESCO Publications, 1971.

Yearbook of Labour Statistics, 1971. Geneva: International Labor Organization, International Labor Office, n.d.

Zéndequi, Guillermo de (ed.). *Image of Haiti.* Washington: Organization of American States, General Secretariat, 1972.

Section II. Political

Bailey, Norman A. *Latin America in World Politics*. New York: Walker, 1967.

Ball, Margaret M. *The OAS in Transition*. Durham: Duke University Press, 1969.

Bellegarde-Smith, Patrick. "Haiti: Notes on Socio-Cultural Development," The American University, 1972 (Unpublished manuscript.).

Binning, William C. "The Nixon Foreign Aid Policy for Latin America," *Inter-American Economic Affairs*, XXV, No. 1, Summer 1972, 31–46.

Brand, W. *Impressions of Haiti*. The Hague: Mouton, 1965.

Burnett, Ben G., and Johnson, Kenneth F. *Political Forces in Latin America*. Belmont, California: Wadsworth, 1968.

Busey, James L. *Latin American Political Guide*. Maniton Springs, California: Juniper Editions, 1972.

Connell-Smith, Gordon. *The Inter-American System*. London: Oxford University Press, 1966.

Corkran, Herbert, Jr. *Patterns of International Cooperation in the Caribbean, 1942–69*. Dallas: Southern Methodist University Press, 1970.

Courlander, Harold, and Bastein, Rémy. *Religion and Politics in Haiti*. (Institute for Cross-Cultural Research Studies I.) Washington: ICR, 1966.

Crassweller, Robert D. *The Caribbean Community: Changing Societies and U.S. Policy*. New York: Praeger, for the Council on Foreign Relations, 1972.

———. "Darkness in Haiti," *Foreign Affairs*, IL, No. 2, January 1971, 315–329.

Edelmann, Alexander T. *Latin American Government and Politics*. Homewood, Illinois: Dorsey Press, 1969.

Fagg, John Edwin. *Cuba, Haiti, and the Dominican Republic*. (The Modern Nations in Historical Perspective.) Englewood Cliffs: Prentice-Hall, 1965.

Gil, Federico. *Latin American-U.S. Relations*. New York: Harcourt, Brace Jovanovich, 1971.

Gingres, Jean-Pierre O. *Duvalier, Caribbean Cyclone: The History of Haiti and its Present Government*. New York: Exposition Press, 1967.

Haiti. *Guide Economique de la République d'Haiti*. Port-au-Prince: 1964.

Haiti. Conseil National de Développement et de Planification. *Plan d'Action Economique et Sociale, 1970–1971*. Port-au-Prince: 1970.

Haiti. Embassy in Washington. *News About Haiti,* I, No. 2, June 1972, entire issue.

"Haiti: Guns Make Friends," *The Economist* [London], CCXLIV, No. 6730, April 19, 1962, 40.

"Haiti: Rhapsody in Jet." Pages 249-274 in Eugene Fodor (ed.), *Fodor's Caribbean, Bahamas and Bermuda.* New York: David McKay, 1971.

Heinl, Robert Debs, Jr. "Haiti: A Case Study in Freedom," *New Republic,* CL, May 16, 1964, 15-21.

————. "Haiti: Next Mess in the Caribbean?" *Atlantic Monthly,* CCXX, November 1967, 83-89.

Herring, Hubert. *A History of Latin America.* (3d ed.) New York: Knopf, 1968.

Herskovits, Melville J. *Life in a Haitian Valley.* New York: Doubleday, Anchor Books, 1971.

Horowitz, Michael M. (ed.) *Peoples and Cultures of the Caribbean.* Garden City: Natural History Press, for the American Museum of Natural History, 1971.

Kantor, Harry. *Patterns of Politics and Political Systems in Latin America.* Chicago: Rand McNally, 1969.

Law and Judicial Systems of Nations. Washington: World Peace Through Law Center, 1968.

Logan, Rayford W. *Haiti and the Dominican Republic.* (Under auspices of Royal Institute of International Affairs.) New York: Oxford University Press, 1968.

Mecham, John Lloyd. *The United States and Inter-American Security: 1889-1960.* Austin: University of Texas Press, 1961.

Munro, Dana. "The American Withdrawal from Haiti, 1929-1934," *Hispanic American Historical Review,* XLIX, No. 1, February 1969, 1-26.

Needler, Martin C. *Political Systems of Latin America.* New York: Van Nostrand Reinhold, 1970.

Organization of American States. *Annual Report of the Secretary General,* Fiscal Year, 1966-67. (OAS Official Records, Ser. D/111.18.) Washington: Pan American Union, 1967.

————. *Image of Haiti.* Washington: General Secretariat, March 1972.

Peaslee, Amos J. *Constitutions of Nations,* II. The Hague: Martinus Nijhoff, 1956.

The Political and Socio-Economic Role of the Military in Latin America, Appendix, III. Coral Gables: University of Miami, Center for Advanced International Studies, 1971.

"Report on Haiti," *Latin American Report,* VI, No. 6, May/June 1967, 4-9.

Rotberg, Robert I., and Clague, Christopher K. *Haiti: The Politics of Squalor.* Boston: Houghton Mifflin, 1971.

Schmidt, Hans. *The United States Occupation of Haiti, 1915-1934.* New Brunswick: Rutgers University Press, 1971.

Scofield, John. "Haiti: West Africa in the West Indies," *National Geographic*, CXIX, No. 2, February 1961, 227-260.

Smith, Bradley. *The Guide to the Caribbean*. New York: Knopf, 1961.

U.S. Agency for International Development. *U.S. Overseas Loans and Grants and Assistance from International Organizations; Obligations and Loan Authorizations, July 1, 1945–June 30, 1971*. Washington: GPO, May 24, 1972.

Walton, Richard J. *Beyond Diplomacy: A Background Book on American Military Intervention*. New York: Parents Magazine Press, 1970.

Williams, Eric. *From Columbus to Castro: The History of the Caribbean, 1492–1969*. New York: Harper and Row, 1970.

Wilson, Larman C. "The Foreign Policies of the Dominican Republic and Haiti." Chapter 9 in Harold E. Davis and Larman C. Wilson (eds.), *Latin American Foreign Policies: An Analysis*. The American University, School of International Service (Unpublished manuscript.), 1971 (mimeo.).

(Various issues of the following periodicals were also used in the preparation of this section: *Américas* [Washington], August 1972-February 1973; *Christian Science Monitor*, August 1972-February 1973; *Economist para América Latina* [London], May 1968; *Evening Star* [Washington], April 1971-August 1971; *Guardian Weekly* [Manchester, England], September 1971; *Latin America* [London], May 1968-September 1972; *Miami Herald*, September 1972; *Newsweek* [New York] May 1972; *New York Times*, April 1971-August 1972; *Quarterly Economic Review: Cuba, Dominican Republic, Haiti, Puerto Rico* [London], July 1969-January 1972; *Times of the Americas* [Washington], May 1968-March 1972; *Wall Street Journal* [New York], December 1971-April 1972; *Washington Daily News*, March 1970-October 1971; *Washington Post*, April 1971-August 1972.)

Section III. Economic

"At a Bargain Price: Help for the Underfed," *U.S. News & World Report*, LXVI, No. 5, February 3, 1969, 84-85.

Balance of Payments Yearbook, 1966-70, XXIII. Washington: International Monetary Fund, 1972.

Chamberlain, Greg. "French Launch 'Invasion of Haiti'," *Guardian Weekly* [Manchester, England], CVII, No. 19, November 4, 1972, 10.

Cole, J. P. *Latin America: An Economic and Social Geography*. London: Butterworths, 1970.

Comhaire-Sylvain, S. and Comhaire-Sylvain, J. "A Statistical Note on the Kenscoff Market System, Haiti," *Social and Economic Studies* [Kingston], XIII, No. 3, September, 1964, 397-404.

Conway Research, Inc. *Latin America's Industrial Incentives*. Atlanta: 1967.

Crassweller, Robert D. *The Caribbean Community: Changing Societies and U.S. Policy*. New York: Praeger, for the Council on Foreign Relations, 1972.

The Europa Yearbook, 1971, II. London: Europa Publications, 1971.

Fagg, John Edwin. *Cuba, Haiti, and the Dominican Republic*. (The Modern Nations in Historical Perspective.) Englewood Cliffs: Prentice-Hall, 1965.

Food and Agriculture Organization. *Enquêtes sur les terres et les eaux dans la Plaine des Gonaïves et le Département du Nord-Ouest: Haïti*, I-V. Rome: FAO, 1969.

Gildea, Ray Y. "Haiti," *Focus*, XVII, No. 9, May 1967, 1-6.

Haidar, Walter, and Alvarez, Ray. "Basic Data on the Economy of Haiti," U.S. Department of Commerce. Bureau of International Commerce. *Overseas Business Reports* (OBR 70-13.) Washington: GPO, April, 1970.

————. "Foreign Trade Regulations of Haiti" U.S. Department of Commerce. Bureau of International Commerce. *Overseas Business Reports*. (OBR 70-24). Washington: GPO, June, 1970.

Haiti. *Budget de Fonctionnement de l'Exercise 1969-1970: Octobre 1969-Septembre 1970*. Port-au-Prince: Le Moniteur, 1969.

Haiti. Administration Générale des Douanes. *Rapport Annuel de l'Administration Générale des Douanes pour l'Exercise, Octobre 1969-September 1970*. Port-au-Prince: n.d.

Haiti. Commissariat National du Tourisme. *Le Tourisme en Haïti*. Port-au-Prince: n.d.

Haiti. Conseil National de Développement et de Planification. *Plan d'Action Economique et Sociale, 1970–1971.* Port-au-Prince: 1970.

Haiti. Département de l'Agriculture, des Ressources Naturelles et du Développement Rural. *Rapport de la Commission Nationale Pour la Conservation des Ressources Naturelles Renouvelables.* Port-au-Prince: Imprimerie de l'Etat, 1960.

Haiti. Presses Nationales d'Haiti. *Priorités de la Planification et Projections Quinquennales,* I. Port-au-Prince: 1972.

Haiti. Service de la Population. *Les Fluctuations Cycliques de l'Economie Haïtienne* (Etudes Démographiques, Economiques et Sociologiques, Publication 2.) Port-au-Prince: Imprimerie de l'Etat, n.d.

Haiti. Département des Finances et des Affaires Economiques. Institut Haïtien de Statistique. *Bulletin de Statistique Supplément Annuel 1967–1969.* Port-au-Prince: n.d.

———. *Bulletin Trimestriel de Statistique, 1969,* LXXIV. Port-au-Prince: n.d.

———. *Guide Economique de la République d'Haïti.* Port-au-Prince: 1964.

"Haiti Continues Marked Recovery from 1960's Slump," *Commerce Today,* II, No. 25, September 18, 1972, 47–48.

"Haiti's Steadily Improving Industry Now Provides Over One-Third of Country's Exports to U.S.," *International Commerce,* LXXV, No. 41, October 13, 1969, 27–28.

Haney, Emil B., Jr. *The Nature of Shifting Cultivation in Latin America.* (Land Tenure Center, No. 45.) Madison: University of Wisconsin, LTC, May 1968.

Holly, Marc Aurele. *Agriculture in Haiti.* New York: Vantage Press, 1955.

Hurt, Leslie C. "U.S. Sugar Act Extended—New Quotas Established," *Foreign Agriculture,* IX, No. 43, October 25, 1971, 12.

Inter-American Committee for Agricultural Development. *Inventory of Information Basic to the Planning of Agricultural Development in Latin America: Haiti.* Washington: Pan American Union, 1963.

Inter-American Development Bank. *Social Progress Trust Fund: Fifth Annual Report, 1965.* Washington: 1966.

———. *Socio-Economic Progress in Latin America. Annual Report, 1971.* Washington: 1972.

———. *Socio-Economic Progress in Latin America: Social Progress Trust Fund: Sixth Annual Report, 1966.* Washington: 1967.

———. *Socio-Economic Progress in Latin America: Social Progress Trust Fund: Seventh Annual Report, 1967.* Washington: 1968.

———. *Socio-Economic Progress in Latin America: Social Progress Trust Fund: Eighth Annual Report, 1968.* Washington: 1969.

———. *Socio-Economic Progress in Latin America: Social Progress Trust Fund: Ninth Annual Report, 1969.* Washington: 1970.

———. *Socio-Economic Progress in Latin America: Social Progress Trust Fund: Tenth Annual Report, 1970.* Washington: 1971.

International Monetary Fund. *International Financial Statistics: December 1972.* Washington: 1972.

―――. *Twenty-Third Annual Report on Exchange Restrictions, 1972.* Washington: 1972.

Legerman, Caroline J. "Kin Groups in a Haiti Market." Pages 382–390 in Michael M. Horowitz (ed.), *Peoples and Cultures of the Caribbean.* Garden City: Natural History Press, for the American Museum of Natural History, 1971.

Leyburn, James G. *The Haitian People* (Rev. ed.) New Haven: Yale University Press, 1966.

Manigat, Leslie F. *Haiti of the Sixties, Object of International Concern.* Washington: Washington Center of Foreign Policy Research, 1964.

Métraux, Alfred. "Cooperative Labor Groups in Haiti." Pages 318–339 in Michael M. Horowitz (ed.), *Peoples and Cultures of the Caribbean.* Garden City: Natural History Press, for the American Museum of Natural History, 1971.

Minerals Yearbook, 1968, IV: Area Reports: International. Washington: GPO, for U.S. Department of the Interior, Bureau of Mines, 1970.

Minerals Yearbook, 1969, IV: Area Reports: International. Washington: GPO, for U.S. Department of the Interior, Bureau of Mines, 1971.

Moore, O. Ernest. *Haiti: Its Stagnant Society and Shackled Economy.* (An Exposition-University Book.) New York: Exposition Press, 1972.

Organization of American States. General Secretariat. *Haiti.* (American Republic Series No. 12.) Washington: 1963 (reprint 1971.).

Organization of American States. Department of Legal Affairs. General Legal Division. *Mining and Petroleum Legislation in Latin America* (2d ed.) Washington: Pan American Union, 1969.

Organization of American States. General Secretariat. Department of Information and Public Affairs. *Seven Basic Export Products.* Washington: 1972.

Organization of American States. Inter-American Economic and Social Council. Inter-American Committee on the Alliance for Progress (CIAP). *Domestic Efforts and the Needs for External Financing for the Development of Haiti.* (OEA/SER .H/XIV CIAP/29.) Washington: Pan American Union, July 26, 1966.

―――. *Technical Assistance Mission to Haiti, August, 1967.* Washington: Pan American Union, January 18, 1968.

Pan American Coffee Bureau. *Annual Coffee Statistics.* (No. 35, 1971.) New York: 1972.

Pan American Union. *Cacao: The Chocolate Tree.* (Commodity Series.) Washington: 1968.

Pan American Union. Division of Laws and Treaties. Department of International Law. *A Statement of the Laws of Haiti in Matters Affecting Business* (2d ed.) Washington: 1955.

Petruc, T. C. *Rapport au Gouvernement d'Haiti sur Bases pour une Planification Agricole.* (U.N. FAO, Report No. 2957.) Rome: FAO, 1971.

Pick's Currency Yearbook, 1971. New York: Pick Publishing, 1971.

Pierre-Charles, Gérard. *l'Economie haïtienne et sa voie de développement.* Paris: Editions G. P. Maisonneuve et Larose, 1967.

————. "Haiti: Esencia y realidad del desarrollo," *Revista Mexicana de Sociología* [Mexico City], XXXI, No. 3, 1969, 589–608.

"Political Charges, New Power Plant Brightens Haiti's Economic Prospects." *Commerce Today*, II, No. 1, October 18, 1971, 49–50.

Puga, William B. (ed.) *Electrical World: A Directory of Electric Utilities in Latin America, Bermuda and the Caribbean Islands.* (1969–70 ed.) New York: McGraw-Hill, 1969.

"Report on Haiti." *Latin American Report*, VI, No. 6, May/June 1967, 4–9.

Robinson, Harry. *Latin America: A Geographical Survey.* New York: Praeger, 1967.

Schaedel, Richard P. *An Essay in the Human Resources of Haiti.* Port-au-Prince: U.S. Agency for International Development/Haiti, 1962.

Scofield, John. "Haiti: West Africa in the West Indies," *National Geographic Magazine*, CXIX, No. 2, February 1961, 227–260.

Smith, Bradley. *Escape to the West Indies.* New York: Alfred A. Knopf, 1961.

The South American Handbook, 1970. London: Trade and Travel Publications, 1970.

The Statesman's Year-Book, 1972–1973. London: Macmillan, 1972.

Street, John M. *Historical and Economic Geography of the Southwest Peninsula of Haiti.* Berkeley: University of California, Department of Geography, 1960.

Underwood, Frances W. "Land and its Manipulation Among the Haitian Peasantry." Pages 469–482 in Ward H. Goodenough (ed.), *Explorations in Cultural Anthropology.* New York: McGraw-Hill, 1964.

United Nations. Department of Economic and Social Affairs. *World Economic Survey, 1969–1970: The Developing Countries in the 1960's and the Problem of Appraising Progress.* New York: 1971.

United Nations. Economic Commission for Latin America. *Estudio Económico de América Latina, 1969.* New York: 1970.

United Nations. Industrial Development Organization. *Small-Scale Industry in Latin America.* New York: 1969.

U.S. Agency for International Development. *Status of Loan Agreements as of March 31, 1971.* Washington: 1971.

U.S. Department of State. *Republic of Haiti: Background Notes.* (Publication No. 8287.) Washington: GPO, November 1970.

U.S. Embassy in Port-au-Prince. *Haiti: Post Report.* Port-au-Prince: 1972.

U.S. Export-Import Bank of the United States. *Cumulative Record by Country, February 12, 1954 to June 30, 1970.* Washington: 1970.

U.S. National Council on Marine Resources and Engineering Development. *Marine Science Activities of the Nations of Latin America.* Washington: GPO, 1968.

U.S. Office of the Coordinator of Inter-American Affairs. Research Division. "Rural Haiti." Washington: 1943 (mimeo.).

U.S. Department of Agriculture. Economic Research Service. *The Agricultural Situation in the Western Hemisphere—Review of 1970 and Outlook for 1971.* (ERS-Foreign 312.) Washington: GPO, 1971.

———. *Haiti's Agriculture and Trade.* (ERS-Foreign 283.) Washington: n.d.

U.S. Agency for International Development. Bureau for Program and Policy Coordination. Office of Statistics and Reports. *AID Economic Data Book: Latin America.* Washington: July 1971.

———. *U.S. Overseas Loans and Grants and Assistance from International Organizations.* Washington: 1970.

Valles, M.T. *Les Idéologies Coopérativistes et Leurs Applicabilités en Haiti.* Paris: G. P. Maisonneuve et Larose, 1967.

Westbrook, John T. "Socio-economic Factors Related to Success and Failure in Agrarian Reform: the 'Caracul' Project, República Dominicana." Pages 293–325 in F. M. Andic and T. G. Mathews (eds.), *The Caribbean in Transition: Papers on Social, Political and Economic Development.* Río Piedras: University of Puerto Rico, 1965.

Wilson, Ruth Danenhower. *Here is Haiti.* New York: Philosophical Library, 1957.

Wood, Harold A. *Northern Haiti: Land, Land Use, and Settlement.* Toronto: University of Toronto Press, 1963.

The World and Its Peoples: The Caribbean Region and Central America. New York: Greystone Press, 1969.

Worldmark Encyclopedia of the Nations, III: Americas. (Ed., Louis Barron.) New York: Worldmark Press, Harper and Row, 1967.

(Various issues of the following periodicals were also used in the preparation of this section: *Alliance for Progress Weekly Newsletter* [Washington], March 15, 1971–October 23, 1972; *Américas* (Washington), August 1972–February 1973; *Business Latin America* (New York), February 20, 1969–October 26, 1972; *Christian Science Monitor,* August 1972–February 1973; *Economist* [London], August 1972–February 1973; *Guardian Weekly* [Manchester, England], August 1972–February 1973; *IMF Survey,* August 14, 1972–November 27, 1972; *Inter-American Center of Tax Administrators Newsletter* [Panama], December 1968–August, 1972; *Latin America* [London], January 9, 1970–November 2, 1972; *Monthly Bulletin of Agricultural Economics and Statistics* (FAO) [Rome], June 1972–October 1972; *News About Haiti* [Washington], June 1972–August 1972; *New York Times,* August 1972–February 1973; *NOTICIAS: Weekly Digest of Hemisphere Reports* [New York], April 9, 1969–October 25, 1972; *Quarterly Economic Review: Cuba, Dominican Republic, Haiti, Puerto Rico* [London], July 3, 1969–July 1972; *Times of the Americas* [Washington], May 29, 1972–November 15, 1972;

Translations on Latin America [Washington], December 14, 1966–November 29, 1972; *U.S. Embassy in Port-au-Prince. Various reports,* December 1, 1970–January, 1972; *U.S. Embassy in Santo Domingo. Various Reports,* March 11, 1971–January 1972; *Wall Street Journal* [New York], August 1972–February 1973; *Washington Post,* August 1972–February 1973; *Washington Star and Evening News,* August 1972–February 1973; *World Agricultural Production and Trade: Statistical Report* [Washington], July 1972–October 1972.)

Section IV. National Security

"Discussions Regarding Military and Naval Cooperation Between the United States and Haiti." Pages 1090–1106 in *Foreign Relations of the United States, 1945,* IX: The American Republic. Washington: GPO, 1945.

Haiti. Conseil National de Développement et de Planification. *Plan d'Action Economique et Sociale, 1970–1971.* Port-au-Prince: 1970.

Haiti. Laws, Statutes, etc.
  Code d'Instruction Criminelle. Port-au-Prince: Editions Henri Deschamps, 1958.
  Code Pénal. Port-au-Prince: Editions Henri Deschamps, 1948.

Haiti. Département des Finances et des Affaires Economiques. Institut Haïtien de Statistique. *Bulletin Trimestriel de Statistique, 1969:* LXXIV. Port-au-Prince: n.d.

"Haiti." In *Enciclopedia Universal Ilustrada* (Europeo-Americana), XXVII. Barcelona: n.pub., 1925.

Manigat, Leslie F. *Haiti of the Sixties, Object of International Concern.* Washington: Washington Center of Foreign Policy Research, 1964.

Métraux, Alfred. *Haiti: Black Peasants and Voodoo.* (Trans., Peter Lengyel.) New York: Universe Books, 1960.

The Political and Socio-Economic Role of the Military in Latin America. Appendix, III. Coral Gables: University of Miami, Center for Advanced International Studies, 1971.

Street, John M. *Historical and Economic Geography of the Southwest Peninsula of Haiti.* Berkeley: University of California, Department of Geography, 1960.

U.S. Department of State. Bureau of Intelligence and Research. *World Strength of the Communist Party Organizations. 23rd Annual Report.* (1971 ed.) Washington: 1971.

U.S. United States Arms Control and Disarmament Agency. Bureau of Economic Affairs. *World Military Expenditures, 1970.* Washington: 1970.

Yearbook on Latin American Communist Affairs, 1971. Stanford: Hoover Institution Press, Stanford University, 1971.

GLOSSARY

baccalauréat—Certificate of completion of four-year upper cycle in secondary school.

bamboche—Secular celebration or spree.

bocor—Voodoo sorcerer.

cacoism—Involvement of peasant guerrillas in revolutionary activities.

CAMEP—Centrale Autonome Metropolitaine d'Eau Potable (Autonomous Metropolitan Potable Water Center). Responsible for water supply in Port-au-Prince metropolitan area.

COALEP—Coopérative pour l'Alimentation en Eau Potable Pour les Comunités du Arrier-Pays (Cooperative for Potable Water Supply to Communities of the Interior). Provides water-supply installations for areas not able to finance the resulting services.

combite(s)—A working party of rural neighbors summoned by farmers for tasks such as working in fields during peak periods or constructing a house. Work is followed by feasting and dancing.

Creole—Language that arose as a pidginized form of French maritime and West African dialects during the colonial period; is spoken by all Haitians and is the only language of the peasant masses.

creolized French—French influenced by Creole.

cult of the dead—Complex of voodoo beliefs and practices honoring the dead.

gourde—Monetary unit. Symbol is G. Official rate in 1972 was 5 gourdes equal US$1. This rate had been in effect for more than thirty years.

gros habitant(s)—Haitian term for wealthy and powerful peasant.

houngan(s)—Voodoo priest.

loa (pl., *loa*)—Anthropomorphic spirits or gods in voodoo; of Haitian or African origin and subordinate to Christian God.

mambo(s)—Voodoo priestess.

méringue—A popular dance.

négritude—Glorification of Afro-Haitian heritage.

rara—A band of musicians that performs during latter part of Lent.

SHRH—Service Hydraulique du République d'Haïti (Hydraulic Service of the Republic of Haiti). An agency of the Secretariat of State for Public Works, Transportation and Communications, which is generally responsible for public water supply.

ville(s) de province—Provincial town. Any urban center other than Port-au-Prince.

INDEX

Published Country Studies

(Area Handbook Series)

550–84	Rwanda	550–89	Tunisia
550–51	Saudi Arabia	550–80	Turkey
550–70	Senegal	550–74	Uganda
550–180	Sierra Leone	550–97	Uruguay
550–184	Singapore	550–71	Venezuela
550–86	Somalia	550–57	Vietnam, North
550–93	South Africa	550–55	Vietnam, South
550–95	Soviet Union	550–183	Yemens, The
550–179	Spain	550–99	Yugoslavia
550–96	Sri Lanka (Ceylon)	550–67	Zaïre
550–27	Sudan	550–75	Zambia
550–47	Syria	550–171	Zimbabwe
550–62	Tanzania		
550–53	Thailand		
550–178	Trinidad and Tobago		

☆ U.S. GOVERNMENT PRINTING OFFICE: 1986 0-490-994